THEA
TEXAS HIGHER EDUCATION ASSESSMENT

THEA
TEXAS HIGHER EDUCATION ASSESSMENT

LEARNINGEXPRESS®

NEW YORK

Copyright © 2005 LearningExpress

All rights reserved under International and Pan-American Copyright Conventions.
Published in the United States by LearningExpress, LLC, New York.

Library of Congress Cataloging-in-Publication Data:
THEA : Texas Higher Education Assessment.
   p. cm.
 ISBN 1-57685-475-2
 1. THEA Test—Study guides. 2. Basic education—Ability testing—Texas—Study guides.
 I. Title: Texas Higher Education Assessment. II. LearningExpress (Organization)
LB2353.7.T37T44 2005
373.126'2—dc22

                                2004016516

Printed in the United States of America

9 8 7 6 5 4 3 2 1

ISBN: 1-57685-475-2

For more information or to place an order, contact LearningExpress at:
 55 Broadway
 8th Floor
 New York, NY 10006

Or visit us at:
 www.learnatest.com

About the CD-ROM ▶

The CD-ROM included free in this book allows you the option of taking a complete test or just selecting some practice questions in any of the three subjects. In addition, the CD-ROM scores the tests for you and (like the book) offers detailed answer explanations.

Our CD-ROM is designed to be user-friendly, however, please consult the "How to Use the CD-ROM" section in the back of this book before you use the program.

Contents

THEA
TEXAS HIGHER EDUCATION ASSESSMENT

1 ▶ What Is the THEA?

CHAPTER SUMMARY

This chapter gives you the basic information you need to know about the THEA: who has to take it, how to register, what is on the test, and how it is scored.

The Texas Higher Education Assessment (THEA) was designed to ensure that students in Texas obtain the reading, math, and writing skills necessary to take on college-level work. The test portion of the program is administered and developed by the Texas Higher Education Coordinating Board (THECB) and National Evaluation Systems, Inc. (NES). It was created to help educators identify students who may need remedial help before pursuing higher-education courses.

▶ Who Must Take the THEA?

All students who plan on enrolling in a Texas public institution of higher learning must take the THEA test. Educational institutions decide what to do with students who do not pass portions of, or the entire test.

The THEA must also be passed by the following:

- those who are entering a public higher education institution in Texas
- those transferring from a private higher education institution in Texas
- those transferring from an out-of-state higher education institution
- those who are teacher education students in institutions in Texas

It is possible to take the THEA test on a computer. If you miss dates for the paper-and-pencil exam, this may be a way for you to take the test on a different date; the Computer-Administered Test (CAT) is given more frequently. The THEA CAT is administered once a week at 12 different locations in Texas. However, keep in mind that seating is limited and the registration fee is higher than the fee for the paper-and-pencil test.

You may not have to take the THEA if one of the following is true of you:

- you have an ACT composite score of 23, with a minimum of 19 on both the English and Math tests
- you have an SAT combined Verbal and Math score of 1070, with a minimum of 500 on both the Verbal and Math tests (NOTE: The SAT is changing in March 2005. These criteria may change.)
- you score 1770 on the Texas Assessment of Academic Skills (TAAS) Writing test; score 89 on the Texas Learning Index on the Reading test; and score 86 on the Texas Learning Index on the Math test
- you enroll in a certificate program of 42 semester credit hours or less at a public community college or technical college
- you have an associate's or baccalaureate degree

NOTE: There are several other exemptions, and institutions may have their own guidelines for exemption. You should understand whether these exemptions apply to you before registering for the exam.

▶ How Do I Register for the THEA?

You may register for the THEA by mail or online. (NOTE: You may only register by phone if you are registering late or are seeking emergency registration.) If you are registering by mail, complete the form found in the THEA Test Registration Bulletin. Your high school guidance office or college admissions office will have free copies of this bulletin. If you are registering online, go to www.thea.nesinc.com. Once you have registered, you will receive a registration receipt, and later an admission ticket to the exam. You must bring your admission ticket with you on exam day.

Registration Fee

There is a registration fee for the THEA test. At the time this book was printed, this fee was $29. If you can't afford the fee and you think you might qualify for a waiver, contact the financial aid office of the institution you wish to attend or your high school guidance office to see if it can be arranged.

▶ Important Contact Information

For questions as to whether you are exempt from taking the THEA test, about registration procedures, test taking, score reports, or alternative dates and places, contact your high school guidance office, college admissions office, or one of the following:

Texas Higher Education Coordinating Board
www.thecb.state.tx.us
Division of Educational Partnerships
The Center for College Readiness
P.O. Box 12788
Austin, TX 78711-2788
512-427-6330

THEA Test
National Evaluation Systems, Inc.
www.thea.nesinc.com
P.O. Box 140347
Austin, TX 78714-0347
512-927-5397

▶ When and Where

The THEA is administered six times throughout the year. Typically, there is one test date in each of the following months: September, November, March, April, June, and July. To find the test center closest to you, check the THEA Test Registration Bulletin.

▶ What Is the THEA Like?

You will have five hours to complete all three sections on the THEA test; the three sections are not timed separately, which means you can take as much time as you need for each section, but your total testing time will not exceed five hours. Each section has from 40 to 50 multiple-choice questions; the Writing section also has an essay. You do not have to complete every section in one sitting. You may concentrate on one or two sections the first time you take the test, re-register, and work solely on the third section at a later date. (However, keep in mind that you will have to pay the registration fee each time you take the test.)

▶ What Is Tested

Three subjects—reading, math, and writing—will be tested. All of the questions on the THEA will be in multiple-choice format, with the exception of the essay-writing portion. Each of the three sections of the test is designed to test specific skills, which are listed below.

Reading

The first section of the THEA is the Reading section. It is made up of 40 to 50 multiple-choice questions based on approximately seven reading selections (300–700 words each). The questions on the Reading section of the test are designed to test your ability to:

- determine the meaning of words and phrases
- understand the main idea and supporting details in written material
- identify an author's purpose, point of view, and intended meaning
- analyze the relationship among ideas in written material
- use critical reasoning skills to evaluate written material
- apply the following study skills to reading assignments: organizing and summarizing information; understanding and following directions; and interpreting graphs, tables, and charts

Mathematics

The Math section of the THEA is also composed of between 40 and 50 multiple-choice questions. The types of math covered include fundamental mathematics, algebra, geometry, and problem solving. Following are skills that are covered in each mathematical discipline on the Math section of the THEA:

- Fundamental Mathematics: Solving word problems with integers, fractions, decimals, and units of measurement; solving problems involving various types of graphs, tables, and charts; solving problems involving mean, median, and mode; and variability.
- Algebra: Graphing numbers and the relationship between numbers; solving equations and word problems with one or two variables; understanding operations involving algebraic expressions; and solving problems involving quadratic equations.
- Geometry: Solving problems involving geometric figures; and solving problems involving geometric concepts such as similarity, congruence, parallelism, and perpendicularity.
- Problem Solving: Using a combination of mathematical and reasoning skills, including deductive and inductive reasoning.

You will not need to memorize any complicated formulas for the Math section; all appropriate formulas will be provided. Certain types of calculators are permitted for the THEA.

Writing

The Writing section is made up of two subsections: a multiple-choice subsection of between 40 and 50 questions, and a writing sample subsection where you will demonstrate your ability to communicate your thoughts in writing. The multiple-choice subsection will test the following skills:

- Elements of composition: Recognizing purpose and audience; recognizing unity, focus, and development in an essay; and recognizing effective organization.
- Sentence structure, usage, and mechanics: Recognizing effective sentences; and recognizing edited standard English.

The following qualities will be taken into consideration when your essay is scored:

- appropriateness
- unity and focus
- development
- organization
- sentence structure
- usage
- mechanical conventions

▶ Test Day

On test day, you should plan to arrive around 30 minutes before the start of your test. You must bring your admission ticket with you. If you are taking a paper-based test, you should have several #2 pencils with you, as well as an eraser. You are allowed to use a basic (non-programmable) calculator on the THEA. Calculators will not be provided to you, and you should check with your testing center to be certain you have the correct type of calculator.

You will also need to have two forms of identification. At least one form of identification must have a recent photograph of you. Some approved forms of identification include:

- driver's license
- passport
- military identification card
- student identification card

▶ What Not to Bring

Here are some items that will not be allowed in the test room:

- cell phones
- pagers
- unapproved calculators
- watches with alarms
- paper
- study aids (dictionaries, books)
- food or drink
- backpacks or large bags

▶ What about Scores?

After about two weeks from the day you take the THEA, you should receive your scores. (If you take the THEA CAT, you will receive unofficial scores immediately. Later, you will receive official scores.) At the time you register for the THEA test, you can request that your scores be sent to one or more colleges or universities. If you fail any portion of the THEA, the university or college you attend will require you to take remedial courses in that subject until you are able to pass that section of the THEA.

▶ How the Test Is Scored

The multiple-choice sections of the exam will be scored electronically. There is no penalty for guessing, so it is in your best interest to fill in an answer, rather than leaving a blank, even when you are unsure.

The writing sample is actually scored by human beings, rather than by a computer. The scaled score for the essay is from 1 to 4 points—4 being the highest. Your essay will be read by two different people, so your essay will receive a final score between 2 and 8. If you score 6 or above, you automatically pass the entire Writing section; your multiple-choice writing subsection is not even considered in the overall score. If you score a 4 or below, you fail the entire Writing section, regardless of your score on the multiple-choice subsection. If you score a 5 on the essay, then you must answer 70% of the writing multiple-choice questions correctly in order to pass the Writing section. In other words, whether or not you pass the Writing section depends most heavily on the quality of your essay, so you should concentrate most of your study time on learning to write a good essay.

▶ Where Do I Begin?

You should begin your study program with Chapter 2, "The LearningExpress Test Preparation System." This chapter will help you devise a study schedule for yourself. If you stick to it, and devote yourself to improving those areas in which you need help, you will be on your way to passing the THEA.

CHAPTER

The LearningExpress Test Preparation System

CHAPTER SUMMARY

Taking the THEA can be tough. It demands a lot of preparation if you want to achieve a top score. Your academic future depends on your passing the exam. The LearningExpress Test Preparation System, developed exclusively for LearningExpress by leading test experts, gives you the discipline and attitude you need to be a winner.

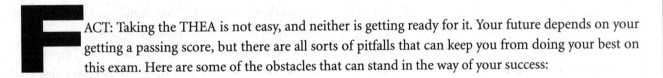

FACT: Taking the THEA is not easy, and neither is getting ready for it. Your future depends on your getting a passing score, but there are all sorts of pitfalls that can keep you from doing your best on this exam. Here are some of the obstacles that can stand in the way of your success:

- being unfamiliar with the format of the exam
- being paralyzed by test anxiety
- leaving your preparation to the last minute
- not preparing at all!
- not knowing vital test-taking skills: how to pace yourself through the exam, how to use the process of elimination, and when to guess
- not being in tip-top mental and physical shape
- messing up on test day by arriving late at the test site, having to work on an empty stomach, or shivering through the exam because the room is cold

What's the common denominator in all these test-taking pitfalls? One word: control. Who's in control, you or the exam?

Here's some good news: The LearningExpress Test Preparation System puts you in control. In nine easy-to-follow steps, you will learn everything you need to know to make sure that you are in charge of your preparation and your performance on the exam. Other test-takers may let the test get the better of them; other test-takers may be unprepared or out of shape, but not you. You will have taken all the steps you need to take to get a high score on the THEA.

Here's how the LearningExpress Test Preparation System works: Nine easy steps lead you through everything you need to know and do to get ready to master your exam. Each of the steps listed below includes both reading about the step and one or more activities. It's important that you do the activities along with the reading, or you won't be getting the full benefit of the system. Each step tells you approximately how much time that step will take you to complete.

Step 1. Get Information	50 minutes
Step 2. Conquer Test Anxiety	20 minutes
Step 3. Make a Plan	30 minutes
Step 4. Learn to Manage Your Time	10 minutes
Step 5. Learn to Use the Process of Elimination	20 minutes
Step 6. Know When to Guess	20 minutes
Step 7. Reach Your Peak Performance Zone	10 minutes
Step 8. Get Your Act Together	10 minutes
Step 9. Do It!	10 minutes
Total	**3 hours**

We estimate that working through the entire system will take you approximately three hours, though it's perfectly OK if you work faster or slower. If you take an afternoon or evening, you can work through the whole LearningExpress Test Preparation System in one sitting. Otherwise, you can break it up, and do just one or two

steps a day for the next several days. It's up to you—remember, you are in control.

▶ Step 1: Get Information

Time to complete: 50 minutes

Activity: Read Chapter 1, "What Is the THEA?"

Knowledge is power. The first step in the Learning-Express Test Preparation System is finding out everything you can about the THEA. Once you have your information, the next steps in the LearningExpress Test Preparation System will show you what to do about it.

Part A: Straight Talk about the THEA

Why should you have to go through a rigorous exam? It is simply an attempt to be sure you have the knowledge and skills necessary to succeed in school.

It is important for you to remember that your score on the THEA does not determine how smart you are or even whether you will make a good student. There are all kinds of things an exam like this can't test, like whether you have the drive, determination, and dedication to succeed. Those kinds of things are hard to evaluate, while a test is easy to evaluate.

This is not to say that the exam is not important! The knowledge tested on the exam is knowledge you will need to succeed in college. Your ability to become a college student depends on your passing this exam. That's why you are here—using the LearningExpress Test Preparation System to achieve control over the exam.

Part B: What's on the Test

If you haven't already done so, stop here and read Chapter 1 of this book, which gives you an overview of the exam. Then, go to the Internet and read the most up-to-date information about your exam directly from the test developers.

▶ Step 2: Conquer Test Anxiety

Time to complete: 20 minutes

Activity: Take the Test Stress Test

Having complete information about the exam is the first step in getting control of the exam. Next, you have to overcome one of the biggest obstacles to test success: test anxiety. Test anxiety not only impairs your performance on the exam itself; but also keeps you from preparing! In Step 2, you will learn stress management techniques that will help you succeed on your exam. Learn these strategies now, and practice them as you work through the exams in this book, so they will be second nature to you by exam day.

Combating Test Anxiety

The first thing you need to know is that a little test anxiety is a good thing. Everyone gets nervous before a big exam—and if that nervousness motivates you to prepare thoroughly, so much the better. It is said that Sir Laurence Olivier, one of the foremost British actors of the last century, felt ill before every performance. His stage fright didn't impair his performance; in fact, it probably gave him a little extra edge—just the kind of edge you need to do well, whether on a stage or in an examination room.

At the bottom of the page is the Test Stress Test. Stop and answer the questions, to find out whether your level of test anxiety is something you should worry about.

Your Test Stress Score

Here are the steps you should take, depending on your score. If you scored:

Below 3, your level of test anxiety is nothing to worry about; it's probably just enough to give you that little extra edge.

Between 3 and 6, your test anxiety may be enough to impair your performance, and you should practice the stress management techniques listed in this section to try to bring your test anxiety down to manageable levels.

Test Stress Test

You only need to worry about test anxiety if it is extreme enough to impair your performance. The following questionnaire will provide a diagnosis of your level of test anxiety. In the blank before each statement, write the number that most accurately describes your experience.

0 = Never   1 = Once or twice   2 = Sometimes   3 = Often

_____ I have gotten so nervous before an exam that I simply put down the books and didn't study for it.

_____ I have experienced disabling physical symptoms such as vomiting and severe headaches because I was nervous about an exam.

_____ I have simply not showed up for an exam because I was scared to take it.

_____ I have experienced dizziness and disorientation while taking an exam.

_____ I have had trouble filling in the little circles because my hands were shaking too hard.

_____ I have failed an exam because I was too nervous to complete it.

_____ **Total: Add up the numbers in the blanks above.**

Above 6, your level of test anxiety is a serious concern. In addition to practicing the stress management techniques listed in this section, you may want to seek additional, personal help. Talk to your guidance counselor. Tell the counselor that you have a level of test anxiety that sometimes keeps you from being able to take an exam. The counselor may be willing to help you or may suggest someone else you should talk to.

Stress Management Before the Test

If you feel your level of anxiety getting the best of you in the weeks before the test, here is what you need to do to bring the level down again:

Get prepared. There is nothing like knowing what to expect and being prepared for it to put you in control of test anxiety. That is why you are reading this book. Use it faithfully, and remind yourself that you are better prepared than most of the people taking the test.

Practice self-confidence. A positive attitude is a great way to combat test anxiety. This is no time to be humble or shy. Stand in front of the mirror and say to your reflection, "I am prepared. I am full of self-confidence. I am going to ace this test. I know I can do it." Say it into a tape recorder and play it back once a day. If you hear it often enough, you will believe it.

Fight negative messages. Every time someone starts telling you how hard the exam is or how it's almost impossible to get a high score, start telling them your self-confidence messages above. Don't listen to the negative messages. Turn on your voice recorder and listen to your self-confidence messages.

Visualize. Imagine yourself on your first day on a university or college campus. Visualizing success can help make it happen—and it reminds you of why you are going to all this work in preparing for the exam.

Exercise. Physical activity helps calm your body down and focus your mind. Besides, being in good physical shape can actually help you do well on the exam. Go for a run, lift weights, go swimming—and do it regularly.

Stress Management on Test Day

There are several ways you can bring down your level of test anxiety on test day. They will work best if you practice them in the weeks before the test, so you know which ones work best for you.

Deep breathing. Take a deep breath while you count to five. Hold it for a count of one, then let it out on a count of five. Repeat several times.

Move your body. Try rolling your head in a circle. Rotate your shoulders. Shake your hands from the wrist. Many people find these movements very relaxing.

Visualize again. Think of the place where you are most relaxed: lying on the beach in the sun, walking through the park, or whatever. Now close your eyes and imagine you are actually there. If you practice in advance, you will find that you only need a few seconds of this exercise to experience a significant increase in your sense of well-being.

When anxiety threatens to overwhelm you right there during the exam, there are still things you can do to manage your stress level:

Repeat your self-confidence messages. You should have them memorized by now. Say them silently to yourself, and believe them!

Visualize one more time. This time, visualize yourself moving smoothly and quickly through the test; answering every question right and finishing just before time is up. Like most visualization techniques, this one works best if you have practiced it ahead of time.

Find an easy question. Find an easy question, and answer it. Getting even one question finished gets you into the test-taking groove.

Take a mental break. Everyone loses concentration once in a while during a long test. It is normal, so you shouldn't worry about it. Instead, accept what has happened. Say to yourself, "Hey, I lost it there for a minute. My brain is taking a break." Put down your pencil, close your eyes, and do some deep breathing for a few seconds. Then you are ready to go back to work.

Try these techniques ahead of time, and see if they work for you!

▶ Step 3: Make a Plan

Time to complete: 30 minutes

Activity: Construct a study plan

Maybe the most important thing you can do to get control of yourself and your exam is to make a study plan. Too many people fail to prepare simply because they fail to plan. Spending hours on the day before the exam poring over sample test questions not only raises your level of test anxiety, it also is simply no substitute for careful preparation and practice over time.

Don't fall into the cram trap. Take control of your preparation time by mapping out a study schedule. On the following pages are two sample schedules, based on the amount of time you have before you take the THEA. If you are the kind of person who needs deadlines and assignments to motivate you for a project, here they are. If you are the kind of person who doesn't like to follow other people's plans, you can use the suggested schedules here to construct your own.

Even more important than making a plan is making a commitment. You have to set aside some time every day for study and practice. Try for at least 20 minutes a day. Twenty minutes daily will do you much more good than two hours on Saturday.

Don't put off your study until the day before the exam. Start now. A few minutes a day, with half an hour or more on weekends, can make a big difference in your score.

Schedule A: The 30-Day Plan

If you have at least a month before you take the THEA, you have plenty of time to prepare—as long as you don't waste it! If you have less than a month, turn to Schedule B.

TIME	PREPARATION
Days 1–4	Skim over any other study materials you may have. Make a note of 1) areas you expect to be emphasized on the exam and 2) areas you don't feel confident in. On Day 4, concentrate on those areas.
Day 5	Take the first practice exam in Chapter 3.
Day 6	Score the first practice exam. Identify two areas that you will concentrate on before you take the second practice exam.
Days 7–10	Study one of the areas you identified as your weak point. Don't forget, there are reviews of Reading, Mathematics, and Writing in Chapters 4, 5, and 6. Review one of these topics in detail to improve your score on the next practice test.
Days 11–14	Study the other area you identified as your weak point. Don't forget to use the review information in Chapters 4, 5, and 6. Review one of the skills in these chapters to improve your score on the next practice test.
Day 15	Take the second practice exam in Chapter 7.
Day 16	Score the second practice exam. Identify one area to concentrate on before you take the third practice exam.
Days 17–22	Study the one area you identified for review. Again, use Chapters 4, 5, and 6 for help.
Day 22	Take the last practice exam in Chapter 8.
Day 23	Score the test. Note how much you have improved.
Days 24–28	Study any remaining topics you still need to review. Use the review chapters for help.
Days 29	Take an overview of all your study materials, consolidating your strengths and improving on your weaknesses.
Day before the exam	Relax. Do something unrelated to the exam and go to bed at a reasonable hour.

Schedule B: The 10-Day Plan

If you have two weeks or less before you take the exam, use this 10-day schedule to help you make the most of your time.

TIME	PREPARATION
Day 1	Take the first practice exam in Chapter 3 and score it using the answer key at the end. Note which topics you need to review most.
Day 2	Review one area that gave you trouble on the first practice exam. Use Chapters 4, 5, and 6 to review one skill and to improve your score on the next practice test.
Day 3	Review another skill area that gave you trouble on the first practice exam. Again, use the review chapters to help you.
Day 4	Take the second practice exam in Chapter 7 and score it.
Day 5	If your score on the second practice exam doesn't show improvement on the two areas you studied, review them. If you did improve in those areas, choose a new weak area to study today.
Day 6–7	Continue to use the review chapters to improve some skills and reinforce others.
Day 8	Take the third practice exam in Chapter 8 and score it.
Day 9	Choose your weakest area from the third practice exam to review.
Day 10	Use your last study day to brush up on any areas that are still giving you trouble. Use the review chapters.
Day before the exam	Relax. Do something unrelated to the exam and go to bed at a reasonable hour.

► Step 4: Learn to Manage Your Time

Time to complete: 10 minutes to read, many hours of practice!

Activities: Practice these strategies as you take the sample tests in this book

Steps 4, 5, and 6 of the LearningExpress Test Preparation System put you in charge of your exam by showing you test-taking strategies that work. Practice these strategies as you take the sample tests in this book, and then you will be ready to use them on test day.

First, you will take control of your time on the exam. It feels terrible to know there are only five minutes left when you are only three-quarters of the way through the test. Here are some tips to keep that from happening to *you.*

Follow directions. Read the directions carefully and ask questions before the exam begins if there is anything you don't understand.

Pace yourself. If there is a clock in the testing room, keep an eye on it. This will help you pace yourself. For example, when one-quarter of the time has elapsed, you should be a quarter of the way through the test, and so on. If you are falling behind, pick up the pace a bit.

Keep moving. Don't waste time on one question. If you don't know the answer, skip the question and move on. You can always go back to it later.

Don't rush. Though you should keep moving, rushing won't help. Try to keep calm and work methodically and quickly.

▶ Step 5: Learn to Use the Process of Elimination

Time to complete: 20 minutes

Activity: Complete worksheet on Using the Process of Elimination

After time management, your next most important tool for taking control of your exam is using the process of elimination wisely. It's standard test-taking wisdom that you should always read all the answer choices before choosing your answer. This helps you find the right answer by eliminating wrong answer choices. And, sure enough, that standard wisdom applies to your exam, too.

You should always use the process of elimination on tough questions, even if the right answer jumps out at you. Sometimes the answer that jumps out isn't right after all. You should always proceed through the answer choices in order. You can start with answer choice **a** and eliminate any choices that are clearly incorrect.

If you are taking the test on paper, like the practice exams in this book, it's good to have a system for marking good, bad, and maybe answers. We're recommending this one:

    X = bad
    ✓ = good
    ? = maybe

If you don't like these marks, devise your own system. Just make sure you do it long before test day—while you're working through the practice exams in this book—so you won't have to worry about it just before the exam.

Even when you think you are absolutely clueless about a question, you can often use the process of elimination to get rid of one answer choice. If so, you are better prepared to make an educated guess, as you will see in Step 6. More often, the process of elimination allows you to get down to only two possibly right answers. Then you are in a strong position to guess. And sometimes, even though you don't know the right answer, you find it simply by getting rid of the wrong ones.

Try using your powers of elimination on the questions in the Using the Process of Elimination worksheet on the next page. The questions aren't about a specific topic; they're just designed to show you how the process of elimination works. The answer explanations for this worksheet show one possible way you might use the process to arrive at the right answer.

The process of elimination is your tool for the next step, which is knowing when to guess.

▶ Step 6: Know When to Guess

Time to complete: 20 minutes

Activity: Complete worksheet on Your Guessing Ability

Armed with the process of elimination, you are ready to take control of one of the big questions in test-taking: Should I guess? The first and main answer is Yes. The number of questions you answer correctly yields your raw score. So you have nothing to lose by guessing. The worksheet is found on page 17.

Use the process of elimination to answer the following questions.

1. Ilsa is as old as Meghan will be in five years. The difference between Ed's age and Meghan's age is twice the difference between Ilsa's age and Meghan's age. Ed is 29. How old is Ilsa?
   a. 4
   b. 10
   c. 19
   d. 24

2. "All drivers of commercial vehicles must carry a valid commercial driver's license whenever operating a commercial vehicle." According to this sentence, which of the following people need NOT carry a commercial driver's license?
   a. a truck driver idling his engine while waiting to be directed to a loading dock
   b. a bus operator backing her bus out of the way of another bus in the bus lot
   c. a taxi driver driving his personal car to the grocery store
   d. a limousine driver taking the limousine to her home after dropping off her last passenger of the evening

3. Smoking tobacco has been linked to
   a. increased risk of stroke and heart attack.
   b. all forms of respiratory disease.
   c. increasing mortality rates over the past ten years.
   d. juvenile delinquency.

4. Which of the following words is spelled correctly?
   a. incorrigible
   b. outragous
   c. domestickated
   d. understandible

Answers

Here are the answers, as well as some suggestions as to how you might have used the process of elimination to find them.

1. d. You should have eliminated answer **a** off the bat. Ilsa can't be four years old if Meghan is going to be Ilsa's age in five years. The best way to eliminate other answer choices is to try plugging them in to the information given in the problem. For instance, for answer **b**, if Ilsa is 10, then Meghan must be 5. The difference in their ages is 5. The difference between Ed's age, 29, and Meghan's age, 5, is 24. Is 24 two times 5? No. Then answer **b** is wrong. You could eliminate answer **c** in the same way and be left with answer **d**.

2. c. Note the word *not* in the question, and go through the answers one by one. Is the truck driver in choice **a** "operating a commercial vehicle"? Yes, idling counts as "operating," so he needs to have a commercial driver's license. Likewise, the bus operator in answer **b** is operating a commercial vehicle; the question doesn't say the operator has to be on the street. The limo driver in **d** is operating a commercial vehicle, even if it doesn't have a passenger in it. However, the cabbie in answer **c** is *not* operating a commercial vehicle, but his own private car.

3. a. You could eliminate answer **b** simply because of the presence of the word *all*. Such absolutes hardly ever appear in correct answer choices. Choice **c** looks attractive until you think a little about what you know—aren't *fewer* people smoking these days, rather than more? So how could smoking be responsible for a higher mortality rate? (If you didn't know that *mortality rate* means the rate at which people die, you might keep this choice as a possibility, but you would still be able to eliminate two answers and have only two to choose from.) And choice **d** is not logical, so you could eliminate that one, too. You are left with the correct choice, **a**.

4. a. How you used the process of elimination here depends on which words you recognized as being spelled incorrectly. If you knew that the correct spellings were *outrageous*, *domesticated*, and *understandable*, then you were home free. You probably knew that at least one of those words was wrong!

▶ Step 7: Reach Your Peak Performance Zone

Time to complete: 10 minutes to read; weeks to complete!

Activity: Complete the Physical Preparation Checklist

To get ready for a challenge like a big exam, you have to take control of your physical, as well as your mental, state. Exercise, proper diet, and rest will ensure that your body works with, rather than against, your mind on test day, as well as during your preparation.

Exercise

If you don't already have a regular exercise program going, the time during which you are preparing for an exam is actually an excellent time to start one. And if you are already keeping fit—or trying to get that way—don't let the pressure of preparing for an exam fool you into quitting now. Exercise helps reduce stress by pumping wonderful hormones called endorphins into your system. It also increases the oxygen supply throughout your body, including your brain, so you will be at peak performance on test day.

A half hour of vigorous activity—enough to raise a sweat—every day should be your aim. If you are really pressed for time, every other day is OK. Choose an activity you like and get out there and do it. Jogging with a friend always makes the time go faster, or take a radio.

But don't overdo it. You don't want to exhaust yourself. Moderation is the key.

Diet

First of all, cut out the junk. Go easy on caffeine and nicotine, and eliminate alcohol and any other drugs from your system at least two weeks before the exam. Promise yourself a treat the night after the exam, if need be.

What your body needs for peak performance is simply a balanced diet. Eat plenty of fruits and vegetables, along with protein and carbohydrates. Foods that are high in lecithin (an amino acid), such as fish and beans, are especially good "brain foods."

The night before the exam, you might "carbo-load" the way athletes do before a contest. Eat a big plate of spaghetti, rice and beans, or whatever your favorite carbohydrate is.

The following are ten really hard questions. You are not supposed to know the answers. Rather, this is an assessment of your ability to guess when you don't have a clue. Read each question carefully, just as if you did expect to answer it. If you have any knowledge at all of the subject of the question, use that knowledge to help you eliminate wrong answer choices.

1. September 7 is Independence Day in
   a. India.
   b. Costa Rica.
   c. Brazil.
   d. Australia.

2. Which of the following is the formula for determining the momentum of an object?
   a. $p = mv$
   b. $F = ma$
   c. $P = IV$
   d. $E = mc^2$

3. Because of the expansion of the universe, the stars and other celestial bodies are all moving away from each other. This phenomenon is known as
   a. Newton's first law.
   b. the big bang.
   c. gravitational collapse.
   d. Hubble flow.

4. American author Gertrude Stein was born in
   a. 1713.
   b. 1830.
   c. 1874.
   d. 1901.

5. Which of the following is NOT one of the Five Classics attributed to Confucius?
   a. the *I Ching*
   b. the *Book of Holiness*
   c. the *Spring and Autumn Annals*
   d. the *Book of History*

6. The religious and philosophical doctrine that holds that the universe is constantly in a struggle between good and evil is known as
   a. Pelagianism.
   b. Manichaeanism.
   c. neo-Hegelianism.
   d. Epicureanism.

7. The third Chief Justice of the U.S. Supreme Court was
   a. John Blair.
   b. William Cushing.
   c. James Wilson.
   d. John Jay.

8. Which of the following is the poisonous portion of a daffodil?
   a. the bulb
   b. the leaves
   c. the stem
   d. the flowers

9. The winner of the Masters golf tournament in 1953 was
   a. Sam Snead.
   b. Cary Middlecoff.
   c. Arnold Palmer.
   d. Ben Hogan.

10. The state with the highest per capita personal income in 1980 was
   a. Alaska.
   b. Connecticut.
   c. New York.
   d. Texas.

Answers

Check your answers against the correct answers below.

1. c.
2. a.
3. d.
4. c.
5. b.
6. b.
7. b.
8. a.
9. d.
10. a.

How Did You Do?

You may have simply gotten lucky and actually known the answer to one or two questions. In addition, your guessing was more successful if you were able to use the process of elimination on any of the questions. Maybe you didn't know who the third Chief Justice was (question 7), but you knew that John Jay was the first. In that case, you would have eliminated answer **d** and therefore improved your odds of guessing right from one in four to one in three.

According to probability, you should get $2\frac{1}{2}$ answers correct, so getting either two or three right would be average. If you got four or more right, you may be a really terrific guesser. If you got one or none right, you may be a really bad guesser.

Keep in mind, though, that this is only a small sample. You should continue to keep track of your guessing ability as you work through the sample questions in this book. Circle the numbers of questions you guess on as you make your guess; or, if you don't have time while you take the practice exams, go back afterward and try to remember which questions you guessed at. Remember, on an exam with four answer choices, your chances of getting a right answer is one in four. So keep a separate "guessing" score for each exam. How many questions did you guess on? How many did you get right? If the number you got right is at least one-fourth of the number of questions you guessed on, you are at least an average guesser, maybe better—and you should always go ahead and guess on the real exam. If the number you got right is significantly lower than one-fourth of the number you guessed on, you would, frankly, be safe in guessing anyway, but maybe you would feel more comfortable if you guessed only selectively, when you can eliminate a wrong answer or at least feel good about one of the answer choices.

Rest

You probably know how much sleep you need every night to be at your best, even if you don't always get it. Make sure you do get that much sleep, though, for at least a week before the exam. Moderation is important here, too. Extra sleep will just make you groggy.

If you are not a morning person and your exam will be given in the morning, you should reset your internal clock so that your body doesn't think you are taking an exam at 3 A.M. You have to start this process well before the exam. The way it works is to get up half an hour earlier each morning, and then go to bed half an hour earlier that night. Don't try it the other way around; you will just toss and turn if you go to bed early without having gotten up early. The next morning, get up another half an hour earlier, and so on. How long you will have to do this depends on how late you are used to getting up. Use the Physical Preparation Checklist on the next page to make sure you are in tip-top form.

Physical Preparation Checklist

For the week before the exam, write down 1) what physical exercise you engaged in and for how long and 2) what you ate for each meal. Remember, you are trying for at least half an hour of exercise every other day (preferably every day) and a balanced diet that is light on junk food.

Exam minus 7 days

Exercise: _____ for _____ minutes

Breakfast: _____

Lunch: _____

Dinner: _____

Snacks: _____

Exam minus 6 days

Exercise: _____ for _____ minutes

Breakfast: _____

Lunch: _____

Dinner: _____

Snacks: _____

Exam minus 5 days

Exercise: _____ for _____ minutes

Breakfast: _____

Lunch: _____

Dinner: _____

Snacks: _____

Exam minus 4 days

Exercise: _____ for _____ minutes

Breakfast: _____

Lunch: _____

Dinner: _____

Snacks: _____

Exam minus 3 days

Exercise: _____ for _____ minutes

Breakfast: _____

Lunch: _____

Dinner: _____

Snacks: _____

Exam minus 2 days

Exercise: _____ for _____ minutes

Breakfast: _____

Lunch: _____

Dinner: _____

Snacks: _____

Exam minus 1 day

Exercise: _____ for _____ minutes

Breakfast: _____

Lunch: _____

Dinner: _____

Snacks: _____

▶ Step 8: Get Your Act Together

Time to complete: 10 minutes to read; time to complete will vary

Activity: Complete Final Preparations worksheet

You are in control of your mind and body; you are in charge of test anxiety, your preparation, and your test-taking strategies. Now it's time to take charge of external factors, like the testing site and the materials you need to take the exam.

Find Out Where the Exam Is and Make a Trial Run

Do you know how to get to the testing site? Do you know how long it will take to get there? If not, make a trial run, preferably on the same day of the week at the same time of day. Make note, on the Final Preparations worksheet that follows, of the amount of time it will take you to get to the exam site. Plan on arriving 30–45 minutes early so you can get the lay of the land, use the bathroom, and calm down. Then figure out how early you will have to get up that morning, and make sure you get up that early every day for a week before the exam.

Gather Your Materials

The night before the exam, lay out the clothes you will wear and the materials you have to bring with you to the exam. Plan on dressing in layers; you won't have any control over the temperature of the examination room. Have a sweater or jacket you can take off if it's warm. Use the following checklist on the Final Preparations worksheet to help you pull together what you will need.

Don't Skip Breakfast

Even if you don't usually eat breakfast, do so on exam morning. A cup of coffee doesn't count. Don't do doughnuts or other sweet foods, either. A sugar high will leave you with a sugar low in the middle of the exam. A mix of protein and carbohydrates is best: cereal with milk and just a little sugar, or eggs with toast, will do your body a world of good.

Final Preparations

Getting to the Exam Site

Location of exam site: _____

Date: _____

Departure time: _____

Do I know how to get to the exam site?

    Yes _____ No _____

If no, make a trial run.

Time it will take to get to exam site: _____

Things to Lay Out the Night Before

Clothes I will wear   _____

Sweater/jacket   _____

Watch   _____

Photo ID   _____

No. 2 pencils   _____

_____   _____

_____   _____

▶ Step 9: Do It!

Time to complete: 10 minutes, plus test-taking time

Activity: Ace the THEA!

Fast forward to exam day. You are ready. You made a study plan and followed through. You practiced your test-taking strategies while working through this book. You are in control of your physical, mental, and emotional state. You know when and where to show up and what to bring with you. In other words, you are better prepared than most of the other people taking the exam. You are psyched.

Just one more thing. When you are done with the exam, you will have earned a reward. Plan a celebration. Call up your friends and plan a party, or have a nice dinner for two—whatever your heart desires. Give yourself something to look forward to.

And then do it. Go into the exam, full of confidence, armed with the test-taking strategies you have practiced until they're second nature. You are in control of yourself, your environment, and your performance on the exam. You are ready to succeed. So do it. Go in there and ace the exam. And look forward to your future success!

CHAPTER

3 ▶ THEA Practice Exam 1

CHAPTER SUMMARY

This is the first of the three practice tests in this book based on the Texas Higher Education Assessment (THEA). Use this test to see how you would do if you were to take the exam today.

This practice exam is of the same type as the real Texas Higher Education Assessment you will be taking. It is divided into three sections:

- Reading, 42 multiple-choice questions
- Mathematics, 48 multiple-choice questions
- Writing, 40 multiple-choice questions and one essay

The THEA is timed, but for now, don't worry too much about timing. Just take this first practice test in as relaxed a manner as you can to find out your strengths and weaknesses.

The answer sheet you should use for the multiple-choice questions is on the following page. You should write your essay on a separate piece of paper. When you finish answering the questions and writing your essay, you will find complete answer explanations.

▶ Answer Sheet

SECTION 1: READING

1. ⓐ ⓑ ⓒ ⓓ
2. ⓐ ⓑ ⓒ ⓓ
3. ⓐ ⓑ ⓒ ⓓ
4. ⓐ ⓑ ⓒ ⓓ
5. ⓐ ⓑ ⓒ ⓓ
6. ⓐ ⓑ ⓒ ⓓ
7. ⓐ ⓑ ⓒ ⓓ
8. ⓐ ⓑ ⓒ ⓓ
9. ⓐ ⓑ ⓒ ⓓ
10. ⓐ ⓑ ⓒ ⓓ
11. ⓐ ⓑ ⓒ ⓓ
12. ⓐ ⓑ ⓒ ⓓ
13. ⓐ ⓑ ⓒ ⓓ
14. ⓐ ⓑ ⓒ ⓓ
15. ⓐ ⓑ ⓒ ⓓ
16. ⓐ ⓑ ⓒ ⓓ
17. ⓐ ⓑ ⓒ ⓓ
18. ⓐ ⓑ ⓒ ⓓ
19. ⓐ ⓑ ⓒ ⓓ
20. ⓐ ⓑ ⓒ ⓓ
21. ⓐ ⓑ ⓒ ⓓ
22. ⓐ ⓑ ⓒ ⓓ
23. ⓐ ⓑ ⓒ ⓓ
24. ⓐ ⓑ ⓒ ⓓ
25. ⓐ ⓑ ⓒ ⓓ
26. ⓐ ⓑ ⓒ ⓓ
27. ⓐ ⓑ ⓒ ⓓ
28. ⓐ ⓑ ⓒ ⓓ
29. ⓐ ⓑ ⓒ ⓓ
30. ⓐ ⓑ ⓒ ⓓ
31. ⓐ ⓑ ⓒ ⓓ
32. ⓐ ⓑ ⓒ ⓓ
33. ⓐ ⓑ ⓒ ⓓ
34. ⓐ ⓑ ⓒ ⓓ
35. ⓐ ⓑ ⓒ ⓓ
36. ⓐ ⓑ ⓒ ⓓ
37. ⓐ ⓑ ⓒ ⓓ
38. ⓐ ⓑ ⓒ ⓓ
39. ⓐ ⓑ ⓒ ⓓ
40. ⓐ ⓑ ⓒ ⓓ
41. ⓐ ⓑ ⓒ ⓓ
42. ⓐ ⓑ ⓒ ⓓ

SECTION 2: MATH

1. ⓐ ⓑ ⓒ ⓓ
2. ⓐ ⓑ ⓒ ⓓ
3. ⓐ ⓑ ⓒ ⓓ
4. ⓐ ⓑ ⓒ ⓓ
5. ⓐ ⓑ ⓒ ⓓ
6. ⓐ ⓑ ⓒ ⓓ
7. ⓐ ⓑ ⓒ ⓓ
8. ⓐ ⓑ ⓒ ⓓ
9. ⓐ ⓑ ⓒ ⓓ
10. ⓐ ⓑ ⓒ ⓓ
11. ⓐ ⓑ ⓒ ⓓ
12. ⓐ ⓑ ⓒ ⓓ
13. ⓐ ⓑ ⓒ ⓓ
14. ⓐ ⓑ ⓒ ⓓ
15. ⓐ ⓑ ⓒ ⓓ
16. ⓐ ⓑ ⓒ ⓓ
17. ⓐ ⓑ ⓒ ⓓ
18. ⓐ ⓑ ⓒ ⓓ
19. ⓐ ⓑ ⓒ ⓓ
20. ⓐ ⓑ ⓒ ⓓ
21. ⓐ ⓑ ⓒ ⓓ
22. ⓐ ⓑ ⓒ ⓓ
23. ⓐ ⓑ ⓒ ⓓ
24. ⓐ ⓑ ⓒ ⓓ
25. ⓐ ⓑ ⓒ ⓓ
26. ⓐ ⓑ ⓒ ⓓ
27. ⓐ ⓑ ⓒ ⓓ
28. ⓐ ⓑ ⓒ ⓓ
29. ⓐ ⓑ ⓒ ⓓ
30. ⓐ ⓑ ⓒ ⓓ
31. ⓐ ⓑ ⓒ ⓓ
32. ⓐ ⓑ ⓒ ⓓ
33. ⓐ ⓑ ⓒ ⓓ
34. ⓐ ⓑ ⓒ ⓓ
35. ⓐ ⓑ ⓒ ⓓ
36. ⓐ ⓑ ⓒ ⓓ
37. ⓐ ⓑ ⓒ ⓓ
38. ⓐ ⓑ ⓒ ⓓ
39. ⓐ ⓑ ⓒ ⓓ
40. ⓐ ⓑ ⓒ ⓓ
41. ⓐ ⓑ ⓒ ⓓ
42. ⓐ ⓑ ⓒ ⓓ
43. ⓐ ⓑ ⓒ ⓓ
44. ⓐ ⓑ ⓒ ⓓ
45. ⓐ ⓑ ⓒ ⓓ
46. ⓐ ⓑ ⓒ ⓓ
47. ⓐ ⓑ ⓒ ⓓ
48. ⓐ ⓑ ⓒ ⓓ

SECTION 3: WRITING PART A

1. ⓐ ⓑ ⓒ ⓓ
2. ⓐ ⓑ ⓒ ⓓ
3. ⓐ ⓑ ⓒ ⓓ
4. ⓐ ⓑ ⓒ ⓓ
5. ⓐ ⓑ ⓒ ⓓ
6. ⓐ ⓑ ⓒ ⓓ
7. ⓐ ⓑ ⓒ ⓓ
8. ⓐ ⓑ ⓒ ⓓ
9. ⓐ ⓑ ⓒ ⓓ
10. ⓐ ⓑ ⓒ ⓓ
11. ⓐ ⓑ ⓒ ⓓ
12. ⓐ ⓑ ⓒ ⓓ
13. ⓐ ⓑ ⓒ ⓓ
14. ⓐ ⓑ ⓒ ⓓ
15. ⓐ ⓑ ⓒ ⓓ
16. ⓐ ⓑ ⓒ ⓓ
17. ⓐ ⓑ ⓒ ⓓ
18. ⓐ ⓑ ⓒ ⓓ
19. ⓐ ⓑ ⓒ ⓓ
20. ⓐ ⓑ ⓒ ⓓ
21. ⓐ ⓑ ⓒ ⓓ
22. ⓐ ⓑ ⓒ ⓓ
23. ⓐ ⓑ ⓒ ⓓ
24. ⓐ ⓑ ⓒ ⓓ
25. ⓐ ⓑ ⓒ ⓓ
26. ⓐ ⓑ ⓒ ⓓ
27. ⓐ ⓑ ⓒ ⓓ
28. ⓐ ⓑ ⓒ ⓓ
29. ⓐ ⓑ ⓒ ⓓ
30. ⓐ ⓑ ⓒ ⓓ
31. ⓐ ⓑ ⓒ ⓓ
32. ⓐ ⓑ ⓒ ⓓ
33. ⓐ ⓑ ⓒ ⓓ
34. ⓐ ⓑ ⓒ ⓓ
35. ⓐ ⓑ ⓒ ⓓ
36. ⓐ ⓑ ⓒ ⓓ
37. ⓐ ⓑ ⓒ ⓓ
38. ⓐ ⓑ ⓒ ⓓ
39. ⓐ ⓑ ⓒ ⓓ
40. ⓐ ⓑ ⓒ ⓓ

▶ Section 1: Reading

Questions 1–6 are based on the following passage.

(1) The atmosphere forms a gaseous, protective envelope around Earth. It protects Earth from the cold of space, from harmful ultraviolet light, and from all but the largest meteors. After traveling over 93 million miles, solar energy strikes the atmosphere and Earth's surface, warming the planet and creating what is known as the biosphere, which is the region of Earth capable of sustaining life. Solar radiation, in combination with the planet's rotation, causes the atmosphere to circulate. Atmospheric circulation is one important reason that life on Earth can exist at higher latitudes because equatorial heat is transported poleward, moderating the climate.

(2) The equatorial region is the warmest part of the Earth because it receives the most direct, and therefore strongest, solar radiation. The plane in which the Earth revolves around the Sun is called the ecliptic. Earth's axis is inclined $23\frac{1}{2}$ degrees with respect to the ecliptic. This inclined axis is responsible for our changing seasons because, as seen from the Earth, the Sun oscillates back and forth across the equator in an annual cycle. About June 21 each year the Sun reaches the Tropic of Cancer, $23\frac{1}{2}$ degrees north latitude. This is the northernmost point where the Sun can be directly overhead. About December 21 of each year the Sun reaches the Tropic of Capricorn, $23\frac{1}{2}$ degrees south latitude. This is the southernmost point at which the Sun can be directly overhead. The polar regions are the coldest parts of the Earth because they receive the least direct, and therefore the weakest, solar radiation. Here solar radiation strikes at a very oblique angle and thus spreads the same amount of energy over a greater area than in the equatorial regions. A static envelope of air surrounding the Earth would produce an extremely hot, unlivable equatorial region while the polar regions would remain unlivably cold.

(3) The transport of water vapor in the atmosphere is an important mechanism by which heat energy is redistributed poleward. When water evaporates into the air and becomes water vapor it absorbs energy. At the equator, water vapor-saturated air rises high into the atmosphere where winds aloft carry it poleward. As this moist air approaches the polar regions, it cools and sinks back to Earth. At some point the water vapor condenses out of the air as rain or snow, releasing energy in the process. The now dry polar air flows back toward the equator to repeat the convection cycle. In this way, heat energy absorbed at the equator is deposited at the poles and the temperature gradient between these regions is reduced.

(4) The circulation of the atmosphere and the weather it generates is but one example of the many complex, interdependent events of nature. The web of life depends for its continued existence on the proper functioning of these natural mechanisms. Global warming, the hole in the atmosphere's ozone layer, and increasing air and water pollution pose serious, long-term threats to the biosphere. Given the high degree of nature's interconnectedness, it is quite possible that the most serious threats have yet to be recognized.

1. Which of the following best expresses the main idea of the passage?
   a. The circulation of atmosphere—now threatened by global warming, the hole in the ozone layer, and pollution—protects the biosphere and makes life on Earth possible.
   b. If the protective atmosphere around the Earth is too damaged by human activity, all life on Earth will cease.
   c. Life on Earth is the result of complex interdependent events of nature, events which are being interfered with at the current time by harmful human activity.
   d. The circulation of atmosphere is the single most important factor in keeping the biosphere alive, and it is constantly threatened by harmful human activity.

2. Which of the following best represents the organization of the passage?

   a. I.   definition and description of the circulation of the atmosphere

       II. how the atmosphere affects heat and water in the biosphere

      III. how the circulation of the atmosphere works

     IV. what will happen if human activity destroys the atmosphere and other life-sustaining mechanisms

   b. I.   origin of the atmosphere and ways it protects the biosphere

       II. how the circulation of the atmosphere affects the equator and the poles

      III. how the circulation of the atmosphere interrelates with other events in nature to protect life on Earth

     IV. threats to life in the biosphere

   c. I.   definition and description of the circulation of the atmosphere

       II. protective functions of the circulation of the atmosphere

      III. relationship of the circulation of the atmosphere to other life-sustaining mechanisms

     IV. threats to nature's interconnectedness in the biosphere

   d. I.   the journey of the atmosphere 93 million miles through space

       II. how the atmosphere circulates and protects the biosphere

      III. how the atmosphere interrelates with weather in the biosphere

     IV. how damage to the biosphere threatens life on Earth

3. Which of the following is the best definition of *biosphere* as it is used in the passage?

   a. the protective envelope formed by the atmosphere around the living Earth

   b. that part of the Earth and its atmosphere in which life can exist

   c. the living things on Earth whose existence is made possible by circulation of the atmosphere

   d. the circulation of the atmosphere's contribution to life on Earth

4. Which of the following sentences from the passage best supports the author's point that circulation of the atmosphere is vital to life on Earth?

   a. "The equatorial region is the warmest part of the Earth because it receives the most direct, and therefore strongest, solar radiation."

   b. "The circulation of the atmosphere and the weather it generates is but one example of the many complex, interdependent events of nature."

   c. "[The atmosphere] protects Earth from the cold of space, from harmful ultraviolet light, and from all but the largest meteors."

   d. "A static envelope of air surrounding the Earth would produce an unlivably hot equatorial region while the polar regions would remain unlivably cold."

5. Based on the passage, which of the following is directly responsible for all temperature changes on Earth?

   a. variations in the strength of solar radiation

   b. variations in the amount of ultraviolet light

   c. variation of biologic processes in the biosphere

   d. variation in global warming

6. The first paragraph of the passage deals mainly with which of the following effects of the atmosphere on the Earth?
a. its sheltering effect
b. its reviving effect
c. its invigorating effect
d. its cleansing effect

Questions 7–12 are based on the following passage.

(1) The coast of the State of Maine is one of the most _____ in the world. A straight line running from the southernmost city in Maine, Kittery, to the northernmost coastal city, Eastport, would measure about 225 miles. If you followed the coastline between the same two cities, you would travel more than ten times as far. This ruggedness is the result of what is called a "drowned coastline." The term comes from the glacial activity of the Ice Age. At that time, the whole area that is now Maine was part of a mountain range that towered above the sea. As the glacier descended, however, it expended enormous force on those mountains and they sank into the sea.

(2) As the mountains sank, ocean water charged over the lowest parts of the remaining land, forming a series of twisting inlets and lagoons, of contorted grottos and nooks. Once the glacier receded, the highest parts of the former mountain range that were nearest the shore remained as islands. Although the mountain ranges were never to return, the land rose somewhat over the centuries. On Mt. Desert Island, one of the most famous of the islands the glacier left behind in its retreat from the coast of Maine, marine fossils have been found at 225 feet above today's sea level, indicating that level was once the shoreline.

(3) The 2,500-mile-long rocky and jagged coastline of Maine keeps watch over nearly 2,000 islands. Many of these islands are tiny and uninhabited, but many are home to thriving communities.

Mt. Desert Island is one of the largest—sixteen miles long and nearly twelve miles wide—and one of the most beautiful of the Maine coast islands. Mt. Desert very nearly formed as two distinct islands. It is split almost in half by Somes Sound, a very deep and very narrow stretch of water seven miles long. On the east side of the island, Cadillac Mountain rises fifteen hundred and thirty two feet, making it the highest mountain on the Atlantic seaboard.

(4) For years, Mt. Desert Island, particularly its major settlement, Bar Harbor, afforded summer homes for the wealthy. Recently, Bar Harbor has made a name for itself as a burgeoning arts community as well. But there is much more to Mt. Desert Island than a sophisticated and wealthy playground. A majority of the island is unspoiled forest land, and it makes up the greatest part of Acadia National Park. Mt. Desert Island sits on the boundary line between the temperate and sub-Arctic zones. Therefore, the island supports the flora and fauna of both zones, as well as beach, inland, and alpine plants. And Mt. Desert Island lies in a major bird migration lane; all kinds of migratory birds pass over the island. All this is in addition to its geological treasures!

(5) The establishment of Acadia National Park in 1916 means that this diversity of nature will be preserved and that it will be available to all people, not just the wealthy who once had exclusive access to the island's natural beauty. Today, visitors to Acadia may receive nature instruction from the park naturalists, in addition to enjoying the beauty of the island by camping, hiking, cycling, or boating. Or, visitors may choose to spend time at the archeological museum, learning about the Stone Age inhabitants of the island. The best view on Mt. Desert Island, though, is from the top of Cadillac Mountain. From the summit, you can gaze back toward the mainland or out over the Atlantic Ocean and contemplate the beauty created by a retreating glacier.

7. Which of the following lists of topics best outlines the information in the passage?

  a.   I.   ice-age glacial activity
      II.   the Islands of Casco Bay
      III. formation of Cadillac Mountain
      IV.   summer residents of Mt. Desert Island

  b.   I.   formation of a drowned coastline
      II.   the topography of Mt. Desert Island
      III. the environment of Mt. Desert Island
      IV.   tourist attractions on Mt. Desert Island

  c.   I.   mapping the Maine coastline
      II.   the arts community at Bar Harbor
      III. history of the National Park system
      IV.   climbing Cadillac Mountain

  d.   I.   the effect of glaciers on small islands
      II.   stone-age dwellers on Mt. Desert Island
      III. the importance of bio-diversity
      IV.   hiking in Acadia National Park

8. Which of the following statements best expresses the main idea of paragraph 4 of the passage?
  a. The wealthy residents of Mt. Desert Island selfishly kept it to themselves.
  b. Acadia National Park is one of the smallest of the national parks.
  c. On Mt. Desert Island, there is great tension between the year-round residents and the summer tourists.
  d. Due to its location and environment, Mt. Desert Island supports incredibly diverse animal and plant life.

9. According to the passage, the large number of small islands along the coast of Maine are the result of
  a. glaciers forcing a mountain range into the sea.
  b. Maine's location between the temperate and sub-Arctic zones.
  c. the irregularity of the Maine coast.
  d. the need for summer communities for wealthy tourists and artists.

10. The content of paragraph 5 indicates that the writer believes that
  a. the continued existence of national parks is threatened by budget cuts.
  b. the best way to preserve the environment on Mt. Desert Island is to limit the number of visitors.
  c. national parks allow large numbers of people to visit and learn about interesting wilderness areas.
  d. Mt. Desert Island is the most interesting tourist attraction in Maine.

11. According to the passage, the coast of Maine is approximately
  a. 2,500 miles long.
  b. 2,000 miles long.
  c. 225 miles long.
  d. 235 miles long.

12. In the context of paragraph 1, which of the following words best fits in the blank?
  a. beautiful
  b. irregular
  c. hazardous
  d. well-traveled

Questions 13–17 are based on the following passage.

(1) Businesses today routinely use large amounts of both financial and non-financial information. Sales departments keep track of current and potential customers, marketing departments keep track of product details and regional demographics, and accounting departments keep track of financial data and issue reports. To be effective, this data must be organized into a meaningful and useful system. Such a system is called a management information system, abbreviated MIS. The financial hub of the MIS is the accounting information system.

(2) Accounting is the information system that records, analyzes, and reports economic transactions, enabling decision makers to make informed choices when allocating scarce economic resources. It is a tool that enables the user, whether a business entity or an individual, to make wiser, more informed economic choices. It is an aid to planning, controlling, and evaluating a broad range of activities. Bookkeeping, often confused with accounting, is actually a subset of accounting. It is the component of accounting that does the mechanical, repetitive record keeping; but it does not include the analysis or reporting of economic information. Modern accounting is usually separated into either managerial accounting or financial accounting. A managerial accounting system is intended only for internal use by management. The primary guideline for implementing a managerial accounting system is that the information must be "useful." A financial accounting system is intended for use by both management and those outside the organization. Because it is important that financial accounting reports be interpreted correctly, financial accounting is subject to a set of _____ guidelines called "generally accepted accounting principles" (GAAP).

(3) Accounting is based on the double-entry system of bookkeeping that originated during the Renaissance. Fundamental to the double-entry system is the concept of duality. All economic events have two components that offset and thus balance each other: cost and benefit, work and reward, asset and equity, debit and credit. Business transactions are the building blocks of the accounting system. In order to properly record transactions they must be measured with a common yardstick. Money is the measure of all business transactions and is the link which enables economic data to be compared. There are three basic criteria for measuring a business transaction: a) When is the transaction recognized? Traditionally, a transaction is recognized when legal title passes from seller to buyer and an obligation to pay results. b) What is the value of a transaction?

Value is generally agreed to be the original cost of a good or service. c) How is a transaction to be classified? Correct classification places information about the transaction into the proper account for storage and later use. A simple account has three parts: a title and two columns. The left column is called the "debit" column. The right column is called the "credit" column. A debit could represent an increase or a decrease to the account, depending on how the account is classified. The same is true for a credit.

(4) Although records of the exchange of goods and services have existed for centuries, it was the creation of the double-entry system of accounting that enabled the development of the modern, highly sophisticated methods of business control and administration in use today.

13. This passage is most likely taken from
   a. a newspaper column.
   b. an essay about modern business.
   c. a legal brief.
   d. a business textbook.

14. The word that would best fit into the blank in the final sentence of the second paragraph is
   a. discretionary.
   b. convenient.
   c. austere.
   d. stringent.

15. According to the information in the passage, which of the following is LEAST likely to be a function of accounting?
   a. helping business people make sound judgments
   b. producing reports of many different kinds of transactions
   c. assisting with the marketing of products
   d. assisting companies in important planning activities

16. The word *debit* as it is used in the third paragraph of the passage most nearly means
  a. losses in a transaction.
  b. an increase or decrease to the account.
  c. a decrease to the account only.
  d. an expenditure which lessens the amount in the account.

17. The main purpose of paragraph 3 is to
  a. define *duality* as it relates to business transactions.
  b. describe the double-entry system in keeping track of financial transactions.
  c. describe the common yardstick used to measure financial transactions.
  d. outline the evolution of the double-entry system since the Renaissance.

Questions 18–24 are based on the following passage.

(1) Light pollution is a growing problem worldwide. Like other forms of pollution, light pollution degrades the quality of the environment. Our ability to see and appreciate the night sky is being steadily diminished by the ever-increasing use of inappropriate night lighting. Where once it was possible to look up at the night sky and see thousands of stars twinkling in the blackness, one now sees little more than the yellow glare of urban sky glow.

(2) A basic component of light pollution is glare. Glare occurs when light from a bright source shines directly into the eyes. It is usually caused by an unshielded, or improperly shielded, light source. It can make driving on rainy, slick streets very hazardous. Glare that crosses property boundaries and creates a nuisance, is called "light trespass." Light trespass is becoming an important issue in many suburban and rural communities because of the increasing use of cheap, improperly shielded, 175-watt, dusk-to-dawn mercury vapor light fixtures. Typically, they are installed in an effort to improve home security, on the theory that more light equals

more safety. This is a false belief for two important reasons. First, the excessively bright light creates deep shadows, perfect hiding places for criminals. _____, the light showcases one's possessions and reveals the layout of the property, _____ inviting theft. The combined effect of glare from all urban sources creates "sky glow," that yellowish white glow seen in the urban night sky. This is a very recent phenomena in the history of mankind, beginning with Thomas Edison's invention of the incandescent light bulb. Before this invention, cities were illuminated first by torches and then by gaslight, neither of which contributed much to the overall brightening of the night sky.

(3) Not only is light pollution a nuisance but it is also harmful to life forms whose rhythms depend on celestial events. Birds migrating at night use stars to navigate and can become lost when flying through a heavily light polluted region that obscures their vision of the night sky. Newly hatched sea turtles have become confused by the urban glow of a nearby coastal city and instead of moving toward the sea's luminance, crawl toward the city's glow and their death. The circadian rhythms of plants and animals are also affected by a twenty-four-hours-a-day regimen of light. Birds that normally sing at dawn can now be heard singing in the middle of the urban night. Plants will retain their leaves longer near a strong night light and thus will not be properly prepared for the arrival of winter.

(4) When we lose the ability to connect visually with the vastness of the universe by looking up at the night sky, we lose our connection with something profoundly important to the human spirit, our sense of wonder. Fortunately, this situation does not have to be. Unlike other forms of pollution where it may take years to repair the damage, light pollution disappears immediately when corrective action is taken. In the long run, it is cheaper to install and maintain quality lighting that does not waste energy by shining light that is too bright, where it is not needed, and where it is not wanted.

18. The passage implies that the most serious damage done by light pollution is to our
   a. artistic appreciation.
   b. sense of physical well-being.
   c. cultural advancement.
   d. spiritual selves.

19. According to the passage, light trespass is increasingly a problem
   a. for criminals who are hiding in the shadows.
   b. in suburban and rural areas.
   c. in rainy weather.
   d. for migrating birds.

20. Which of the following words or phrases, if inserted into the blanks in the passage, would help the reader understand the sequence of the author's ideas?
   a. Second . . . thus
   b. Then . . . finally
   c. Therefore . . . as a result
   d. On the other hand . . . still

21. The author's main purpose in writing this passage is to
   a. explain why bright exterior lights do not deter burglars.
   b. describe the circadian rhythms of plants and animals.
   c. highlight the growing problem of light pollution.
   d. review the history of the electric light.

22. Which of the following statements from the passage indicate the writer's opinion, rather than fact?
   a. Glare that crosses property boundaries and creates a nuisance is called "light trespass."
   b. Not only is light pollution a nuisance but it is also harmful to life forms whose rhythms depend on celestial events.
   c. Unlike other forms of pollution, the damage of which may take years to repair, light pollution disappears immediately when corrective action is taken.
   d. When we lose the ability to connect visually with the night sky, we lose our connection with something profoundly important to the human spirit.

23. The passage maintains that light pollution can be dangerous to species other than human beings because it tends to hide
   a. the stars.
   b. predators.
   c. food sources.
   d. places of shelter.

Questions 24–29 are based on the following passage.

(1) The Sami are an indigenous people living in the northern parts of Norway, Sweden, Finland, and Russia's Kola peninsula. Their traditional homelands once extended well onto the Scandinavian peninsula, but the pressure of increased colonization, mining operations, logging, and the construction of hydroelectric power plants have pushed the Sami steadily north until today they are mostly found north of the Arctic Circle. The Sami are more commonly known as "Lapps" and their homeland is often called "Lapland." However, they object to being called "Lapps" and consider this to be a derogatory term because the word *lapp* means "a

patch of cloth used for mending." This implies that the Sami wear patched clothing and therefore that they are poor people.

(2) There are several theories which seek to explain the Sami's origin but none have been proven conclusively. One theory is that the Sami belong to a much larger indigenous group of "circumpolar tribes" who inhabit the northernmost part of Europe and Asia. These circumpolar tribes once had similar hunter/gatherer lifestyles and cultures. However, the arrival of other peoples using firearms, a more efficient hunting method, greatly reduced the population of wild reindeer herds and other game on which these circumpolar tribes depended. In order to survive, some of these native peoples became herders of reindeer, others became fishermen, and still others adopted the ways of the newcomers and became farmers. Another theory of Sami origin is that they are the descendants of reindeer hunters who immigrated up from the south. Proponents of a third theory believe the Sami have inhabited the Scandinavian peninsula since before the last Ice Age and lived in warmer coastal areas during this glacial period. The latter theory is supported by genetic studies that conclude the Sami have lived in isolation from other European peoples for tens of thousands of years.

(3) Generally, there are three categories of Sami. The Forest Sami are semi-nomadic and live by hunting and fishing in coniferous forests. They make limited use of reindeer for transportation and fur. Most of the Swedish and Finnish Sami belong to this group. The Sea Sami, who live on Norway's northern coast, are also semi-nomadic, hunting in winter and fishing on the sea in summer. The Reindeer Sami, who are nomads and make extensive use of reindeer, tend their herds in the northern regions of Sweden and Norway. Although this group is regarded as the most typical form of Sami culture, it is, in fact, not as common as the Forest Sami culture.

(4) Originally, the Sami religion was _____, which means nature and natural objects have a conscious life, a spirit. One is expected to move quietly in the wilderness and avoid making a disturbance out of courtesy to these spirits. Ghengis Khan is said to have declared that the Sami were one people he would never try to fight again. Since the Sami were not warriors and didn't believe in war, they simply disappeared in times of conflict. They were known as "peaceful retreaters." Even though the Sami today are struggling to preserve their cultural identity and way of life, there is hope, for, as one Sami is quoted as saying, "We adapt our ways to fit the times."

24. Which of the following words would best fit into the blank in paragraph 4?
   a. superstitious
   b. fallacious
   c. fictitious
   d. animistic

25. Based on the tone of the passage, which of the following words best describes the author's attitude toward the Sami people?
   a. admiring
   b. pitying
   c. contemptuous
   d. patronizing

26. Which of the following is NOT a reason for the Sami people moving steadily north?
   a. increased colonization
   b. government relocation policy
   c. mining operations
   d. hydroelectric power plants

27. According to the passage, indigenous people living in the northern parts of Norway, Sweden, Finland, and Russia's Kola peninsula prefer to be called
   a. Lapps.
   b. Scandinavians.
   c. Sami.
   d. Laplanders.

28. It can be inferred from the passage that the Sami were known as "peaceful retreaters" because they
   a. were afraid of foreign invaders.
   b. were not citizens of any country and therefore could not be drafted.
   c. refused to learn to use modern weapons and so were easily defeated.
   d. would simply disappear in wartime.

29. Which of the following is NOT a category of the Sami people?
   a. the Forest Sami
   b. the Sea Sami
   c. the Mountain Sami
   d. the Reindeer Sami

Questions 30–35 are based on the following passage.

(1) Milton Hershey was born near the small village of Derry Church, Pennsylvania, in 1857. It was a _____ beginning that did not foretell his later popularity. Milton only attended school through the fourth grade; at that point, he was apprenticed to a printer in a nearby town. Fortunately for all chocolate lovers, Milton did not excel as a printer. After a while, he left the printing business and was apprenticed to a candy maker in Lancaster, Pennsylvania. It was apparent he had found his calling in life and, at the age of eighteen, he opened his own candy store in Philadelphia. In spite of his talents as a candy maker, the shop failed after six years.

(2) It may come as a surprise to Milton Hershey's fans today that his first candy success came with the manufacture of caramel. After the failure of his Philadelphia store, Milton headed for Denver, where he learned the art of making caramels. There he took a job with a local manufacturer who insisted on using fresh milk in making his caramels; Milton saw that this made the caramels especially tasty. After a time in Denver, Milton once again attempted to open his own candy-making businesses, in Chicago, New Orleans, and New York City. Finally,

in 1886, he went to Lancaster, Pennsylvania, where he raised the money necessary to try again. This company—the Lancaster Caramel Company—made Milton's reputation as a master candy maker.

(3) In 1893, Milton attended the Chicago International Exposition, where he saw a display of German chocolate-making implements. Captivated by the equipment, he purchased it for his Lancaster candy factory and began producing chocolate, which he used for coating his caramels. By the next year, production had grown to include cocoa, sweet chocolate, and baking chocolate. The Hershey Chocolate company was born in 1894 as a subsidiary of the Lancaster Caramel Company. Six years later, Milton sold the caramel company, but retained the rights, and the equipment, to make chocolate. He believed that a large market of chocolate consumers was waiting for someone to produce reasonably priced candy. He was right.

(4) Milton Hershey returned to the village where he had been born, in the heart of dairy country, and opened his chocolate manufacturing plant. With access to all the fresh milk he needed, he began producing the finest milk chocolate. The plant that opened in a small Pennsylvania village in 1905 is today the largest chocolate factory in the world. The confections created at this facility are favorites in the United States and internationally.

(5) The area where the factory is located is now known as Hershey, Pennsylvania. Within the first decades of its existence, the town of Hershey thrived, as did the chocolate business. A bank, a school, churches, a department store, even a park and a trolley system all appeared in short order; the town soon even had a zoo. Today, a visit to the area reveals the Hershey Medical Center, Milton Hershey School, and Hershey's Chocolate World, a theme park where visitors are greeted by a giant Reese's Peanut Butter Cup. All of these things—and a huge number of happy chocolate lovers—were made possible because a caramel maker visited the Chicago Exposition of 1893!

30. According to information contained in the passage, the reader can infer which of the following?

    a. Chocolate is popular in every country in the world.

    b. Reese's Peanut Butter Cups are manufactured by the Hershey Chocolate Company.

    c. Chocolate had never been manufactured in the U.S. before Milton Hershey did it.

    d. The Hershey Chocolate Company now makes more money from Hershey's Chocolate World than from the manufacture and sale of chocolate.

31. Which of the following best defines the word *subsidiary* as used in paragraph 3?

    a. a company owned entirely by one person

    b. a company founded to support another company

    c. a company that is not incorporated

    d. a company controlled by another company

32. The writer's main purpose in this passage is to

    a. recount the founding of the Hershey Chocolate Company.

    b. describe the process of manufacturing chocolate.

    c. compare the popularity of chocolate to other candies.

    d. explain how apprenticeships work.

33. According to the passage, Milton Hershey sold his caramel company in

    a. 1894.

    b. 1900.

    c. 1904.

    d. 1905.

34. The mention of the Chicago International Exposition of 1893 in the passage indicates that

    a. the exposition in Chicago is held once every three years.

    b. the theme of the exposition of 1893 was "Food from Around the World."

    c. the exposition contained displays from a variety of countries.

    d. the site of the exposition is now a branch of the Hershey Chocolate Company.

35. Which of the following words best fits in the blank in paragraph 1 of the passage?

    a. dramatic

    b. modest

    c. undignified

    d. rewarding

Questions 36–42 are based on the following passage.

(1) Scientists have developed (a/an) _____ procedure that reveals details of tissues and organs that are difficult to see by conventional magnetic resonance imaging (MRI). By using "hyperpolarized" gases, scientists have taken the first clear MRI pictures of human lungs and airways. Researchers hope the new technique will aid the diagnosis and treatment of lung disorders, and perhaps lead to improved visualization of blood flow.

    (2) The air spaces of the lungs have been notoriously difficult for clinicians to visualize. Chest X rays can detect tumors or inflamed regions in the lungs but provide poor soft-tissue contrast and no clear view of air passages. Computed-tomography, a cross-sectional X ray scan, can provide high resolution images of the walls of the lungs and its airways but gives no measure of function. Conventional MRI, because it images water protons, provides poor images of the lungs, which are filled with air, not water.

(3) The new MRI technique detects not water, but inert gases whose nuclei have been strongly aligned, or hyperpolarized, by laser light. Initially this technique seemed to have no practical application, but exhaustive research has proven its potential. Scientists plan to further refine this technology with animal and human studies, in part because they have yet to produce a viable three-dimensional image of human lungs.

(4) By 1995 researchers had produced the first three-dimensional MRI pictures of a living animal's lungs. In the first human test, a member of the research team inhaled hyperpolarized helium-3. His lungs were then imaged using a standard MRI scanner that had been adjusted to detect helium. The results were impressive, considering that the system had yet to be optimized and there was only a relatively small volume of gas with which to work.

(5) When a standard MRI is taken, the patient enters a large magnet. Many of the body's hydrogen atoms (primarily the hydrogen atoms in water) align with the magnetic field like tiny bar magnets, and the nucleus at the center of each atom spins constantly about its north-south axis. Inside the MRI scanner, a radio pulse temporarily knocks the spinning nuclei out of position, and as their axes gradually realign within the magnetic field, they emit faint radio signals. Computers convert these faint signals into an image.

(6) The new gas-based MRI is built around similar principles. But circularly polarized light, rather than a magnet, is used to align spinning nuclei, and the inert gases helium-3 or xenon-129 (rather than hydrogen) provide the nuclei that emit the image-producing signals. The laser light polarizes the gases through a technique known as spin exchange. Helium-3 and xenon-129 are ideal for gas-based MRI because they take hours to lose their polarization. Most other gases readily lose their alignment. The clarity of an MRI picture depends in part on the volume of aligned nuclei.

36. The MRI innovation is different from the standard MRI in that it
   a. distinguishes gases rather than water.
   b. uses magnets rather than light.
   c. has a range of useful applications.
   d. provides better images of blood circulation.

37. The inability to generate satisfactory images of air routes is a deficiency of
   a. computed tomography.
   b. the spin exchange process.
   c. three-dimensional pictures.
   d. X rays.

38. MRIs transmit radio signals
   a. before nuclei rotate on an axis.
   b. before atoms align with magnets.
   c. after nuclei are aligned by magnetism.
   d. after signals are transformed into pictures.

39. The word that can best be interchanged with *hyperpolarization* in the passage is
   a. visualization.
   b. alignment.
   c. emission.
   d. tomography.

40. The use of which of the following is substituted for the use of a magnet in one of the MRI techniques?
   a. light
   b. hydrogen
   c. helium-3
   d. X rays

41. An image lacking in clarity is likely to be the result of
   a. a high number of aligned nuclei.
   b. hydrogen being replaced with xenon.
   c. an abbreviated period of alignment.
   d. nuclei regaining their aligned position.

42. Which of the following words would fit best in the blank in the first paragraph of the passage?
   a. explicit
   b. costly
   c. innovative
   d. clever

▶ Section 2: Mathematics

1. A company makes several items, including filing cabinets. One-third of their business consists of filing cabinets, and 60% of their filing cabinets are sold to businesses. What percent of their total business consists of filing cabinets sold to businesses?

$1/3 \times 0.60 = 0.20$

   a. 20%
   b. 33%
   c. 40%
   d. 60%

2. If the speed of light in air is 3.00×10^8 meters per second, how far would a beam of light travel in 2,000 seconds?
   a. 1.50×10^5 meters
   b. 6.00×10^5 meters
   c. 1.50×10^{11} meters
   d. 6.00×10^{11} meters

3. Lefty keeps track of each length of the fish that he catches. Below are the lengths in inches of the fish that he caught one day:
   12, 13, 8, 10, 8, 9, 17
   What is the median fish length that Lefty caught that day?
   a. 8 inches
   b. 10 inches
   c. 11 inches
   d. 12 inches

Questions 4 and 5 are based on the following graph.

Rainfall 2002–2004

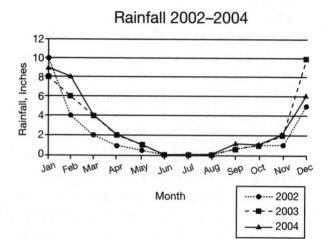

4. According to the graph, what month in 2003 had the most rainfall?
   a. January
   b. February
   c. November
   d. December

5. What was the average (mean) rainfall in February for the three years?
   a. 4 inches
   b. 5 inches
   c. 6 inches
   d. 7 inches

6. The Chen family traveled 75 miles to visit relatives. If they traveled $43\frac{1}{3}$ miles before they stopped at a gas station, how far was the gas station from their relatives' house?
   a. $31\frac{2}{3}$ miles
   b. $32\frac{2}{3}$ miles
   c. 35 miles
   d. $38\frac{1}{3}$ miles

7. Julie counts the cars passing her house, and finds that 2 of every 5 cars are foreign. If she counts for an hour, and 60 cars pass, how many of them are likely to be domestic?

a. 12
b. 24
c. 30
d. 36

$$\frac{3}{5} \times 60 = \frac{180}{5}$$

$$\begin{array}{r} 60 \\ \times 3 \\ \hline 180 \end{array}$$

8. A steel beam 15 feet long is cut into 4 pieces. The first piece consists of $\frac{1}{3}$ of the beam, the second is $\frac{1}{6}$ of the beam, and the third piece is $\frac{1}{10}$ of the beam. How long is the remaining piece of the beam?

a. $1\frac{1}{2}$ feet
b. $2\frac{1}{2}$ feet
c. 6 feet
d. 9 feet

5   9
2.5
1.5   6

9. A bag of jellybeans contains 8 black beans, 10 green beans, 3 yellow beans, and 9 orange beans. What is the probability of selecting either a yellow or an orange bean?

a. $\frac{1}{10}$
b. $\frac{2}{5}$
c. $\frac{4}{15}$
d. $\frac{3}{10}$

$$\frac{12}{30} = \frac{6}{15} = \frac{2}{5}$$

$$\begin{array}{r} 15 \\ 2\overline{\smash{\big)}30} \\ \underline{-2} \\ 10 \end{array}$$

10. Dimitri has 40 math problems to do for homework. If he does 40% of the assignment in one hour, how long will it take for Dimitri to complete the whole assignment?

a. 1.5 hours
b. 2.0 hours
c. 2.5 hours
d. 4.0 hours

$$2.5$$
$$16\overline{\smash{\big)}340}$$
$$\begin{array}{r} 32 \\ \hline 80 \\ 80 \\ \hline 0 \end{array}$$

Question 11 is based on the following table.

STEVE'S BIRDWATCHING PROJECT

DAY	NUMBER OF RAPTORS SEEN
Monday	
Tuesday	7
Wednesday	12
Thursday	11
Friday	4
Mean	8

11. The table above shows the data Steve collected while watching birds for one week. How many raptors did Steve see on Monday?

a. 6
b. 8
c. 10
d. 12

$$\begin{array}{r} 8 \\ \times 5 \\ \hline 40 \end{array}$$

$$40 - 34 = 6$$

12. Which of the following numbers is NOT between −0.02 and 1.02?

a. −0.15
b. −0.015
c. 0
d. 0.02

Question 13 is based on the following table.

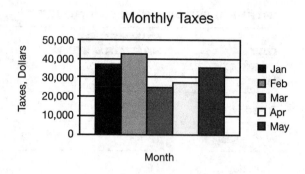

Monthly Taxes

13. What were the total taxes collected for January, February, and April?
- **a.** $78,000
- **b.** $98,000
- **c.** $105,000
- **d.** $115,000

38,000
41,000°
+ 26,000
105,000

Question 14 is based on the following table.

BLUE ROUTE BUS SCHEDULE

	DEPOT	WASHINGTON ST.
Bus 1	6:00	6:53
Bus 2	6:30	7:23
Bus 3	7:00	7:53
Bus 4	7:20	
Bus 5	7:40	8:33

14. According to the table, what time is Bus 4 scheduled to arrive at Washington Street?
- **a.** 8:03
- **b.** 8:10
- **c.** 8:13
- **d.** 8:18

15. Membership dues at Arnold's Gym are $53 per month this year, but were $50 per month last year. What was the percent increase in the gym's prices?
- **a.** 5.5%
- **b.** 6.0%
- **c.** 6.5%
- **d.** 7.0%

Question 16 is based on the following diagram.

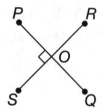

16. In the figure, angle *POS* measures 90 degrees. What is the measure of angle *ROQ*?
- **a.** 30 degrees
- **b.** 45 degrees
- **c.** 90 degrees
- **d.** 180 degrees

Questions 17–19 are based on the following graph of wildfire trends.

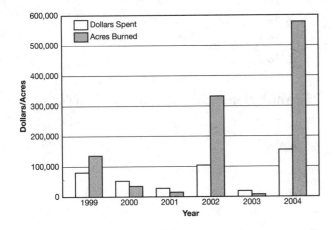

Questions 20–22 are based on the following graph, which compares the average annual rainfall with the actual rainfall for one year in a particular city.

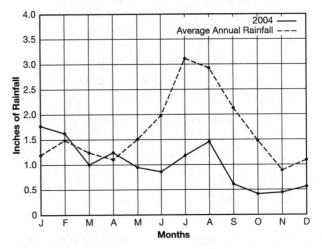

17. According to the graph, in which of the following years were the fewest acres burned?
   a. 2000
   b. 2001
   c. 2002
   d. 2003

18. According to the graph, about how much money was spent fighting wildfires during 2002?
   a. $ 90,000
   b. $100,000
   c. $110,000
   d. $300,000

19. According to the graph, in which of the following years was the cost per acre of fighting wildfires the lowest?
   a. 2001
   b. 2002
   c. 2003
   d. 2004

20. According to the graph, in which of the following months during 2004 was the rainfall nearest normal?
   a. April
   b. May
   c. June
   d. July

21. What is the average rainfall amount for the month of September?
   a. 0.5 inches
   b. 0.7 inches
   c. 2.0 inches
   d. 2.1 inches

22. During 2004, how many months had above-average rainfall amounts?
   a. 2
   b. 3
   c. 6
   d. 9

23. Which of these has a 9 in the thousandths place?
a. 3.00950 *(circled)*
b. 3.09050
c. 3.90050
d. 3.00590

24. James has a length of rope that he measures with a yardstick to be 28 inches long. By laying the yardstick end-to-end with the rope, what is the longest distance that he can measure accurately?
a. 28 inches
b. 36 inches
c. 50 inches
d. 64 inches *(circled)*

handwritten: 36 < yardstick   28 + 36 = 64

25. The number of red blood corpuscles in one cubic millimeter is about 5,000,000 and the number of white blood corpuscles in one cubic millimeter is about 8,000. What, then, is the ratio of white blood corpuscles to red blood corpuscles?
a. 1:400
b. 1:625 *(circled)*
c. 1:40
d. 4:10

handwritten: 5,000,000 : 8,000   8 : 5,000   1 : 625

26. A piece of ribbon 3 feet 4 inches long was divided in 5 equal parts. How long was each part?
a. 11 inches
b. 10 inches
c. 9 inches
d. 8 inches *(circled)*

handwritten: 36 + 4 = 40   5 | 40 - 40 = 0 → 8

27. If candy bars cost $0.40 and soft drinks cost $0.50, what is the cost of four candy bars and three soft drinks?
a. $2.10
b. $2.30
c. $2.60
d. $3.10 *(circled)*

handwritten: $1.60 + $1.50 = $3.10

28. What is 56.73647 rounded to the nearest hundredth?
a. 100
b. 57
c. 56.7
d. 56.74 *(circled)*

29. Which of the following is between $\frac{1}{3}$ and $\frac{1}{4}$?
a. $\frac{1}{2}$
b. $\frac{1}{5}$
c. $\frac{2}{3}$
d. $\frac{2}{7}$ *(circled)*

30. The population of Smithtown increases at a rate of 3% annually. If the population is currently 2,500, what will the population be at the same time next year?
a. 2,530
b. 2,560
c. 2,575 *(circled)*
d. 2,800

handwritten: 2,500 × .03   7500 + 0000 = 75.00   2,500 + 75 = 2,575

31. How many feet of ribbon will a theatrical company need to tie off a performance area that is 34 feet long and 20 feet wide?
a. 54
b. 68
c. 88
d. 108 *(circled)*

handwritten: 2L + 2w   40   34(2) + 20(2) = 108

32. A university has 36,042 total students. Of these students, 16,534 are male. Approximately how many more women attend the university than men?
a. 1,500
b. 2,000
c. 3,000 *(circled)*
d. 4,000

handwritten: 36,042 - 16,534 = 19,508   19,500 - 16,500 = 3,000

33. A machine on a production line produces parts that are not acceptable by company standards 4% of the time. If the machine produces 500 parts, how many will be defective?

a. 4
b. 10
c. 16
d. 20 (circled)

34. About how many liters of water will a 5-gallon container hold? (1 liter = 1.06 quarts)

a. 5
b. 11
c. 19 (circled)
d. 20

35. Nationwide, in one year there were about 21,500 residential fires associated with furniture. Of these, 11,350 were caused by smoking materials. About what percent of the residential furniture fires were smoking-related?

a. 47%
b. 49%
c. 50%
d. 53% (circled)

$$\frac{11,350}{21,500} = \frac{x}{100}$$
$$1135000 = 21,500 x$$
$$x = 52.79$$

36. Rashaard went fishing six days in the month of June. He caught 11, 4, 0, 5, 4, and 6 fish respectively. On the days that Rashaard fished, what was his average catch?

a. 4
b. 5 (circled)
c. 6
d. 7

$$\frac{a}{b} = \frac{x}{100}$$
b = total
a = derivative

37. Jerry was $\frac{1}{3}$ as young as his grandfather 15 years ago. If the sum of their ages is 110, how old is Jerry's grandfather?

a. 80
b. 75 (circled)
c. 65
d. 60

$110 = J + G$ $J = 110 - G$
$J - 15 = \frac{1}{3}(G - 15)$
$110 - G - 15 = \frac{1}{3}G - 5$
$100 = \frac{4}{3}G$ $G = 75$

38. Solve for x in the following equation: $\frac{1}{3}x + 3 = 8$.

a. 33
b. 15 (circled)
c. 11
d. 3

$\frac{1}{3}x + 3 = 8$
$\frac{1}{3}x = 5$
$x = 15$

39. Which of the following is a simplification of $\frac{(x^2 + 4x + 4)}{(x + 2)}$?

a. $x - 2$
b. $x + 4$
c. $x^2 + 3x + 2$
d. $x + 2$ (circled)

$\frac{(x + 2)(x + 2)}{(x + 2)}$

40. A line passes through the points (0,−1) and (2,3). What is the equation for the line?

a. $y = \frac{1}{2}x - 1$
b. $y = \frac{1}{2}x + 1$
c. $y = 2x - 1$
d. $y = 2x + 1$ (circled)

$\frac{y_2 - y_1}{x_2 - x_1} = \frac{3 + 1}{2 - 0} = \frac{4}{2} = 2$
$y + 1 = 2(x - 0)$
$y = 2x + 1$

41. What is the slope of the line passing through (4,2) and (−2,−1)?

a. $\frac{1}{2}$ (circled)
b. $-\frac{1}{2}$
c. 2
d. −2

$\frac{y_2 - y_1}{x_2 - x_1} = \frac{-1 - 2}{-2 - 4} = \frac{3}{6} = \frac{1}{2}$

42. Which of the following is a solution to
$3x^2 + 9x + 9$?

a. 3

b. 2

c. $3 \pm \sqrt{\frac{(-3)}{2}}$

d. $3 \pm \sqrt{\frac{3}{2}}$

$x = \dfrac{9 \pm \sqrt{9^2 - 4(3)(9)}}{2(3)}$

$x = 9 \pm 3\sqrt{(-3)}$ over 2

43. Which of the following values should be placed in each set of parentheses below in order to solve the equation by completing the square?
$x^2 + 4x + (?) = 7 + (?)$

a. –4

b. 2

c. –2

d. 4

$\dfrac{4}{2} = 2$

$2^2 = 4$

Question 44 is based on the following graph.

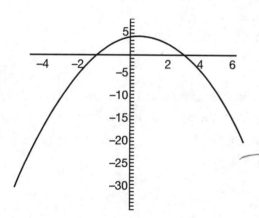

44. Which equation is represented by the graph above?

a. $y = -x^2 + 2x + 4$

b. $y = -x^2 + 2x - 4$

c. $y = x^2 + 2x + 4$

d. $y = x^2 + 2x - 4$

Question 45 is based on the following graph.

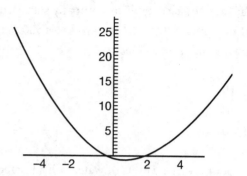

45. Which of the following inequalities is represented by the graph above?

a. $y \geq x^2 + 2$

b. $y \geq x^2 - 2$

c. $y \geq x^2 + 2x$

d. $y \geq x^2 - 2x$

46. If $f(x) = 3x^2 - \frac{1}{2}x + 7$, what is $f(\frac{1}{2})$?

a. $\frac{15}{2}$

b. $\frac{-15}{2}$

c. 8

d. $\frac{17}{2}$

47. What is the value of y when $x = 3$ and $y = 5 + 4x$?

a. 6

b. 9

c. 12

d. 17

$y = 5 + 4(3) = 17$

48. After three days, a group of hikers discovers that they have used $\frac{2}{5}$ of their supplies. At this rate, how many more days can they go forward before they have to turn around?

a. 0.75 days

b. 1.5 days

c. 3.75 days

d. 4.5 days

► Section 3: Writing (Part A— Multiple-Choice)

Questions 1–3 are based on the following passage.

(1) Greyhound racing is the sixth most popular spectator sport in the United States. (2) Over the last decade, a growing number of racers have been adopted to live out retirement as household pets, once their racing career is over.

(3) Many people hesitate to adopt a retired racing greyhound because they think only very old dogs are available. (4) People also worry that the greyhound will be more nervous and active than other breeds and will need a large space to run. (5) _____. (6) In fact, racing greyhounds are put up for adoption at a young age; even champion racers, who have the longest careers, only work until they are about three-and-a-half years old. (7) Since greyhounds usually live to be 12–15 years old, their retirement is much longer than their racing careers. (8) Far from being nervous dogs, greyhounds have naturally sweet, mild dispositions, and, while they love to run, they are sprinters rather than distance runners and are sufficiently exercised with a few laps around a fenced-in backyard everyday.

(9) Greyhounds do not make good watchdogs, but they are very good with children, get along well with other dogs (and usually cats as well), and are very affectionate and loyal. (10) A retired racing greyhound is a wonderful pet for almost anyone.

1. Which part, if inserted in the blank space labeled Part 5, would best help to focus the writer's argument in the second paragraph?
   a. Even so, greyhounds are placid dogs.
   b. These worries are based on false impressions and are easily dispelled.
   c. Retired greyhounds do not need race tracks to keep in shape.
   d. However, retired greyhounds are too old to need much exercise.

2. Which of the following changes is needed in the first paragraph?
   a. Part 2: Change *growing* to *increasing*.
   b. Part 2: Change *their* to *there*.
   c. Part 1: Change *is* to *was*.
   d. Part 2: Change *have* to *has*.

3. Which of the following parts, if added between Parts 9 and 10 of the third paragraph, would be most consistent with the writer's purpose, tone, and intended audience?
   a. Former racing dogs make up approximately 0.36% of all dogs owned as domestic pets in the United States.
   b. Despite the fact that greyhounds make excellent domestic pets, there are still a large number of former racers who have not been adopted.
   c. Good-natured and tolerant dogs, greyhounds speedily settle into any household, large or small; they are equally at ease in an apartment or a private home.
   d. It is imperative that people overcome the common myths they harbor about greyhounds that are preventing them from adopting these gentle dogs.

Questions 4–6 are based on the following passage.

(1) Following a recent series of arson fires in public-housing buildings, the mayor of Crasonville has decided to expand the city's Community Patrol, made up of 18- to 21-year-olds, to about 400 people. (2) The Community Patrol has been an important part of the city's efforts to reduce the number of arson crimes.

(3) In addition to the expanded patrol, the city also has decided to reduce the seriousness of these fires, most often set in stairwells, by stripping the paint from the stairwell walls. (4) Fed by the thick layers of oil-based paint, these arson fires race up the stairwells at an alarming speed. (5) Fire retardant

failed to work in almost all cases. (6) When the city attempted to control the speed of these fires by covering walls with a flame retardant. (7) In the most recent fire, the flames raced up ten stories after the old paint under the newly applied fire retardant ignited. (8) Because the retardant failed to stop the flames, the city has decided to stop applying it and will now strip the stairwells down to the bare walls.

4. Which part in the second paragraph is not standard written English?
   a. Part 8
   b. Part 6
   c. Part 5
   d. Part 7

5. Which of the following changes should be made to Part 3 of the passage?
   a. Remove the word *also*.
   b. Change *patrol* to *patrols*.
   c. Change *has decided* to *decided*.
   d. Remove the word *these*.

6. Which of the following parts, if inserted between Part 2 and Part 3 of the passage, would best develop the ideas in the first paragraph?
   a. The Community Patrol keeps up a twenty-four hour a day watch of derelict buildings in four of the city's boroughs.
   b. The additional Community Patrol members effectively increases the Patrol's size by 25 percent.
   c. The Community Patrol has already reduced arson fires by 20% in certain neighborhoods; increasing the Patrol numbers will allow the city to extend this protection to all city boroughs.
   d. The increase in the Community Patrol also helps to lower unemployment among Crasonville's youth; this makes the increase a popular decision, enhancing the mayor's reputation with voters.

Questions 7 and 8 are based on the following passage.

(1) Yesterday I was exposed to what was called, in a recent newspaper ad for Dilly's Deli, "a dining experience like no other." (2) I decided on the hamburger steak special, the other specials were liver and onions and tuna casserole. (3) Each special is offered with two side dishes, but there was no potato salad left and the green beans were cooked nearly beyond recognition. (4) I chose the gelatin of the day and what turned out to be the blandest coleslaw I have ever eaten.

(5) At Dilly's you sit at one of the four long tables. (6) The couple sitting across from me was having an argument. (7) The truck driver sitting next to me told me more than I wanted to know about highway taxes. (8) <u>After tasting</u> each of the dishes on my plate, it was time to leave; at that moment, one of the people working behind the counter yelled at me to clean up after myself. (9) Throwing away that plate of food was the most enjoyable part of dining at Dilly's.

7. Which of the following changes should be made to Part 2 of the first paragraph?
   a. Replace *were* with *are*.
   b. Replace the comma with a dash.
   c. Replace *I decided* with *Deciding*.
   d. Replace the comma with a semicolon.

8. Which of the following words or phrases should replace the underlined words in Part 8 of the second paragraph?
   a. Having tasted
   b. After I tasted
   c. Tasting
   d. After having tasted

Questions 9–11 are based on the following passage.

(1) Although most people are exercising regularly, experts note that eating right is also a key to good health. (2) Nutritionists recommend the "food pyramid" as a simple guide to eating the proper foods. (3) At the base of the food pyramid are grains and fiber. (4) People should eat six to eleven servings of bread, cereal, rice, and pasta everyday. (5) Servings of vegetables and fruit, the next level up the pyramid should be eaten five to nine times per day. (6) The next pyramid level is the dairy group. (7) Two or three servings a day of milk, yogurt, or cheese help maintain good nutrition. (8) Moving up the pyramid, the next level is the meat, poultry, fish, beans, eggs, and nuts group, of which everyone should eat only two to three servings a day. (9) At the very top of the pyramid is fats, oils, and sweets; these foods should be eaten only infrequently.

(10) _____.

(11) If they follow the pyramid's guidelines, people do not have to shop in health food or specialty stores. (12) People need only stay in the outer two or three aisles of the supermarket, where the healthiest foods are located.

9. Which of the following revisions is necessary in Part 9 of the passage?

  a. At the very top of the pyramid is fats, oils and sweets; these foods should be eaten only infrequently.

  b. At the very top of the pyramid are fats, oils, and sweets; these foods should be eaten only infrequently.

  c. At the very top of the pyramid is fats, oils, and sweets; these foods must be eaten only infrequently.

  d. At the very top of the pyramid is fats, oils, and sweets; only these foods should be eaten infrequently.

10. Which of the following parts, if inserted in the blank line numbered Part 10, would be most consistent with development and grammar of the paragraph?

  a. The nutrition plan set out in the food pyramid was designed to make it easy to fit good nutrition habits into your already too complicated lives.

  b. Unlike fad diets and weighty books of calorie counts, the food pyramid is a clear visual aid that will help people remember the essentials of healthy eating.

  c. While the food pyramid can help you learn how to eat more healthily, it cannot replace the necessity of exercise.

  d. The nutrition plan set out in the food pyramid was designed to make it easy to fit good nutrition habits into people's already too complicated lives.

11. Which of the following changes is needed in the above passage?

  a. Part 5: Insert comma after *pyramid*.

  b. Part 1: Replace *most* with *more*.

  c. Part 8: Replace *of which* with *which*.

  d. Part 8: Insert a colon after *is*.

Questions 12 and 13 are based on the following passage.

(1) Police officers must read suspects their Miranda rights upon taking them into custody. (2) When a suspect who is merely being questioned <u>incriminates</u> himself, he might later claim to have been in custody and seek to have the case dismissed on the grounds of not having been <u>appraised</u> of his Miranda rights.

(3) In such cases, a judge must make a determination as to whether or not a reasonable person would have believed himself to have been in custody, based on certain criteria. (4) Officers must be aware of these <u>criteria</u> and take care not to give suspects

grounds for later claiming they believed themselves to be in custody.

(5) The judge must <u>ascertain</u> whether the suspect was questioned in a threatening manner (for example, if the suspect was seated while both officers remained standing) and whether the suspect was aware that he or she was free to leave at any time.

12. Which of the underlined words in the passage should be replaced by a more appropriate, accurate word?
a. incriminates
b. appraised
c. criteria
d. ascertain

13. Which of the following changes would make the sequence of ideas in the passage clearer?
a. Place Part 5 after Part 1.
b. Reverse Parts 3 and 5.
c. Reverse the order of Parts 4 and 5.
d. Delete Part 2.

Questions 14 and 15 are based on the following passage.

(1) An ecosystem is a group of animals and plants living in a specific region and interacting with one another and with their physical environment. (2) Ecosystems include physical and chemical components, such as soils, water, and nutrients that support the organisms living there. (3) These organisms may range from large animals to microscopic bacteria. (4) Ecosystems also can be thought of as the interacting among all organisms in a given habitat; for instance, one species may serve as food for another. (5) People are part of the ecosystems where they live and work. (6) Environmental Groups are forming in many communities. (7) Human activities can harm or destroy local ecosystems unless actions such as land development for housing or businesses are carefully planned to conserve and sustain the ecology

of the area. (8) An important part of ecosystem management involves finding ways to protect and enhance economic and social well-being while protecting local ecosystems.

14. Which of the following numbered parts is LEAST relevant to the main idea of the paragraph?
a. Part 1
b. Part 6
c. Part 7
d. Part 8

15. Which of the following changes is needed in the passage?
a. Part 5: Place a comma after *live*.
b. Part 2: Remove the comma after *water*.
c. Part 6: Use a lower case g for the word *Group*.
d. Part 8: Change *involves* to *involved*.

Questions 16 and 17 are based on the following passage.

(1) Courts allow hearsay evidence (secondhand reporting of a statement) only when the truth of the statement is irrelevant. (2) Hearsay that depends on the statement's truthfulness, is inadmissible because the witness does not appear in court and swear an oath to tell the truth. (3) Because his demeanor when making the statement is not visible to the jury, the accuracy of the statement cannot be tested under cross-examination, and to introduce it would deprive the accused of the constitutional right to confront the accuser. (4) The courtroom demeanor of a witness is crucial to a lawyer's convincing a jury of the veracity of his case. (5) Hearsay is admissible, however, when the truth of the statement is unimportant. (6) For example, if a defendant claims he was unconscious at a certain time, but a witness claims that the defendant spoke to her at that time, this evidence would be admissible because the truth of what the defendant said is irrelevant.

16. Which of the following numbered parts is LEAST relevant to the main idea of the paragraph?
a. Part 4
b. Part 6
c. Part 1
d. Part 5

17. Which of the following changes is needed in the passage?
a. Part 5: Remove the comma after *however*.
b. Part 3: Remove the comma after *jury*.
c. Part 2: Remove the comma after *truthfulness*.
d. Part 1: Remove the comma after *statement*.

Questions 18 and 19 are based on the following passage.

(1) There are two types of diabetes, insulin-dependent and non-insulin-dependent. (2) Between 90 and 95 percent of the estimated 13 to 14 million people in the United States with diabetes have non-insulin-dependent, or Type II, diabetes. (3) Because this form of diabetes usually begins in adults over the age of 40 and is most common after the age of 55, it used to be called adult-onset diabetes. (4) _____ its symptoms often develop gradually and are hard to identify at first, _____, nearly half of all people with diabetes do not know they have it. (5) _____, someone who has developed Type II diabetes may more feel tired or ill without knowing why. (6) This can be particularly dangerous because untreated diabetes can cause damage to the heart, blood vessels, eyes, kidneys, and nerves. (7) While the causes, short-term effects, and treatments of the two types of diabetes differ, both types can cause the same long-term health problems.

18. Which of the following parts of the paragraph contains an incomplete or illogical comparison?
a. Part 7
b. Part 5
c. Part 3
d. Part 2

19. Which sequence of words, if inserted into the blanks in the paragraph, helps the reader understand the sequence and logic of the writer's ideas?
a. Since . . . therefore . . . For example
b. While . . . however . . . Next
c. Moreover . . . as a result . . . Eventually
d. Because . . . nevertheless . . . Thus

Questions 20–22 are based on the following passage.

(1) By using tiny probes as neural prostheses, scientists may be able to restore nerve function in quadriplegics, make the blind see, or the deaf hear. (2) Thanks to advanced techniques, an implanted probe can stimulate individual neurons electrically or chemically and then record responses. (3) Preliminary results suggest that the microprobe telemetry systems can be permanently implanted and replace damaged or missing nerves.

(4) The tissue-compatible microprobes represent an advance over the typically aluminum wire electrodes used in studies of the cortex and other brain structures. (5) Previously, researchers data was accumulated using traditional electrodes, but there is a question of how much damage they cause to the nervous system. (6) Microprobes, since they are slightly thinner than a human hair, cause minimal damage and disruption of neurons when inserted into the brain because of their diminutive width.

(7) In addition to recording nervous system impulses, the microprobes have minuscule channels that open the way for delivery of drugs, cellular growth factors, neurotransmitters, and other neuroactive compounds to a single neuron or to groups of neurons. (8) The probes usually have up to four channels, each with its own recording/stimulating electrode.

20. Which of the following changes is needed in the passage?
a. Part 8: Change *its* to *it's*.
b. Part 6: Change *their* to *its*.
c. Part 6: Change *than* to *then*.
d. Part 5: Change *researchers* to *researchers'*.

21. Which of the following parts uses an adverb incorrectly?
a. Part 2
b. Part 8
c. Part 6
d. Part 4

22. Which of the following numbered parts should be revised to reduce unnecessary repetition?
a. Part 5
b. Part 6
c. Part 2
d. Part 8

Questions 23–25 are based on the following passage.

(1) Loud noises on buses not only irritate passengers but also create unsafe situations. (2) They are prohibited by law and by agency policy. (3) Therefore, bus operators are expected to follow the procedures outlined below.

(4) A passenger-created disturbance is by playing excessively loud music or creating loud noises in some other manner. (5) In the event a passenger creates a disturbance, the bus operator will politely ask the passenger to turn off the music or stop making the loud noise. (6) If the passenger refuses to comply, the bus operator will tell the passenger that he or she is in violation of the law and bus policy and will have to leave the bus if he or she will not comply to the request. (7) If police assistance is requested, the bus operator will stay at the location

from which the call to the Command Center was placed or the silent alarm used. (8) The bus operator will wait there until the police arrive, will allow passengers off the bus at this point, and no passengers are allowed on until the situation is resolved.

23. Which of the following numbered parts contains a sentence fragment?
a. Part 4
b. Part 7
c. Part 3
d. Part 6

24. Which of the following is the best revision of the sentence numbered Part 8 in the passage?
a. Bus operators will wait there until the police arrive, will allow passengers off the bus at this point, and no passengers will be allowed on until the situation is resolved.
b. Bus operators will wait there until the police arrive, will allow passengers off the bus at this point, and, until the situation is resolved, no passengers are allowed on.
c. Bus operators will wait there until the police arrive, will allow passengers off the bus at this point, and will not allow passengers on until the situation is resolved.
d. Bus operators will wait there until the police arrive, will allow passengers off the bus at this point, and no passengers will be allowed on until the situation is resolved.

25. Which of the following numbered parts uses a preposition incorrectly?
a. Part 2
b. Part 6
c. Part 3
d. Part 8

Questions 26–28 are based on the following passage.

(1) In 1519, Hernando cortez led his army of Spanish Conquistadors into Mexico. (2) <u>Equipped</u> with horses, shining armor, and the most advanced weapons of the sixteenth century, he fought his way from the flat coastal area into the mountainous highlands. (3) Cortez <u>was looking</u> for gold, and he were sure that Indian groups in Mexico had mined large amounts of the precious metal. (4) First, he <u>conquered</u> the groups and then <u>seized</u> their precious gold using very organized methods.

26. Which of the underlined words in the passage above could be replaced with a more precise verb?
- **a.** was looking
- **b.** equipped
- **c.** conquered
- **d.** seized

27. Which of the following sentences uses the verb incorrectly?
- **a.** Part 1
- **b.** Part 2
- **c.** Part 3
- **d.** Part 4

28. Which of the following changes needs to be made to the above passage?
- **a.** Part 2: Delete the comma after *horses*.
- **b.** Part 1: Capitalize the *c* in *Cortez*.
- **c.** Part 3: Insert a comma after *groups*.
- **d.** Part 4: Place a semicolon after *groups*.

Questions 29 and 30 are based on the following passage.

(1) A report on dropout rates in the United States released by the U.S. Department of Education's National Center for Education Statistics found that more young adults are completing high school through alternative methods, such as the GED.

(2) "Alternative programs that give young people a second chance are a growing phenomena," says U.S. Secretary of Education Richard W. Riley. (3) "We need to develop more, higher-quality, alternative programs than meet this rising demand. (4) Young people at risk should not just be left on their own to hang out on the street. (5) New attention needs to be paid to finding ways to encourage many more dropouts to drop back in to school so that they have a real chance at living a decent life. (6) When young people drop out, they do more than just give up their education, they are, too often, giving up on themselves."

29. Which of the following changes needs to be made to the passage?
- **a.** Part 3: Remove the comma after *more*.
- **b.** Part 1: Insert a comma after *statistics*.
- **c.** Part 4: Change *their* to *there*.
- **d.** Part 3: Change *than* to *that*.

30. Which of the following numbered parts contains a run-on sentence?
- **a.** Part 5
- **b.** Part 6
- **c.** Part 1
- **d.** Part 2

Questions 31 and 32 are based on the following passage.

(1) Kwanzaa is a holiday celebrated by many African-Americans from December 26 through January 1. (2) It pays tribute to the rich cultural roots of Americans of African ancestry, and celebrates family, community, and culture, Kwanzaa means the first or the first fruits of the harvest and is based on the ancient African first-fruit harvest celebration. (3) The modern holiday of Kwanzaa was founded in 1966 by Dr. Maulana Karenga, a professor at Callifornia State University in Long Beach, California. (4) The seven-day celebration encourages people to think about their African roots as well as their life in present day America.

31. Which of the following sentences would be the best topic sentence for a second paragraph on the same subject?

a. The seven fundamental principles on which Kwanzaa is based are referred to as the *Nguzo Saba.*

b. These rules consist of unity, self-determination, collective work and responsibility, cooperative economics, purpose, creativity, and faith.

c. Each of its seven candles represents a distinct principle beginning with unity, the center candle.

d. Participants celebrate by performing rituals such as lighting the kinara.

32. Which of the following numbered parts in the passage contains a nonstandard sentence?

a. Part 4

b. Part 3

c. Part 1

d. Part 2

Questions 33–35 are based on the following passage.

(1) A metaphor is a poetic device that deals with comparison. (2) It compares similar qualities of two dissimilar objects. (3) With a simple metaphor, one object becomes the other: *Love is a rose.* Although this doesn't sound like a particularly rich image, a metaphor can communicate so much about a particular image, that poets utilize them more than any other type of figurative language. (4) The reason for this is that a poet composes poetry to express emotional experience. (5) <u>Succinctly</u>, what the poet imagines love to be may or may not be our perception of love. (6) Therefore, the poet's job is to enable us to *experience* it and feel it the same way. (7) You should be able to nod in agreement and say, "Yes, that's it! (8) I understand precisely where this guy is coming from."

33. The tone of this passage is very formal; the last sentence is not. Which of the following would be more consistent with the tone of the passage?

a. This guy is right on.

b. I can relate to the poet's experience.

c. I know this feeling.

d. This poem gets right to the point.

34. Which of the following numbered parts contains a nonstandard use of a pronoun?

a. Part 3

b. Part 5

c. Part 6

d. Part 7

35. Which of the following adverbs should replace the underlined word in Part 5?

a. Consequently

b. Normally

c. Occasionally

d. Originally

Questions 36–38 are based on the following passage.

(1) If you have little time to care for your garden, be sure to select hardy plants, such as phlox, comfrey, and peonies. (2) These will, with only a little care, keep the garden brilliant with color all through the growing season. (3) Sturdy sunflowers and hardy species of roses are also good selections. (4) As a thrifty gardener, you should leave part of the garden free for the planting of herbs such as lavender, sage, thyme, and parsley.

(5) If you have a moderate amount of time, growing vegetables and a garden culture of pears, apples, quinces, and other small fruits can be an interesting occupation, which amply rewards the care languished on it. (6) Even a small vegetable and fruit garden may yield radishes, celery, beans, and strawberries that will be delicious on the family table. (7) _____.

(8) When planting seeds for the vegetable garden, you should be sure that they receive the proper amount of moisture, that they are sown at the right season to receive the right degree of heat, and that the seed is placed near enough to the surface to allow the young plant to reach the light easily.

36. Which of the following changes would best help to clarify the ideas in the first paragraph?
   a. Omit the phrase, *with only a little care*, from Part 2.
   b. Reverse the order of Parts 2 and 3.
   c. Add a sentence after Part 4 explaining why saving room for herbs is a sign of thrift in a gardener.
   d. Add a sentence about the ease of growing roses after Part 3.

37. Which of the following sentences, if inserted in the blank line numbered Part 7, would be most consistent with the writer's development of ideas in the second paragraph?
   a. When and how you plant is important to producing a good yield from your garden.
   b. Very few gardening tasks are more fascinating than growing fruit trees.
   c. Of course, if you have saved room for an herb garden, you will be able to make the yield of your garden even more tasty by cooking with your own herbs.
   d. Growing a productive fruit garden may take some specialized and time-consuming research into proper grafting techniques.

38. Which of the following changes needs to be made in the passage?
   a. Part 8: Change *sown* to *sewn*.
   b. Part 5: Change *languished* to *lavished*.
   c. Part 2: Change *through* to *threw*.
   d. Part 8: Change *surface* to *surfeit*.

Questions 39 and 40 are based on the following passage.

This selection is from Willa Cather's short story, "Neighbor Rosicky."

(1) On the day before Christmas the weather set in very cold; no snow, but a bitter, biting wind that whistled and sang over the flat land and lashed one's face like fine wires. (2) There was baking going on in the Rosicky kitchen all day, and Rosicky sat inside, making over a coat that Albert had outgrown into an overcoat for John. (3) Mary's big red geranium in bloom for Christmas, and a row of Jerusalem cherry trees, full of berries. (4) It was the first year she had ever grown these; Doctor Ed brung her the seeds from Omaha when he went to some medical convention. (5) They reminded Rosicky of plants he had seen in England; and all afternoon, as he stitched, he sat thinking about the two years in London, which his mind usually shrank from even after all this while.

39. Which of the following numbered parts uses a verb form incorrectly?
   a. Part 5
   b. Part 2
   c. Part 4
   d. Part 3

40. Which of the following numbered parts contains a sentence fragment?
   a. Part 4
   b. Part 3
   c. Part 2
   d. Part 5

▶ Section 3: Writing (Part B— Writing Sample)

Carefully read the writing topic that follows, then prepare a multiple-paragraph writing sample of 300–600 words on that topic. Make sure your essay is well-organized and that you support your central argument with concrete examples.

Bob Maynard has said that "Problems are opportunities in disguise."

Write an essay describing a time in your life when a problem became an opportunity. How did you transform the situation? Explain what you did to turn the problem into an opportunity and how others can benefit from your experience.

► Answer Explanations

Section 1: Reading

1. a. Choice **b** emphasizes only damage to the atmosphere; the passage encompasses more than that. Choice **c** does not mention the atmosphere, which is the main focus of the passage. Choice **d** is too narrow—the final paragraph of the passage emphasizes that the circulation of the atmosphere is but one example of the complex events that keeps the Earth alive.

2. c. Choice **a** is incorrect because the passage does not explain exactly what will happen as a result of damage to the atmosphere and other life-sustaining mechanisms. Choice **b** is incorrect because the passage does not explain the origin of the atmosphere. Choice **d** is incorrect because it is solar energy that travels 93 million miles through space, not the atmosphere.

3. b. The biosphere, as defined in the first paragraph, is a region (or part) of the Earth; it is not the envelope around the Earth, the living things on Earth, or the circulation of the atmosphere (choices **a**, **c**, and **d**).

4. d. Choice **a** deals with solar radiation, not with circulation of the atmosphere. Choice **b** is an assertion without specific supporting detail. Choice **c** describes how the atmosphere protects Earth but does not speak of the circulation of the atmosphere. Only choice **d** explains that conditions would be unlivable at the equator and poles without the circulation of the atmosphere; therefore, it is the best choice.

5. a. The second paragraph deals with how variations in the strength with which solar radiation strikes the Earth affects temperature. None of the other choices is discussed in terms of all temperature changes on Earth.

6. a. There is no mention in the first paragraph of any reviving or cleansing effect the atmosphere may have (choices **b** and **d**). In a sense, enabling the Earth to sustain life is invigorating; however, choice **a** is a better choice because the first two sentences talk about how the atmosphere protects the Earth from harmful forces.

7. b. Choice **b** includes the main points of the passage and is not too broad. Choice **a** features minor points from the passage. Choice **c** also features minor points, with the addition of History of the National Park system, which is not included in the passage. Choice **d** lists points that are not discussed in the passage.

8. d. The information in choices **a**, **b**, and **c** is not expressed in paragraph 4.

9. a. Reread the second sentence of paragraph 2. Choices **b** and **c** are mentioned in the passage but not as causing the islands; choice **d** is not mentioned in the passage.

10. c. Paragraph 5 discusses the visitors to Acadia National Park, whereas choices **a**, **b**, and **d** are not mentioned in the passage.

11. a. The first sentence of paragraph 3 states that the length of the Maine coastline is 2,500 miles.

12. b. The other choices could possibly be true, but only choice **b** fits in the context of the sentence that follows it, which describes the ruggedness of the coast and implies that the coast does not lie in a straight line.

13. d. The passage contains objective information about accounting such as one might find in a textbook. There is nothing new or newsworthy in it (choice **a**). The passage does not contain the significant amount of personal opinion one would expect to find in an essay (choice **b**). It does not deal with matters that might involve litigation (choice **c**).

14. d. The final sentence of the second paragraph emphasizes the importance of correct interpretation of financial accounting. Choice **a** is incorrect because something so important would not be discretionary (optional). Choice **b** may be true, but it is not as important for guidelines to be convenient as it is for them to rigorous. Choice **c** is incorrect because the word *austere* connotes sternness; people may be stern, but inanimate entities, such as guidelines, cannot be.

15. c. Choices **a**, **b**, and **d** are all listed in the passage as functions of accounting. On the other hand, the second sentence of the passage speaks of a marketing department, separate from the accounting department.

16. b. The final sentence of paragraph 3 states: *A debit could represent an increase or a decrease to the account, depending on how the account is classified.*

17. b. Choice **a** is too vague to be the purpose of the paragraph. The common yardstick (choice **c**) refers to money; the paragraph does not emphasize money, it emphasizes the double-entry system of accounting. The evolution of the double-entry system (choice **d**) is not discussed in the passage.

18. d. The passage says that in the face of light pollution we lose our connection with something profoundly important to the human spirit, our sense of wonder. The other choices are not mentioned in the passage.

19. b. The passage says that light trespass is becoming an important issue in many suburban and rural communities. Choice **a** is refuted in the passage, as light trespass can actually help criminals. Choices **c** and **d** are mentioned in other contexts.

20. a. This sentence follows a sentence introduced with the word *first*, indicating this sentence needs to begin with a placement introduction; either *second* (choice **a**) or *then*, (choice **b**) would be appropriate. The second blank precedes a conclusion; so *thus* (choice **a**) is the better option.

21. c. While **a**, **b**, and **d** are all topics that are mentioned in the passage, the main point of the passage is to discuss the growing problem of light pollution.

22. d. In the sentences in answers **a**, **b**, and **c**, the writer reports facts that can be verified by research. Choice **d** best reflects an opinion of the writer which is difficult or impossible to verify with facts.

23. a. Paragraph 3 states that *birds migrating at night use stars to navigate and can become lost when flying through a heavily light polluted region. . . .* The other choices may represent real dangers but are not mentioned in the passage.

24. d. *Animistic* has as its root the Latin *anima*, which means soul; think also of the word *animate*. Choices **a** and **b** are incorrect because the author's discussion of the Sami religion does not pass negative judgment. Choice **c** means untrue or false, which does not fit the definition given.

25. a. To depict the Sami, the author uses words that point to their gentleness, which is an admirable quality: They move quietly, display courtesy to the spirits of the wilderness, and were known as peaceful retreaters. There is nothing pitying, contemptuous, or patronizing in the language of the passage.

26. b. Choice **b** is the only option not mentioned in the passage.

27. c. The passage specifically notes that the Sami do not like the name *Lapps* (choice **a**). Choices **b** and **d** are not options mentioned in the passage; the preferred term appears to be Sami, choice **c**.

28. d. See the last paragraph of the passage. The other choices are not indicated in the passage.

29. c. According to the passage, there are three categories of Sami people, the Forest, Sea, and Reindeer Sami. There is no mention of Mountain Sami (choice **c**).

30. b. Because the writer indicates that visitors to Hershey's Chocolate World are greeted by a giant Reese's Peanut Butter Cup, it would be logical to assume that these are manufactured by Hershey. Although the writer mentions the popularity of chocolate internationally, it is too broad to assume that it is popular in every country (choice **a**); nor is there any indication that Milton Hershey was the first person to manufacture chocolate in the United States (choice **c**). Choice **d** is not discussed in the passage at all.

31. d. In paragraph 3, the passage says the Hershey Chocolate company was born in 1894 *as a subsidiary of the Lancaster Caramel Company*. This indicates that a subsidiary company is one controlled by another company, choice **d**.

32. a. This is the best choice because it is the most complete statement of the material. Choices **c** and **d** focus on small details of the passage; choice **b** is not discussed in the passage.

33. b. Paragraph 3 states that Hershey sold the caramel company six years after the founding of the chocolate company. The chocolate company was founded in 1894; the correct choice is **b**.

34. c. The Chicago International Exposition was where Hershey saw a demonstration of German chocolate making techniques, which indicates, along with the word *international* in its title, that the exposition contained displays from a variety of countries, choice **c**. None of the other choices can be inferred from the information in the passage.

35. b. There is nothing inherently dramatic, undignified, or rewarding discussed in paragraph 1. *Modest* is the word that best fits being born in a small village and having the unremarkable early life described; it is also a word that provides a contrast to the mention of Milton's later popularity.

36. a. According to the first sentence of the third paragraph, the new MRI detects not water but inert gases.

37. d. See the second sentence of the second paragraph, which states that X rays cannot provide a clear view of air passages.

38. c. See the fifth paragraph, which says that radio signals knock nuclei out of position, but as they are realigned they transmit faint radio signals.

39. b. The first sentence of the third paragraph states the equivalency: nuclei are aligned, or hyperpolarized.

40. a. The last paragraph says that light, rather than a magnet, is used to align nuclei, suggesting that the two serve equivalent purposes in the two MRI processes.

41. c. See the last sentence of the passage. Since lesser gases lose their alignment more quickly, a shorter period of alignment would lead to poorer clarity. A higher number of aligned nuclei would theoretically lead to a better image.

42. c. The passage makes clear that the new MRI procedure is new and can reveal details that older procedures could not. Choice **a** (explicit, meaning *clearly stated*) connotes a mode of expression, rather than a procedure. No mention is made of the cost of the procedure (choice **b**). The procedure could be regarded as clever (choice **d**), but the word is inconsistent with the tone of the rest of the passage, which uses more objective, scientific diction.

Section 2: Mathematics

1. a. $\frac{1}{3} \times 0.60 = 0.20 = 20\%$

2. d. Distance traveled is equal to velocity (or speed) multiplied by time. Therefore, 3.00×10^8 meters per second $\times$ 2,000 seconds $= 6.00 \times 10^{11}$ meters.

3. b. The median value is the middle value when the numbers are sorted in descending order. This is 10 inches.

4. d. From the line chart, 2003 is represented by the dotted line with squares at each month. In December 2003, there were 10 inches of rainfall, the most that year.

5. c. The mean is the sum of the values divided by the number of values; $\frac{(8 + 6 + 4)}{3} = 6$ inches.

6. a. If the gas station is $43\frac{1}{3}$ miles from their house, and their relatives live 75 miles away, the numbers are subtracted; $75 - 43\frac{1}{3} = 31\frac{2}{3}$.

7. d. If 2 of 5 cars are foreign, 3 of 5 are domestic; $\frac{3}{5} \times 60$ cars = 36 cars.

8. c. To find the remaining piece, the first 3 pieces are summed and subtracted from one. This gives the proportion of the final piece; $\frac{1}{3} + \frac{1}{6} + \frac{1}{10} = \frac{3}{5}$; $1 - \frac{3}{5} = \frac{2}{5}$; $\frac{2}{5} \times 15$ feet = 6 feet.

9. b. Yellow beans + orange beans = 12. There are 30 total beans; $\frac{12}{30}$ is reduced to $\frac{2}{5}$.

10. c. If Dimitri does 40% of the assignment in one hour, he can do 16 problems per hour. To arrive at the answer, divide 40 by 16; $\frac{40 \text{ problems}}{16 \text{ problems per hour}}$ = 2.5 hours.

11. a. The mean is equal to the sum of values divided by the number of values. Therefore, 8 raptors per day $\times$ 5 days = 40 raptors. The sum of the other six days is 34 raptors; 40 raptors – 34 raptors = 6 raptors.

12. a. –0.15 is less than –0.02, the smallest number in the range.

13. c. January is approximately 38,000; February is approximately 41,000, and April is approximately 26,000. These added together give a total of 105,000.

14. c. The buses arrive 53 minutes after they leave. Therefore, the bus will arrive at 8:13.

15. b. There has been an increase in price of $3; $3 divided by $50 is 0.06. This is an increase of 0.06, or 6%.

16. c. $\overleftrightarrow{PQ}$ and $\overleftrightarrow{RS}$ are intersecting lines. The fact that angle *POR* is a 90-degree angle means that $\overleftrightarrow{PQ}$ and $\overleftrightarrow{RS}$ are perpendicular, indicating that all the angles formed by their intersection, including $\angle ROQ$, measure 90 degrees.

17. d. According to the graph, of the choices given, the fewest acres burned in 2003.

18. c. The bar on the graph is over the $100,000 mark, so the answer would be close to, but more than,

$100,000; the only logical choice is therefore $110,000.

19. d. To answer this question, both Acres Burned and Dollars Spent must be considered. The ratio between the two is greater in 2004 than in the other years.

20. a. In April, the dotted line (representing the average) is closest to the solid line (representing 2004 rainfall).

21. d. Read the dotted line for the total in September.

22. b. The graph shows that during January, February, and April, rainfall amounts were above average.

23. a. In choice **b**, the 9 is in the hundredths place; in **c** it is in the tenths place, and in **d** it is in the ten-thousandths place.

24. d. A yardstick is 36 inches long; add that to the 28 inches of rope, and you will get 64 inches as the longest distance James can measure.

25. b. The unreduced ratio is 8,000:5,000,000 or 8:5,000; 5,000 divided by 8 equals 625, for a ratio of 1:625.

26. d. Three feet equals 36 inches; add 4 inches to get 40 inches total; 40 divided by 5 is 8.

27. d. Solve this problem with the following equation: 4 candy bars $\times$ $0.40 + 3 soft drinks $\times$ $0.50 = $3.10.

28. d. The hundredth is the second digit to the right of the decimal point. Because the third decimal is 6, the second is rounded up to 4.

29. d. Find the answer using the following equations: $\frac{1}{3} = 0.333$; $\frac{1}{4} = 0.25$; $\frac{2}{7} = 0.286$. $\frac{2}{7}$ is between the other two fractions.

30. c. Three percent is equal to 0.03, so multiply 2,500 times 0.03 and add the result to the original 2,500 for a total of 2,575.

31. d. There are two sides 34 feet long and two sides 20 feet long. Using the formula $P = 2L + 2W$ will solve this problem. Therefore, you should multiply 34 times 2 and 20 times 2, and then add the results: 68 + 40 = 108.

32. c. To estimate quickly, the numbers can be rounded to 36,000 and 16,500. 36,000 students minus 16,500 male students is equal to 19,500 female students. 19,500 women minus 16,500 men is equal to 3,000 more women than men.

33. d. Four percent is equal to 0.04; $500 \times 0.04 = 20$.

34. c. The answer to this question lies in knowing that there are four quarts to a gallon. There are therefore 20 quarts in a 5-gallon container. Divide 20 quarts by 1.06 quarts per liter to get 18.8 liters and then round off to 19.

35. d. Division is used to arrive at a decimal, which can then be rounded to the nearest hundredth and converted to a percentage: $\frac{11,350}{21,500} = 0.5279$; 0.5279 rounded to the nearest hundredth is 0.53, or 53%.

36. b. The average is the sum divided by the number of times Rashaard went fishing: $11 + 4 + 0 + 5 + 4 + 6$ divided by 6 is 5.

37. b. This uses two algebraic equations to solve for the age. Jerry (J) and his grandfather (G) have a sum of ages of 110 years. Therefore, $J + G = 110$. Jerry was $\frac{1}{3}$ as young as his grandfather 15 years ago. Therefore, $J - 15 = \frac{1}{3}(G - 15)$. Either equation can be solved for J or G and substituted into the other; $J = 110 - G$; $110 - G - 15 = \frac{1}{3}(G - 5)$; $100 = \frac{4}{3G}$; $G = 75$.

38. b. $\frac{1}{3}x + 3 = 8$. In order to solve the equation, all numbers need to be on one side and all x values on the other. Therefore, $\frac{1}{3}x = 5$; $x = 15$.

39. d. $(x^2 + 4x + 4)$ factors into $(x + 2)(x + 2)$. Therefore, one of the $(x + 2)$ terms can be canceled with the denominator. This leaves $(x + 2)$.

40. c. Slope is equal to the change in y values divided by the change in x values. Therefore, $\frac{(3 - (-1))}{(2 - 0)} = \frac{4}{2} = 2$. The intercept is found by putting 0 in for x in the equation $y = 2x + b$; $-1 = 2(0) + b$; $b = -1$. Therefore, the equation is $y = 2x - 1$.

41. a. Slope is equal to the change in y divided by the change in x. Therefore, $m = \frac{-1 - 2}{(-2 - 4)} + \frac{-3}{-6} = \frac{1}{2}$.

42. c. This must be solved with the quadratic equation, $\frac{b \pm \sqrt{(b^2 - 4ac)}}{2a}$. Therefore, the solution is $\frac{9 \pm \sqrt{(81 - 108)}}{6}$, which simplifies to $\frac{9 \pm 3\sqrt{(-3)}}{6}$. Dividing the numerator and denominator by 3 gives $\frac{3 \pm \sqrt{(-3)}}{2}$.

43. d. To complete the square, one half of the b term is squared and added to each side. Therefore, $\frac{4}{2} = 2$, $2^2 = 4$.

44. a. Because the curve opens downward, it must have a $-x^2$ term in it. Because the curve goes to the point $(0,4)$, the answer must be must be **a**.

45. d. The curve shown is $x^2 - 2x$.

46. a. The fraction $\frac{1}{2}$ must be placed in each x in the function to solve for $f(\frac{1}{2})$. Therefore, $3(\frac{1}{2})^2 - \frac{1}{2}(\frac{1}{2}) + 7 = \frac{3}{4} - \frac{1}{4} + 7 = \frac{15}{2}$.

47. d. Substitute 3 for x in the expression $5 + 4x$ to determine that y equals 17.

48. a. First you find out how long the entire hike can be, based on the rate at which the hikers are using their supplies; $\frac{\frac{2}{5}}{3} = \frac{1}{x}$, where 1 is the total amount of supplies and x is the number of days for the whole hike. Cross-multiplying, you get $\frac{2}{5}x = 3$, so that $x = \frac{(3)(5)}{2}$, or $7\frac{1}{2}$ days for the length of the entire hike. This means that the hikers could go forward for 3.75 days altogether before they would have to turn around. They have already hiked for 3 days; 3.75 minus 3 equals 0.75 for the amount of time they can now go forward before having to turn around.

Section 3: Writing (Part A— Multiple-Choice)

1. b. Paragraph 2 contradicts misconceptions potential adopters of racing greyhounds might have about the breed. Choice **b** states that certain popular beliefs about greyhounds are erroneous and acts as a transition to the facts that follow in the paragraph. Choice **a** does not focus on contradicting the misinformation; also, the phrase, *even so,* appears to agree with the misconceptions rather than contradict them. Choice **c** does not focus on the argument; instead, it repeats information given in the previous sentence. Choice **d**, rather than supporting the main purpose of the paragraph—which is to dispel myths about racing greyhounds—actually contradicts information in Parts 6 and 7.

2. d. The actual subject of the verb *to have* is the word *number,* rather than the word *racers.* It is a third-person singular subject and so must agree with the third-person singular form of the verb *has.* Choice **a** suggests a correction that is unnecessary. Choices **b** and **c** suggest changes that actually cause errors.

3. c. This choice is the best because it retains the writer's informal, reassuring tone and because the information in it furthers the purpose of this paragraph—i.e., the suitability of greyhounds as household pets. Choice **a** is incorrect because the information is not in keeping with the topic of the paragraph; also, the tone set by the inclusion of a precise statistic is too formal. Choice **b** retains the informal tone of the selection but it provides information already given in the first paragraph and is not suitable to the purpose of this paragraph. The tone in choice **d** is argumentative, which defeats the author's purpose of trying to reassure the reader.

4. b. Although choice **b** does include a subject and a verb, it is a dependent clause because it begins with the adverb *when.* Choices **a**, **c**, and **d** are all standard sentences.

5. a. Choice **a** removes the redundancy of Part 3 by taking out the word *also,* which repeats the meaning of the introductory phrase *in addition to.* Choice **b** is incorrect because the passage only mentions one patrol, so making the word plural would not make sense. Choice **c** suggests

an unnecessary correction in verb tense. Choice **d** suggests a change that would imply that the writer is talking about all fires, rather than specifically about the arson fires that are the subject of the passage.

6. c. Choice **c** gives a fact (the percentage of decrease in arson because of the efforts of the Patrol in the past) that supports the statement in the preceding sentence (Part 2) that the Patrol has been effective in reducing arson in the past. This choice also develops the ideas in the paragraph by giving a direct justification of why an increase in the Patrol would help the city achieve its aim of reducing arson. Choice **a** does add information that is on topic, but it fails to connect that activity with its result. Choice **b** adds a factual detail about the size of the increase in the patrol, but it does not develop the idea in Part 2—why the patrol has been important in fighting arson. Choice **d** is off the topic of the paragraph and the passage as a whole.

7. d. Part 2 is an incorrectly punctuated compound sentence, a comma splice. Choice **d** correctly joins the two simple sentences into a compound one by using a semicolon in place of the comma. Choice **a** creates an error in subject-verb agreement. Choice **b** is incorrect because a dash cannot join two simple sentences into a compound one. Choice **c** turns the first phrase of the sentence, *Deciding on the hamburger steak special,* into a dangling modifier.

8. b. This question assesses the ability to recognize the correct use of modifiers. The phrase *after tasting each of the dishes on my plate* is a dangling modifier; the sentence does not have a subject pronoun this phrase could modify. Choice **b** is correct because it supplies the missing subject pronoun *I.* Choices **a**, **c**, and **d** are incorrect because they let the modification error stand; none of them provides a subject pronoun the phrase could modify.

9. b. Choice **b** is correct because it uses the third person plural of the verb to be, *are,* which agrees in number and person with the subject *fats, oils, and sweets.* Choice **a** is incorrect because it does not correct the subject-verb agreement problem; instead it removes an optional comma between *oils* and *and.* Choice **c** is incorrect because it does not correct the agreement error, instead making an unnecessary change in vocabulary from *should* to *must.* Choice **d** is incorrect because it does not correct the agreement problem; instead it creates an error by misplacing the modifier *only* between *sweets* and *these.*

10. d. Choice **d** gives a generalization followed by an example in the next sentence. Choice **a** is incorrect because, although it provides the generalization for the subsequent example, it contains an error in pronoun/antecedent agreement (using the pronoun *you,* which disagrees in person with the antecedent *people*). Choice **b** is incorrect because it adds information irrelevant to the development and order of ideas in the passage. Choice **c** is incorrect because it contains the same pronoun/antecedent agreement problem as choice **a**, and because it returns, in the second paragraph of the passage, to information and ideas that are more appropriate to the first paragraph.

11. a. The comma after the word *pyramid* in Part 5 closes off the parenthetical phrase between the subject, *servings,* and the predicate, *should.* Choice **b** is incorrect because it introduces an incomplete comparison into Part 1. Choice **c** is incorrect because, by removing the preposition *of,* it introduces a faulty subordination in Part 7. Choice **d** is incorrect because a colon after *is* would separate the verb from its object.

12. b. The word *appraised,* meaning judged, does not make sense in the context; the correct word for the context is *apprised,* meaning informed. Choices **a, c,** and **d** are all incorrect because the words *incriminate, criteria,* and *ascertain* are all used correctly in the context of the passage.

13. c. The information in Part 5 continues the description of what judges must ascertain about such cases, which began in Part 3. Skipping next to the responsibilities of officers and back to judges, as happens in the passage as it stands, is confusing. Choice **a** is incorrect because it introduces examples before the passage states what the examples are supposed to show. Choice **b** is incorrect for the same reason choice **a** is incorrect. Choice **d** is incorrect because deleting Part 2 removes the statement from which all the paragraph's examples and information follow.

14. b. The topic of the paragraph is about the ecology of an area; it does not specifically address environmental organizations.

15. c. Since the term *environmental groups* is not a proper noun, it does not need to be capitalized. Choices **a, b,** and **d** are grammatically incorrect.

16. a. The topic of the paragraph is the definition of admissible and inadmissible hearsay evidence. Part 4 introduces material about the how trial lawyers prove their cases, which is off the topic. Choices **b, c,** and **d** are incorrect because they contain information pertinent to the topic of the paragraph.

17. c. This choice removes the comma between the subject *hearsay* and the verb *is.* Choices **a, b,** and **d** are all incorrect because they remove commas that are necessary.

18. b. Part 5 contains the comparative form *more,* but the sentence only includes one side of the comparison. The phrase *someone . . . may feel more tired* is an incomplete comparison because it does not state what people feel more tired than. Choices **a, c,** and **d** are incorrect because these parts do not contain incomplete or faulty comparisons.

19. a. The logical relationships among the sentences are, first, between stated fact and the conclusion or hypothesis drawn from the fact, and, second, between the hypothesis and a particular illustration supporting the hypothesis. Choice **a** is correct because the words it offers direct the reader to the correct relationships. Choice **b** is incorrect because the word *however* introduces a contradiction between a supposed fact and the conclusion drawn from the fact. Choice **c** is incorrect because use of the word *eventually* implies a time sequence in the passage rather than an inferential sequence. Choice **d** is incorrect because the word *nevertheless* introduces a contradiction between a supposed fact and a conclusion drawn from the fact.

20. d. The word *researchers* is a possessive noun, and so an apostrophe must be added. Choices **a** and **c** are incorrect because they substitute misused homonyms for the words given. Choice **b** is incorrect because it contains a faulty pronoun/antecedent—the microprobes have a diminutive width, not the brain.

21. d. In Part 4, the adverb *typically* is misused as an adjective to modify the noun wire. Choices **a**, **b**, and **c** do not contain nonstandard uses of modifiers.

22. b. The phrases *since they* [microprobes] *are slightly thinner than a human hair* and *because of their* [microprobes'] *diminutive width* contain the same information. Choices **a**, **c**, and **d** are incorrect because the sentences indicated in those choices are not redundant.

23. a. The predicate does not match the subject grammatically, which is necessary when using the verb *is*: *A passenger-created disturbance* doesn't match *by playing . . . or creating*. Choices **b**, **c**, and **d** are incorrect because none of them contains nonstandard sentences.

24. c. This choice makes use of parallel structure because the list of the drivers' obligations are all expressed in the same subject/verb grammatical form: Bus drivers will wait, will allow, will not allow. In choices **a**, **b**, and **d**, the parallelism of the list is thrown off by the last item in the list, which changes the subject of its verb from operators to passengers.

25. b. Part 6 contains a nonstandard use of a preposition; in this case it is the unidiomatic use of the preposition *to* with the verb *comply*. The standard idiom is *comply with* rather than *comply to*. Choices **a**, **c**, and **d** do not contain nonstandard uses of prepositions.

26. a. This paragraph is written with powerful verbs. *Was looking* is passive and has little impact in the passage. Choices **b**, **c**, and **d** use the active voice.

27. c. Part 3 says *he were sure*. *He* is singular and takes the verb *was*. Choices **a**, **b**, and **d** are incorrect because all verbs are used correctly.

28. b. *Cortez* is a proper noun and should begin with a capital letter. Choices **a**, **c**, and **d** are incorrect because all punctuation is used correctly.

29. d. In Part 3, the relative pronoun *that* is necessary to properly subordinate the clause *programs that meet this rising demand* to the main clause. Retaining the word *than* would introduce a faulty comparison into the sentence. Choice **a** is incorrect because the comma it seeks to remove is necessary to indicate the restrictive nature of the adjective *more*. Choice **b** is incorrect because no comma is necessary after *statistics*. Choice **c** is incorrect because it erroneously inserts the adverb *there* in a context where the possessive pronoun *their* is required.

30. b. Part 6 contains a run-on sentence. Choices **a**, **c**, and **d** are incorrect because they all contain standard sentences.

31. a. Choice **a** is the most logical sentence because it addresses the principles of the topic—Kwanzaa. Choices **b**, **c**, and **d** would support choice **a**. They would not work as the topic sentence.

32. d. Part 2 contains a run-on sentence. These two sentences should be separated with a period after *culture.* Choices **a**, **b**, and **c** are incorrect because they all contain standard sentences.

33. b. This statement maintains the formal tone established by the rest of the passage. Choices **a**, **c**, and **d** are still too informal.

34. d. In Part 1, the pronoun *you* needs to be changed to *we* to agree in number and person to the antecedents used earlier in the passage. Choices **a**, **b**, and **c** are incorrect because none of these sentences contains a nonstandard use of a pronoun.

35. a. *Consequently* means *as a result of.* The adverbs listed in choices **b**, **c**, and **d** do not address this sequence.

36. c. The first paragraph mentions that saving room for herbs such as lavender, sage, thyme, and parsley is a characteristic of a thrifty gardener, but fails to explain why it is a sign of thrift. Choice **a** is incorrect because it removes information that is vital to explaining why the plants mentioned in Part 1 are appropriate to a gardener who has little time. Choice **b** is incorrect because reversing the order of the sentences moves the demonstrative pronoun *these* in Part 2 too far away from its antecedent. Choice **d** is incorrect because the passage does not indicate that growing roses is easy in general; rather, it suggests that particular types of roses (hardy species) are appropriate to a garden that requires little time for maintenance.

37. a. This sentence creates a transition between the idea of harvesting food from a garden and the proper way of planting in order to achieve a good yield of food. Choice **b** is incorrect because it is redundant, repeating information already stated in Part 5. Choice **c** contains information that is on the subject matter of the first paragraph and is, thus, off-topic in the second. Choice **d** is off-topic and out of keeping with the main idea of the paragraph; it mentions time-consuming work in a paragraph on the subject of gardening that takes a moderate amount of time.

38. b. The word *lavished* should be substituted for a similar-sounding word that makes no sense in the context. Choices **a**, **c**, and **d** are incorrect because they would all substitute words that do not fit in the context.

39. c. Part 4 contains a nonstandard verb form, *brung*, as the past-tense form of *to bring*; the correct verb is *brought*. Choices **a**, **b**, and **d** are incorrect because they do not contain nonstandard usages of verbs.

40. b. Part 3 contains a sentence fragment, for there is no main verb in the sentence. Choices **a**, **c**, and **d** are incorrect because none of them contains nonstandard sentences.

Section 3: Writing (Part B— Writing Sample)

Following are the criteria for scoring THEA essays.

A "4" essay is a well-formed writing sample that addresses the assigned topic and conveys a unified message to its audience. Additionally, it has the following characteristics:

- a clear purpose and focus
- controlled development of a main idea
- clear, concrete, and effective details supporting the main idea
- effective, error-free sentence structure
- precise and careful word choice
- mastery of mechanics such as punctuation and spelling

A "3" essay is an adequate writing sample that addresses the assigned topic and clearly attempts to convey a message to its audience. Generally, it has the following additional characteristics:

- a clear focus and purpose
- organization of ideas that may be vague, incomplete, or only partially effective
- an attempt at development of supporting details, which is only partly realized
- word choice and language usage that are adequate; but with minor errors in sentence structure, usage, and word choice
- mechanical mistakes such as errors in spelling and punctuation

A "2" essay is an incompletely formed writing sample that lacks clear focus. It has the following additional characteristics:

- main topic that is announced but focus on it is not maintained
- unclear purpose
- use of some supporting detail but development and organization unclear
- sentences and paragraphs poorly structured
- distracting errors in sentence structure
- imprecise word usage
- distracting mechanical mistakes such as errors in spelling and punctuation

A "1" essay is an incompletely formed writing sample that fails to convey a unified message. It has the following characteristics:

- an attempt at addressing the topic that fails
- no clear main idea
- language and style that are inappropriate to the audience and purpose
- attempt to present supporting detail which is muddled and unclear
- attempt at organization but failure to present a clear sequence of ideas
- ineffective sentences, very few of which are free of error
- imprecise word usage

- many distracting mechanical mistakes, such as errors in spelling and punctuation

A "U" essay is a writing sample that fails because of one or more of the following:

- failure to address the assigned topic
- illegibility
- written primarily in a language other than English
- length insufficient to score

A "B" essay is a writing sample left completely blank (that is, the test-taker did not respond at all).

Following are examples of scored writing samples. (Note: There are some deliberate errors in all the essays.)

Sample "4" essay

Life is full of problems, but how we approach those problems often determines whether we're happy or miserable. Bob Maynard says that "Problems are opportunities in disguise." If we approach problems with Maynard's attitude, we can see that problems are really opportunities to learn about ourselves and others. They enable us to live happier and more fulfilling lives.

Maynard's quote applies to all kinds of problems. I faced a problem just last week when our family's kitchen sink developed a serious leak. There was water all over our kitchen floor and piles of dishes to be washed. But our landlord was out of town for the week. I come from a big family—I have six brothers and sisters—so we couldn't afford to wait until he got back, and my mom couldn't afford a couple hundred dollars to pay for a plummer on her own. So I took the opportunity to learn how to fix it myself. I went to the library and found a great fix-it-yourself book. In just a few hours, I figured out what was causing the leak and how to stop it. If it weren't for that problem, I probably would have relied on plummers and landlords all my life. Now I know I can handle leaky pipes by myself.

I think it's important to remember that no matter how big a problem is, it's still an opportunity. Whatever kind of situation we face, problems give us the chance to learn and grow, both physically and mentally. For example, when I had a problem with my car and couldn't afford the repairs right away, my problem became an opportunity to get some exercise—something I'd been wanting to do anyway. I had to walk a mile each day to get to the bus stop and back. But in the meantime, I got the chance to start getting back in shape, and I saved a lot on gas.

I've come to realize that problems are really part of what makes life worth living. Problems challenge us and give us the opportunity to do things we have never done before, to learn things we never knew before. They teach us what we are capable of doing. They give us the chance to surprise ourselves.

Sample "3" essay

Just the word "problem" can send some of us into a panic. But problems can be good things, too. Problems are situations that make us think and force us to be creative and resourceful. They can also teach us things we didn't know before.

For example, I had a problem in school a few years ago when I couldn't understand my math class. I started failing my quizzes and homework assignments. I wasn't sure what to do, so finally I went to the teacher and asked for help. She said she would arrange for me to be tutorred by another student who was her best student. In return, though, I'd have to help that student around school. I wasn't sure what she meant by that until I met my tutor. She was handicapped.

My job was to help her carry her books from class to class. I'd never even spoken to someone in a wheelchair before and I was a little scared. But she turned out to be the nicest person I've ever spent time with. She helped me understand everything I need to know for math class and she taught me a lot about what it's like to be handicapped. I learned to appreciate everything that I have, and I also know that people with disabilities are special not because of what they can't do, but because of who they are.

So you see that wonderful things can come out of problems. You just have to remember to look for the positive things and not focus on the negative.

Sample "2" essay

The word "problem" is a negative word but its just an opportunity as Mr. Bob Maynard has said. It can be teaching tool besides.

For example, I had a problem with my son last year when he wanted a bigger allowance. I said no and he had to earn it. He mowed the lawn and in the fall he raked leaves. In the winter he shovelled the walk. After that he apreciated it more.

Its not the problem but the sollution that matters. My son learning the value of work and earning money. (It taught me the value of money to when I had to give him a bigger allowance!) After that he could get what he wanted at the toy store and not have to beg. Which was better for me too. Sometimes we forget that both children and there parents can learn a lot from problems and we can teach our children the value of over-coming trouble. Which is as important as keeping them out of trouble. As well we can teach them the value of money. That is one aspect of a problem that we manytimes forget.

So problems are a good teaching tool as well as a good way to let you're children learn, to look at the silver lining behind every cloud.

Sample "1" essay

I agree with the quote that problems are opportunities in disguise. Sometimes problems are opportunities, too.

I have a lot of problems like anyone else does. Sometimes there very difficult and I don't no how to handle them. When I have a really big problem, I sometimes ask my parents or freinds for advise. Sometimes they help, sometimes they don't, then I have to figure out how to handle it myself.

One time I had a big problem. Where someone stole my wallet and I had to get to a job interview. But I had no money and no ID. This happened in school. So I went to the principles office and reported it. He called the man I was supposed to interview with. Who rescheduled the interview for me. So I still had the opportunity to interview and I'm proud to say I got the job. In fact I'm still working there!

Problems can be opportunities if you just look at them that way. Instead of the other way around.

▶ Scoring

Because it is necessary for you to do well on all three sections of the THEA—Reading, Mathematics, and Writing—you must figure your score on each section separately. The Reading section, the Mathematics section, and the multiple-choice subsection of the Writing section are scored the same way: First find the number of questions you got right in each section. Questions you skipped or got incorrect don't count; just add up how many questions were correct in each section.

In addition to achieving a passing score on the Reading section, Mathematics section, and the multiple-choice subsection of the Writing section, you must receive a passing score on the writing sample subsection of the Writing section of the THEA. On this portion, your writing sample will be scored by two readers who have been especially trained for this task, and the combined score will be used to evaluate your work. (Neither reader will know what score was assigned by the other.) Generally, the essays are scored as follows:

4 = Pass (an excellent and well-formed essay)

3 = Marginal Pass (an average and adequately formed essay)

2 = Marginal Fail (a partially formed but sub-standard essay)

1 = Fail (an inadequately formed essay)

Your score will be a combination of the two readers' judgments, somewhere between a possible high of 8 and a low of 2. If you receive a 6, 7, or 8 on the writing sample subsection, you will automatically pass the Writing portion of the THEA, regardless of your score on the multiple-choice subsection. On the other hand, if you receive a score of 2, 3, or 4, you will not pass the Writing portion, regardless of your score on the multiple-choice subsection. If you receive a score of 5, your performance on the multiple-choice subsection will be used to determine if you pass.

The best way to see how you did on your essay for this practice exam is to give your essay and the scoring criteria to a teacher and ask him or her to score your essays for you.

What is much more important than your scores, for now, is how you did on each of the basic skills tested by the exam. You need to diagnose your strengths and weaknesses so that you can concentrate your efforts as you prepare for the exam.

Use your percentage scores in conjunction with the LearningExpress Test Preparation System in Chapter 2 of this book to help you devise a study plan. Then turn to the review lessons in Chapters 4, 5, and 6 that cover each of the basic skills tested on the THEA. You should plan to spend more time on the chapters that correspond to the questions you found hardest and less time on the chapters that correspond to areas in which you did well. Then, you can go on to the other practice exams in Chapters 7 and 8 to see how much you are improving.

▶ THEA Reading Review

CHAPTER SUMMARY

The THEA Reading Review gives you the essentials you need to pass the Reading test. You will learn about reading strategies, hints for different question types, and tips for answering any question you come across.

The reading comprehension section of the THEA is composed of approximately 40 to 50 multiple-choice questions based on a variety of passages. The passages are similar to materials found in first-year college-level courses or textbooks and may include passages from newspapers, journals, and magazines. The questions are a variety of types. This section explores some general strategies for all kinds of passages and questions. The sections that follow look in detail at each kind of question you might be asked.

▶ Seven Approaches

How do you approach reading comprehension questions? Below are some suggestions from former THEA takers.

- **The Concentrator:** "I read the passage thoroughly before I look at the questions. After concentrating on the passage, I can find the answers to the questions if I don't already know the answer from my careful reading."
- **The Skimmer:** "I skim the passage before looking at the questions. I can always go back and find the answers once I know how the passage is arranged."

- **The Cautious Reader:** "I read the questions first with all their answer choices. I want to know what they will ask me before I read the passage so I can be on the lookout. Then I read the passage two or three times until I am sure I understand it completely."

- **The Game Player:** "I read the questions first and try to answer them from what I already know or can guess. Then I read the passage to see whether I am right. After guessing the answers, I am familiar with the questions enough to recognize the answers when I find them."

- **The Educated Guesser:** "I read the questions first, but not the answers. When I find the answer in the passage, I look for it among the answer choices."

- **The Psychic:** "I believe the test makers would put the questions for the first part of the passage first. So I read the first question and go back to the passage for the answer, and then I do the second question."

- **The Efficiency Expert:** "First I look at the questions and do the questions that have line numbers that indicate where the answer is to be found. Then I skim the passage for the key words I read in the other questions. This way, I sometimes do not even have to read the whole passage."

If you don't already have a preferred method, try some of these approaches as you work through the practice exercises in this book. See which method fits your own mix of talents.

▶ Hints for Reading the Passages

The purpose of a reading comprehension problem is to be as accurate as possible in the allotted time. Practice will help you determine whether you need to read the questions first, the answers first, or some combination thereof. Try some of the shortcuts previously listed to find out which works for you.

Associate with the Passage

Every passage has something to do with real-life situations. Your mission is to discover the answers to such questions as:

- What is the author trying to express?
- Who might the author be?
- Does the author tell readers in the beginning what to expect later in the passage?
- How does the author structure the work to convey meaning?
- Does the author make any statements that might surprise or interest you?
- To what conclusions is the author leading readers?
- What conclusions are stated?

Mark Up the Passage

Some test takers find it helpful to underline text or make notes in the margins to designate the stated subject, supporting facts, conclusions, etc. For others, marking a passage seems a waste of time. You are free to make as many marks as you want on the test booklet, so if marking helps, go for it. If you are not sure, now is the time to try out this method. If you decide to mark a passage, don't mark so much that the bulk of the passage is obscured. Marking a few key words and ideas is more helpful than underlining the majority of the passage.

Notice Transitions

Pay special attention to words that give you an insight into the author's purpose or that change the context of the passage, such as *however*, *nevertheless*, etc. In at least one passage, these words will be left for you to fill in.

▶ Hints for Reading the Questions

Reading the questions carefully is just as important as reading the answers.

Read the Questions as Carefully as the Passage

It is crucial that you read the questions and answers as carefully as you read the passage. Should you read all the answer choices or stop when you have found one that seems right? Test takers differ on this. Some who read all the answers become confused or worry about wasting time. Others feel more secure when they can eliminate every answer but the right one. It is up to you to find the best method.

Know the Question Types

If you answer an inference question as a detail question, you will get the answer wrong, even though the answer you choose is in the passage. The reading strategies in this chapter will show you how to recognize the different question types and how to quickly choose the best answer.

Answer Only from the Passage

Everything you need to know to answer a question has to be somewhere in the passage. While it is helpful to have some knowledge of the subject in order to better understand the author, don't rely on your experience to answer the question. An answer can be true in real life but still not be the correct answer on the test.

Not or *Except*

Look for words in the question such as NOT or EXCEPT, especially if you cannot find your answer, or if there seems to be more than one answer. For example, a question might read: "Which of the following facts is NOT stated in the passage?"

Eliminate

Eliminate all answers that are obviously off the subject or otherwise wrong. Physically cross off the obviously wrong answers in your test booklet so you won't waste time reading them again. Test takers say that they are often left with two close answers. There has to be one answer that is better than the other. Check the passage for clue words that might point to one choice over the other. If, after trying out all the strategies you learn in this book, you are still left with two answers, go ahead and guess, and get on with the next question.

None Left?

If you eliminate all of the answers, go back over the eliminated answers to determine whether there might be another meaning for any of them. Try to find a reason that would make each answer correct. If there is no possible way an answer could be right—for example, if it is completely off the subject—then eliminate that answer. Choose the answer that is the least wrong.

Marking the Unknown Question

Should you mark questions to come back to later? If you do, you will probably have to read the passage again, which can waste valuable time. If an answer jumps out at you after reading the passage once or twice, choose it. Many teachers and test takers recommend going with your first answer, your gut instinct. To save time and avoid dealing with passages more than once, answer all the questions about one passage before continuing on to the next passage.

▶ Using the Steps

The strategies that follow discuss types of reading questions you may encounter on the THEA. They offer sample question beginnings, as well as steps for solving each type of problem. There is no need to memorize all the steps. You may even be able to find the answer by your own methods without looking at the steps—so much the better. The steps are not there to slow you down, but if any of them can help you, use them.

Organization Questions

Passages on the THEA are always organized logically. Studying that organization may give you some ideas on how to organize your essay in the Writing portion of the test. You'll learn about two types of organization questions: structure and misplaced sentences.

▶ Structure Questions

Structure questions usually have stems like these:

- Which of the following best represents the arrangement of the passage?
- Which of the following best describes the organization of the passage?
- The sequence of the passage is best represented by which of the following?

Where to Find Structure Answers in the Passage

To answer structure questions, you need to skim the passage carefully enough to discover the gist of each sentence; that is, whether it is a statistic, an example, a quote, an opinion, or something else.

Practice Passage and Questions

Try the six steps on the structure questions that follow this passage.

Many extended-time programs use heterogeneous grouping of multi-age and/or multi-ability students. Mixed-ability grouping is based on the theory that lower-ability students benefit from working in small groups with their higher-achieving peers, and high-ability students reinforce their knowledge by sharing with their lower-achieving peers. Researchers also have found that multi-age grouping benefits students' mental health as well as academic achievement and contributes to positive attitudes toward school.

Because the voluntary nature of participation in an extended-time program results in a range of student ages and skills, heterogeneous groups may result naturally. Often, however, extended-time program planners arrange groups so that high- and low-ability students work together—with the expectation of cooperative rather than competitive learning. In Chicago's ASPIRA program, students are selected for participation with a goal of mixing high achievers and at-risk participants—and these groups work together closely in all activities.

Six Steps for Structure Questions

1. Skim the passage or read the topic sentences to understand the general topic and the purpose of the passage.
2. Notice the logical sequence of ideas that the author uses.
3. The description of sentences in the answers goes in the same order as the sentences in the passage, so notice the first sentences. Do they state a theory, introduce a topic, or quote a famous person?
4. Look at the answer choices. If the first few sentences state a theory, then the first part of the correct answer should say that the author *states a theory*, *gives a hypothesis*, or other words to that effect. Eliminate any answers that do not match.
5. Apply steps 3 and 4 to the next few sentences in the passage.
6. You should have eliminated at least one or two answers by this step. When only two or three are left, read the next sentences of the passage and find the answer that matches the rest of the structure.

1. Which of the following best describes the structure of the passage?

   a. The passage begins with a hypothesis, and then gives an explanation and support for this theory.

   b. The passage starts with a main idea, gives an example, and then draws a conclusion.

   c. The passage opens with an introduction to the topic, then gives a more detailed account of the topic.

   d. The passage begins with a statement, supports that statement with research, and gives real life examples.

2. Which of the following would be the best outline for the passage?

   a.   I.   Statement
         II. Facts
        III. Quotations

   b.   I.   Theory
         II. Practices

   c.   I.   Research
         II. Discussion
        III. Example

   d.   I.   Question
         II. Answer
        III. Support

Answers

Here is how you could use the six steps to answer question 1.

1. It seems as though the passage is about students of different ages and abilities learning together.

2. The first paragraph tells why and the second tells how students come to be in groups of mixed ability and age.

3. The first sentence states a fact. The other sentences in the paragraph seem to cite research.

The sentence beginning *Researchers also found . . .* implies that research was involved in the theories presented in the second sentence.

4. Choices **c** and **a** are out. The passage does not give much introduction to the topic, and does not present a hypothesis.

5. The next sentences support the topic sentence with research. The answer must be **d**.

6. For this question, you don't need to use this hint.

If you use the same method to answer question 2, you will quickly eliminate answer **d** on the basis of the first few sentences. You eliminate choice **a** because there are no quotations. You are left with choices **b** and **c**, which are very close. Choice **c** contains a vague word, *discussion,* which could be almost any kind of structure. Choice **b** is more precise. The first paragraph in the passage gives the theory, and the second gives the application of the theory. The correct answer is **b**.

▶ Misplaced Sentences

You may be asked to find a sentence that does not logically flow, or that is not necessary to the purpose of the passage. Such questions often start like this:

- Which sentence, if omitted from the passage, would be least likely to interrupt the sequence of ideas?
- Which of the following is least relevant to the main idea of the passage?

Where to Find Misplaced Sentences

In this type of question, you will usually be directed to a particular paragraph. If the first sentence states the main idea of the paragraph, it is unlikely to be the misplaced sentence. Check all others.

Two Steps for Misplaced Sentences

1. Read the passage to determine the main idea.
2. Suspect any sentence that has nothing to do with the main idea.

Practice Passage and Question

Lymph nodes, which measure about 1 to 25 centimeters across, and small vessels called *lymphatics* compose the lymphatic system. The nodes are located in various parts of the body and are connected by the lymphatics. The skin, the largest organ of the human body, is also considered to be a part of the immune system. The nodes work with the body's immune system to fight off infectious agents like bacteria and fungus.

3. Which sentence in the first paragraph is least relevant to the main idea of the paragraph?
   a. Lymph nodes, which measure about 1 to 25 centimeters across, and small vessels called lymphatics compose the lymphatic system.
   b. The nodes are located in various parts of the body and are connected by the lymphatics.
   c. The nodes work with the body's immune system to fight off infectious agents like bacteria and fungus.
   d. The skin, the largest organ of the human body, is also considered to be a part of the immune system.

Answer

The passage describes the lymphatic system's role in fighting off infections. The third sentence has nothing to do with the lymphatic system; therefore, the answer is choice **d**.

Finding the Main Idea

Main idea questions can be put in three categories. The first category asks for a simple sentence or title that includes the main topic of the passage. The second category asks questions about the author and what the author had in mind. Then there are those questions that ask for a paraphrase of all the main ideas in the passage.

Main Idea Questions

Simple main idea questions take a variety of forms:

- What is the main idea of the passage?
- The best title for this passage would be . . .
- What is the theme of the passage?
- The central thought of the passage is . . .

How to Find Main Idea Answers in the Passage

To answer main idea questions, you sometimes do not have to read the whole passage. Often the main idea is stated at the beginning or end of the passage. Sometimes you can identify the main idea by paying attention to the topic sentences of each paragraph of the passage.

Practice Passage and Question

Here is a passage that's similar to one you already read in this chapter.

The immune system, which protects the body from infections, diseases, and other injuries, is composed of the lymphatic system and the skin. Lymph nodes, which measure about 1 to 25 centimeters across, and small vessels called lymphatics compose the lymphatic system. The nodes are located in various parts of the body and are connected by the lymphatics. The nodes work with the body's immune system to fight off infectious agents like bacteria and fungus. When infected, the lymph nodes are often swollen and sensitive.

1. While reading the passage, notice the general topic.
2. Go through the answer choices. Cross out any that are completely off the topic.
3. Cross out any that are too broad for a short passage.
4. Eliminate an answer that is on the general topic but that is not the specific topic of the passage.
5. Cross out any answer choices that only deal with one sentence of a paragraph or one paragraph of a longer passage.
6. If you are still left with two answers that seem to fit most of the sentences in the passage, then choose the one that is most specific.
7. If you have crossed out all choices, check each one again. Consider whether there is another meaning to any of the answer choices. If you're still stumped, go back to the answer that was the most specific and seems to cover more of the passage than the others.

The skin, the largest organ of the human body, is also considered to be a part of the immune system. Hundreds of small nerves in the skin send messages to the brain to communicate pressure, pain, and other sensations. The skin encloses the organs to prevent injuries and forms a protective barrier that repels dirt and water and stops the entry of most harmful chemicals. Sweat glands in the skin help regulate the body's temperature, and other glands release oils that can kill or impede the growth of certain bacteria. Hair follicles in the skin also provide protection, especially of the skull.

4. Which of the following best describes the main topic of the passage?
    a. The immune system is often analyzed and praised by prominent scientists.
    b. The skin and its glands are responsible for preventing most infections.
    c. The lymphatic system and the skin work together to protect the body from infection.
    d. Communication between the lymphatic system and the brain is essential in preventing and fighting infection.

Answer

Use the seven steps to help you answer the question.

1. The general topic seems to have to do with the immune system.
2. It looks as though choice **a** is off the topic because the passage does not mention any prominent scientists.
3. None of the choices seems too broad.
4. Choice **d** seems to be off of the topic of the passage.
5. Choice **b** is too specific because it only refers to one sentence of a paragraph.

You don't have to use steps 6 and 7, because you have one answer left; choice **c** is the only answer that is the main idea of the passage.

Practice Passage and Question

Try another passage and main idea question.

Ballet is an important art form that offers audiences grace and beauty. There are many classic ballets that are still performed today. Many people would agree that *Swan Lake* is among the most popular classic ballets. Indeed, dance companies all over the world still perform this graceful ballet. *Swan Lake* is a story about a beautiful young woman who is transformed by a magician into a swan queen. She is allowed to resume her human form only at midnight, for one brief hour. It is during this precious hour that a handsome prince and his hunting partners find her. As the young woman pleads with the prince not to kill the swans he is hunting, the prince falls deeply in love with her. The young woman, Odette, and the prince perform magical dances during this classic piece.

5. Which of the following would be the best title for the passage?
  a. The Importance of Ballet
  b. *Swan Lake* Is a Popular Classic Ballet
  c. Ballerinas Aspire to Perform the Role of Odette in *Swan Lake*
  d. Anna Pavlova Performs as Odette in *Swan Lake*

Answer

Apply the seven steps.

1. The passage seems to be about the classic ballet *Swan Lake*.
2. Choice **d** appears to be off the topic since Anna Pavlova is not mentioned in the passage.
3. Choice **a** is too broad.
4. Choice **c** is on the general topic of *Swan Lake*, but not on the particular subject of the paragraph.
5. Choice **b** summarizes the main idea of the passage. Although the popularity and appeal of the particular ballet *Swan Lake* is not mentioned until the third sentence, the first two sentences create a broad topic that narrows to the specific, and main, idea. Once again, you did not have to use steps 6 and 7.

▶ Perfect Summary

Paraphrase, or summary, questions are the most troublesome of all the main idea questions because the answer choices are so long. Realize, however, that the test makers had to make three of the choices wrong in some way. Your task is to discover the errors.

Seven Steps for Summary Questions

1. Read or skim the passage, noting or underlining main ideas as they flow from one to the other.
2. Look for phrases that restate the main ideas you underlined.
3. Eliminate answers that contain phrases that contradict ideas in the passage.
4. Eliminate answers that are off the topic or only deal with part of the passage.
5. Eliminate answers that state one or more ideas that the author has not mentioned.
6. If you are left with two choices, choose the most complete one.
7. If you have eliminated all the choices, choose the summary that contains the most ideas that actually appear in the passage.

Summary questions tend to start out like this:

- The best summary of the passage is . . .
- Which of the following best paraphrases the ideas in the passage?
- Which of the following is the best summation of the ideas in the passage?
- Which of the following best restates the main idea of the passage?

How to Find Summary Answers in the Passage

The main idea of the passage can be found in each of the paragraphs, or in sections of the paragraphs. If you can follow the way the author has logically arranged the passage, you are more likely to find the correct answer to a summary question.

Practice Passage and Question

Use the seven steps to answer the question following this passage.

Extended-time programs often feature innovative scheduling, as program staff work to maintain participation and respond to students' and parents' varied schedules and family or employment commitments. Offering students flexibility and some choice regarding when they participate in extended learning may be as simple as offering homework sessions when children need them most—after school and before dinner—as do Kids Crew and the Omaha After-School Study Centers. Or it may mean keeping early and late hours to meet the child care needs of parents who work more than one job or support extended families, as does Yuk Yau Child Development Center. Similarly, the Florida Summer Institute for At-Risk Migrant Students is a residential program so that students' participation does not disrupt their migrant families' travels.

6. Which of the following paraphrases best summarizes the passage above?
   a. After-school programs should help children finish their homework after school.
   b. Kids Crew and other programs meet the needs of children.
   c. There are several ways to schedule programs outside school time to meet the needs of students and families.
   d. Extended-time programs can be innovative, and Yuk Yau Child Development Center is an example of this.

Answer

Go through the seven steps.

1. The flow goes like this: innovative scheduling— family needs—examples: after school, early and late care, residential.
2. Choices a, c, and d have words and ideas noted in step 1.
3. None of the choices is contrary to the passage. (That tactic is usually used with persuasive passages.)
4. The answers are all on topic, but a and b only deal with part of the paragraph.
5. All the ideas are in the passage.
6. You are left with choices c and d. Choice d only mentions one example and the passage gives three. Choice c does not mention any examples specifically, but is broad enough to include all the examples as well as the main idea of the paragraph. You can conclude that the answer is c, and you don't have to use step 7.

▶ About the Author

Authors write to communicate; that is, they want you to understand their ideas and arguments. To that end, they usually will try to write as clearly and logically as possible. To read these passages efficiently, therefore, you need to give the author your undivided attention and try to understand his or her motives and methods in writing the piece. As you read, ask yourself these questions:

- Who is this person?
- Can I detect anything about the author?
- From what perspective does the author write?
- How does the author think?
- What was the author trying to accomplish?
- For whom was the author writing?

Sample question stems for author questions might include the following:

- The author's primary purpose is to . . .
- The author is primarily concerned with . . .
- The main focus of the author is . . .
- In what publication might this passage be found?
- The author is writing primarily for what kind of audience?

- Which best describes the author's relationship with . . .
- Which best describes the feeling of the author toward his subject?
- The attitude of the author toward . . .

▶ How to Find Author Answers in the Passage

You may discover the purpose of the author, like the main idea, in the first or last sentence of the passage, or by looking at the topic sentences of the paragraphs. You can also skim the passage for descriptive words that reveal any bias the author has. The subject of the passage and the absence or presence of technical language are two of the main clues toward discovering the author's intended audience.

Practice Passage and Question

Lincoln's 1863 Thanksgiving Proclamation
It is the duty of nations as well as of men to own their dependence upon the overruling power of God; to confess their sins and transgressions in humble sorrow, yet with assured hope that genuine repentance will lead to mercy and pardon; and to recognize the sublime truth, announced in the Holy

Six Steps for Author Questions

1. For author purpose questions, eliminate answers that do not match the general topic. For questions about the author's intended audience, eliminate audiences that are significantly less or more technical than the author's style.
2. Eliminate answers that say the opposite of what the author is trying to say.
3. Look for a sentence or two that describes the author's purpose or audience.
4. Look for words that indicate a shift in the author's meaning. Sometimes the author's purpose will follow words such as *however*, *although*, or *instead of*.
5. If you are looking for an author's tone, label the answer choices as positive or negative.
6. If you are left with two choices, look at the topic of the passage and decide what might be an appropriate response to the topic.

Scriptures and proven by all history, that those nations are blessed whose God is the Lord.

We know that by His divine law, nations, like individuals, are subjected to punishments and chastisements in this world. May we not justly fear that the awful calamity of civil war which now desolates the land may be a punishment inflicted upon us for our presumptuous sins, to the needful end of our national reformation as a whole people?

We have been the recipients of the choicest bounties of heaven; we have been preserved these many years in peace and prosperity; we have grown in numbers, wealth and power as no other nation has ever grown.

But we have forgotten God. We have forgotten the gracious hand which preserved us in peace and multiplied and enriched and strengthened us, and we have vainly imagined, in the deceitfulness of our hearts, that all these blessings were produced by some superior wisdom and virtue of our own. Intoxicated with unbroken success, we have become too self-sufficient to feel the necessity of redeeming and preserving grace, too proud to pray to the God that made us.

It has seemed to me fit and proper that God should be solemnly, reverently and gratefully acknowledged, as with one heart and one voice, by the whole American people. I do therefore invite my fellow citizens in every part of the United States, and also those who are at sea and those who are sojourning in foreign lands, to set apart and observe the last Thursday of November as a day of Thanksgiving and praise to our beneficent Father who dwelleth in the heavens.

7. Lincoln's purpose in proclaiming a holiday was to
  a. make peace with Native Americans.
  b. promote separation of church and state.
  c. thank God for blessings and favor.
  d. bring complaints as well as thankfulness before God.

Answer
Use the six steps to answer the question.

1. Choice **a** does not match the general topic.
2. Choice **b** says the opposite of what Lincoln meant; he was proposing that all Americans thank God.
3. The last sentence seems to be a climax. Both **c** and **d** contain the idea of thankfulness.
4. The word *but* at the beginning of the fourth paragraph seems to indicate a shift, but that shift is really part of Lincoln's meaning; he is contrasting the blessings America has experienced with Americans' having forgotten God.
5. This isn't a tone question, so you don't need this step.
6. You're left with choices **c** and **d**. The holiday was about thanking God, not bringing complaints. Look again for mention of complaints in the passage. There isn't one, so the closest answer is **c**.

Practice Passage and Questions
Now try the steps on the questions that follow this passage.

The most significant research results produced are as follows: In the area of micro-ecological adaptation and evolutionary process, our research has shown that regardless of the complexity of the selection force and the biological traits, the rate of evolutionary change of the plant populations has been rapid and the results are even better than we expected. Further study of the interactions between plants and their soil environments found that a successful colonization of plant species in soils with elevated toxic levels of soil chemical compounds such as selenium may be achieved in the presence of other chemical compounds (such as sulfate) that could alleviate the toxic effects and improve the conditions for colonization. The knowledge generated by these ecological studies has made it possible to apply the research with more confidence.

8. In what publication might this passage be published?

    a. a book of dissertation abstracts

    b. a general encyclopedia

    c. a bulletin to parents

    d. a science teacher's manual

9. Which of the following can best describe the author's attitude toward the results of the research?

    a. unbiased

    b. satisfied

    c. apologetic

    d. elated

Answers

Here's how you could use the steps on question 8.

1. This is a rather technical passage. Eliminate **c**.
2. Although no choice disagrees with the author, a science teacher's manual would have hints in it for teaching students. There are no clues that this is a teacher's manual. Choice **d** is gone.
3. There is no climax.
4. There are clue words, though they're not easy to find. The author mentions research that is being done. Encyclopedias don't include current research, so **b** is eliminated. That leaves you with choice **a**. This makes sense because a dissertation is someone's research. (You don't need to use steps 5–6.)

For question 9, you have an attitude question.

1. This is a scientific paper so it has to be fairly objective.
2–4. You don't need these steps for an attitude question.

5. From negative to positive, you might rank the answer choices like this: *apologetic, unbiased, satisfied, elated*. There are some clue words; "even better than we expected" and "more confidence" sound as though you should look on the positive side of the list, which includes choices **b** and **d**.
6. This is a research report. *Elated* probably would not be appropriate. The author might be elated, but there are no clues in the passage that the author is that happy. *Satisfied,* choice **b**, seems the closest choice.

▶ Define Details and Context Clues

Most people find detail questions fairly easy to answer, because the answers are right there in the passage. Words in context may be a bit more difficult because you have to look for clues to the word's meaning in the context of the passage. However, you have probably been answering detail questions and figuring out words from context most of your life. These questions mean (relatively) easy points for you. All you need are some strategies to help enhance your speed and accuracy.

Details

Detail questions ask about one specific fact in the passage. They are signaled by question words such as *what, when,* or *where.* You will often find the phrase "according to the passage" in a detail question.

How to Find Detail Answers in the Passage

Detail answers are usually in the body of the paragraphs. Normally they are not in the main idea sentences.

Six Steps for Detail Questions

1. Notice the way the passage is arranged.

2. Search the passage for the detail asked for in the question.

3. Skim for key words. Look for words that are in the question. Once you find the words, find the answer in that sentence.

4. Eliminate answers that contain facts that are not found in the passage. Also eliminate choices that are found in the passage but that do not answer the question.

5. If you are having trouble finding the answer, you may need to review up to five lines above a key word.

6. Do not let technical words stop you from answering the question. You are not being tested on technical language alone. There is always enough information in the passage to answer a detail question without previous knowledge of the topic.

Practice Passage and Questions

Recycling goods gives communities the opportunity to lower their waste output, reduce disposal costs, and most importantly, combat global environmental problems. Recycling paper, glass, plastic, metals, and organic wastes lessens the demand for raw materials and energy. Producing aluminum from scrap instead of raw materials trims air pollution by over 90%. Creating paper from recycled goods reduces the amount of energy needed to process it by over 70%, and it also saves trees. Governmental sources of information about recycling include the Department of Environmental Protection, Solid Waste Management, the Department of Natural Resources, and the Public Works Department.

10. Which fact is NOT found in the passage?
    a. Governmental sources of information about recycling include the Public Works Department.
    b. Producing aluminum from scrap instead of raw materials trims air pollution by over 90%.
    c. Producing plastic from recycled materials lowers air pollution by over 70%.
    d. Recycling glass and metals lessens the demand for raw materials and energy.

11. According to the passage, which substances should be recycled?
    a. paper, glass, rubber, and metals
    b. plastic, colored glass, and newsprint paper
    c. organic wastes, small metal parts, and glass
    d. paper, glass, plastic, metals, and organic wastes

12. With which of the following would the author be most likely to agree?
    a. Americans don't have time to recycle their garbage.
    b. Recycling will help save the earth.
    c. Plastic is a valuable resource, so we shouldn't try to reuse it.
    d. We should recycle even though it costs more and uses more energy to do so.

Answers

For detail questions, you don't necessarily have to work through all the steps. Here are some tips on how you might have answered the questions.

10. Because you are being asked to look up each answer in the passage to see whether it is there, this is really four questions in one. If you decide to take the time to answer this question at all, you should leave it until you have answered the other questions about this passage. By then, you will have discovered how the passage is arranged, and you may have even noticed some of the facts in the passage. Choice **a** is found in the last sentence. Choices **b** and **d** are also contained in the paragraph. You can find all the answers but **c** in the passage. The passage states that producing aluminum (not plastic) from recycled materials lowers air pollution by over 90% (not 70%). The answer is **c**.

11. The answer is **d**. The other choices all contain one or more items that are not discussed in the passage.

12. Use the process of elimination for this question. Choices **a** and **d** are in direct opposition to the other ideas expressed in the passage. Choice **c** is not related to the overall message of the passage and is contrary to the writer's purpose. The answer is **b**. Even though the author doesn't directly say this, it can be inferred from the first sentence of the passage: "Recycling goods gives communities the opportunity to lower their waste output, reduce disposal costs, and most importantly, combat global environmental problems." Another hint is the phrase "it also saves trees."

▶ Words in Context

Another type of question on the THEA has to do with words in context. You will have to look for clues to answer these kinds of questions. Questions on words in context have stems like these:

- What is the best synonym for _____ as it is used in the passage?
- Which of the following is the best meaning of _____ as it is used in the second sentence?

How to Find Words-in-Context Answers

Answers to words-in-context questions are found in the sentences immediately preceding, including, and following the word. Usually there is some explanation nearby—some synonym for the word or paraphrase of its meaning.

Practice Passage and Question

In his famous study of myth, *The Hero With a Thousand Faces*, Joseph Campbell writes about the archetypal hero who has ventured outside the boundaries of the village and, after many trials and adventures, has returned with the boon that will save or enlighten his fellows. Like Carl Jung, Campell believes that the story of the hero is part of the collective unconscious of all human kind. He likens the returning hero to the sacred or tabooed personage described by James Frazier in *The Golden Bough*. Such an individual must, in many instances of myth, be insulated from the rest of society, "not merely for his own sake but for the sake of others; for since the virtue of holiness is, so to say, a powerful explosive which the smallest touch can detonate, it is necessary in the interest of the general safety to keep it within narrow bounds."

There is much similarity between the archetypal hero who has journeyed into the wilderness and the poet who has journeyed into the realm of imagination. Both places are dangerous and full of wonders, and both, at their deepest level, are journeys that take place into the kingdom of the unconscious mind, a place that, in Campbell's words, "goes down into unsuspected Aladdin caves. There not only jewels but dangerous jinn abide . . ."

1. Locate the word and read at least five lines above the word to catch the context. Notice any context clues—words or phrases that explain the meaning of the word.

2. Eliminate all answers that have nothing to do with the passage or the context.

3. If you are lucky, you may encounter an answer choice that is a different part of speech from the word or phrase in question. Think for a minute to make sure this answer choice doesn't have an alternate meaning that is the same part of speech, and if it doesn't, eliminate it.

4. Place the remaining words in the blank and read to see which one fits best.

5. If you think you know the word, make sure the passage uses the word in the same way. Many of the answers will be different possible meanings of the word in question.

6. Look for clues in root words, prefixes, and suffixes.

---

13. Which of the following is the most accurate definition of the word *boon* as it is used in the passage?

    a. present

    b. blessing

    c. charm

    d. curse

Answer

Even if you don't know the definition of the word *boon*, you can determine its meaning from the context of the passage. You can determine that *boon* is a positive term because the passage states that the hero's boon will save or enlighten his fellows. Therefore, you can eliminate choice **d**, *curse*, which is negative. You can also guess from the context of the passage that a *boon* is likely to be intangible and not a concrete *present* or *charm*, (choices **a** and **c**). Choice **b** offers the most accurate definition of *boon*, which is a timely benefit, favor, or blessing.

▶ Inferences and Fill in the Blanks

Inference and fill-in-the-blank questions are both challenging. However, many test takers claim that inference questions are one of the most difficult on the exam. Inference questions are sometimes confused with detail questions. The same answer that might be correct for a detail question, however, will be wrong for an inference question. Knowing how inference questions are likely to be phrased will help you distinguish them from detail questions. Inference question stems usually include words like those highlighted below:

- The author **implies** that . . .
- The author **suggests** that . . .
- It can be **concluded** from this passage that . . .
- The passage **implies** that . . .
- The narrator **hints** that . . .
- It can be **inferred** from the passage that . . .
- Which of the following is **closest** to the author's **outlook** on . . . ?
- The feature that _____ and _____ have in common is . . .

How to Find Inference Answers

Inferences are not directly stated in the passage. If an answer choice can be found in the passage, it is not the right answer. Look, however, for items, people, events, or ideas in the passage that might relate to other items, people, events, or ideas in the passage.

1. Skim the passage to see how it is organized. Find the main ideas.
2. Eliminate any answers that are off the topic.
3. Look for an answer choice that says the same thing in an opposite way.
4. Eliminate any answers that are unreasonable or that cannot be drawn from the facts in the passage.
5. Eliminate any answers that can be concluded from the statements in the passage, but do not answer the question.
6. Choose the answer that is most clearly concluded from the statements in the passage.

Practice Passage and Question

Many educational reformers have focused their efforts over the last decade on instructional practices such as cooperative learning that emphasize problem solving and decision making over solitary reliance on memorization of facts and theories. Furthermore, programs that emphasize problem solving and decision making directly address the national education goal of helping prepare students "for responsible citizenship, further learning, and productive employment in our modern economy." Several programs offer strategies for addressing problem solving and decision making, ranging from in-class discussions and the use of board games to designing and conducting community service activities. For example, tutors at Raising Academic Achievement focus on problem-solving skills and are trained to help students "think, explore, solve, and look back" when working on mathematics problems.

14. Which of the following can be inferred from the information in the passage?
   a. Tutors at Raising Academic Achievement help ensure that students will be productively employed when they become adults.
   b. Cooperative learning emphasizes problem-solving techniques.
   c. Playing board games increases problem-solving skills.
   d. Responsible citizenship should be taught in school.

Answer

Go through the steps.

1. The passage is short and the question offers no topic or location clues.
2. It looks as though **d** is off the topic since the paragraph is not about teaching responsible citizenship; it is only mentioned in passing.
3. Choice **b** is mentioned in the first sentence. Choice **c** is mentioned further on. These two answers can be eliminated. That leaves choice **a**. The passage does not explicitly state that the tutors will help future employment, but it does say tutors help with problem-solving skills and that problem-solving skills will help with future employment. Choice **a** is one step removed from the facts of the passage, so it is the right answer. (You didn't need to use steps 4–6.)

Graphs

Graphs are found in both the reading and the math sections of the THEA. For more information on graphs, please see Chapter 5.

Now that you have reviewed your reading skills, turn to Chapter 5 for a math review.

5 ▶ THEA Math Review

CHAPTER SUMMARY

This review covers the math skills you need to know for the THEA Mathematics test. You will learn about arithmetic, measurement, algebra, geometry, and data analysis.

The THEA Mathematics section measures those mathematical skills and concepts that an educated adult might need. Many of the problems require the integration of multiple skills to achieve a solution. It is composed of between 40 and 50 multiple-choice questions.

▶ Arithmetic

This section covers the basics of mathematical operations and their sequence. It also reviews variables, integers, fractions, decimals, and square roots.

Numbers and Symbols

NUMBERS AND THE NUMBER LINE
- **Counting numbers** (or natural numbers): 1, 2, 3, . . .
- **Whole numbers** include the counting numbers and zero: 0, 1, 2, 3, 4, 5, 6, . . .

- **Integers** include the whole numbers and their opposites. Remember, the opposite of zero is zero: . . . −3, −2, −1, 0, 1, 2, 3, . . .
- **Rational numbers** are all numbers that can be written as fractions, where the numerator and denominator are both integers, but the denominator is not zero. For example, $\frac{2}{3}$ is a rational number, as is $\frac{-6}{5}$. The decimal form of these numbers is either a terminating (ending) decimal, such as the decimal form of $\frac{3}{4}$ which is 0.75; or a repeating decimal, such as the decimal form of $\frac{1}{3}$ which is 0.3333333 . . .
- **Irrational numbers** are numbers that cannot be expressed as terminating or repeating decimals (i.e. non-repeating, non-terminating decimals such as π, $\sqrt{2}$, $\sqrt{12}$).

The number line is a graphical representation of the order of numbers. As you move to the right, the value increases. As you move to the left, the value decreases.

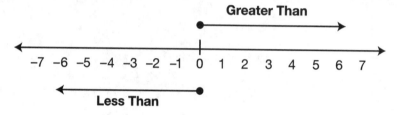

If we need a number line to reflect certain rational or irrational numbers, we can estimate where they should be.

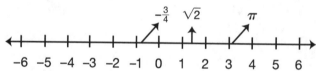

COMPARISON SYMBOLS

The following table will illustrate some comparison symbols:

=	is equal to	5 = 5
≠	is not equal to	4 ≠ 3
>	is greater than	5 > 3
≥	is greater than or equal to	$x \geq 5$ (x can be 5 or any number > 5)
<	is less than	4 < 6
≤	is less than or equal to	$x \leq 3$ (x can be 3 or any number < 3)

SYMBOLS OF ADDITION

In addition, the numbers being added are called **addends**. The result is called a **sum**. The symbol for addition is called a **plus** sign. In the following example, 4 and 5 are addends and 9 is the sum:

$$4 + 5 = 9$$

SYMBOLS OF SUBTRACTION

In subtraction, the number being subtracted is called the **subtrahend**. The number being subtracted FROM is called the **minuend**. The answer to a subtraction problem is called a **difference**. The symbol for subtraction is called a **minus** sign. In the following example, 15 is the minuend, 4 is the subtrahend, and 11 is the difference:

$$15 - 4 = 11$$

SYMBOLS OF MULTIPLICATION

When two or more numbers are being multiplied, they are called **factors**. The answer that results is called the **product**. In the following example, 5 and 6 are factors and 30 is their product:

$$5 \times 6 = 30$$

There are several ways to represent multiplication in the above mathematical statement.

- A dot between factors indicates multiplication:
  $5 \cdot 6 = 30$
- Parentheses around any one or more factors indicate multiplication:
  $(5)6 = 30$, $5(6) = 30$, and $(5)(6) = 30$.
- Multiplication is also indicated when a number is placed next to a variable: $5a = 30$. In this equation, 5 is being multiplied by a.

SYMBOLS OF DIVISION

In division, the number being divided BY is called the **divisor**. The number being divided INTO is called the **dividend**. The answer to a division problem is called the **quotient**.

There are a few different ways to represent division with symbols. In each of the following equivalent expressions, 3 is the divisor and 8 is the dividend:

$$8 \div 3, \quad 8/3, \quad \frac{8}{3}, \quad 3\overline{)8}$$

PRIME AND COMPOSITE NUMBERS

A positive integer that is greater than the number 1 is either prime or composite, but not both.

■ A **prime** number is a number that has exactly two factors: 1 and itself.

> **Examples**
> 2, 3, 5, 7, 11, 13, 17, 19, 23 . . .

■ A **composite** number is a number that has more than two factors.

> **Examples**
> 4, 6, 8, 9, 10, 12, 14, 15, 16 . . .

■ The number 1 is neither prime nor composite since it has only one factor.

Operations

ADDITION

Addition is used when it is necessary to combine amounts. It is easiest to add when the addends are stacked in a column with the place values aligned. Work from right to left, starting with the ones column.

> **Example**
> Add 40 + 129 + 24.

1. Align the addends in the ones column. Since it is necessary to work from right to left, begin to add starting with the ones column. Since the ones column totals 13, and 13 equals 1 ten and 3 ones, write the 3 in the ones column of the answer, and regroup or "carry" the 1 ten to the next column as a 1 over the tens column so it gets added with the other tens:

$$
\begin{array}{r}
\overset{1}{} \\
40 \\
129 \\
+\ 24 \\
\hline
3 \\
\end{array}
$$

2. Add the tens column, including the regrouped 1.

$$
\begin{array}{r}
^{1}\\
40\\
129\\
+\ \ 24\\
\hline
93
\end{array}
$$

3. Then add the hundreds column. Since there is only one value, write the 1 in the answer.

$$
\begin{array}{r}
^{1}\\
40\\
129\\
+\ \ 24\\
\hline
193
\end{array}
$$

SUBTRACTION

Subtraction is used to find the difference between amounts. It is easiest to subtract when the minuend and subtrahend are in a column with the place values aligned. Again, just as in addition, work from right to left. It may be necessary to regroup.

Example

If Becky has 52 clients, and Claire has 36, how many more clients does Becky have?

1. Find the difference between their client numbers by subtracting. Start with the ones column. Since 2 is less than the number being subtracted (6), regroup or "borrow" a ten from the tens column. Add the regrouped amount to the ones column. Now subtract 12 – 6 in the ones column.

$$
\begin{array}{r}
^{4\,1}\\
\not5\not2\\
-\ \ 36\\
\hline
6
\end{array}
$$

2. Regrouping 1 ten from the tens column left 4 tens. Subtract 4 – 3 and write the result in the tens column of the answer. Becky has 16 more clients than Claire. Check by addition: 16 + 36 = 52.

$$
\begin{array}{r}
^{4\,1}\\
\not5\not2\\
-\ \ 36\\
\hline
16
\end{array}
$$

MULTIPLICATION

In multiplication, the same amount is combined multiple times. For example, instead of adding 30 three times, $30 + 30 + 30$, it is easier to simply multiply 30 by 3. If a problem asks for the product of two or more numbers, the numbers should be multiplied to arrive at the answer.

Example

A school auditorium contains 54 rows, each containing 34 seats. How many seats are there in total?

1. In order to solve this problem, you could add 34 to itself 54 times, but we can solve this problem easier with multiplication. Line up the place values vertically, writing the problem in columns. Multiply the number in the ones place of the top factor (4) by the number in the ones place of the bottom factor (4): $4 \times 4 = 16$. Since $16 = 1$ ten and 6 ones, write the 6 in the ones place in the first partial product. Regroup or carry the ten by writing a 1 above the tens place of the top factor.

$$\begin{array}{r} \overset{1}{34} \\ \times\ 54 \\ \hline 6 \end{array}$$

2. Multiply the number in the tens place in the top factor (3) by the number in the ones place of the bottom factor (4); $4 \times 3 = 12$. Then add the regrouped amount $12 + 1 = 13$. Write the 3 in the tens column and the one in the hundreds column of the partial product.

$$\begin{array}{r} \overset{1}{34} \\ \times\ 54 \\ \hline 136 \end{array}$$

3. The last calculations to be done require multiplying by the tens place of the bottom factor. Multiply 5 (tens from bottom factor) by 4 (ones from top factor); $5 \times 4 = 20$, but since the 5 really represents a number of tens, the actual value of the answer is 200 ($50 \times 4 = 200$). Therefore, write the two zeros under the ones and tens columns of the second partial product and regroup or carry the 2 hundreds by writing a 2 above the tens place of the top factor.

$$\begin{array}{r} \overset{2}{34} \\ \times\ 54 \\ \hline 136 \\ 00 \end{array}$$

4. Multiply 5 (tens from bottom factor) by 3 (tens from top factor); $5 \times 3 = 15$, but since the 5 and the 3 each represent a number of tens, the actual value of the answer is 1,500 ($50 \times 30 = 1,500$). Add the two additional hundreds carried over from the last multiplication: $15 + 2 = 17$ (hundreds). Write the 17 in front of the zeros in the second partial product.

$$
\begin{array}{r}
{}^{2} \\
34 \\
\times\ 54 \\
\hline
136 \\
1,700
\end{array}
$$

5. Add the partial products to find the total product:

$$
\begin{array}{r}
{}^{2} \\
34 \\
\times\ 54 \\
\hline
136 \\
+\ 1,700 \\
\hline
1,836
\end{array}
$$

Note: It is easier to perform multiplication if you write the factor with the greater number of digits in the top row. In this example, both factors have an equal number of digits, so it does not matter which is written on top.

DIVISION

In division, the same amount is subtracted multiple times. For example, instead of subtracting 5 from 25 as many times as possible, $25 - 5 - 5 - 5 - 5 - 5$, it is easier to simply divide, asking how many 5s are in 25; $25 \div 5$.

Example

At a road show, three artists sold their beads for a total of $54. If they share the money equally, how much money should each artist receive?

1. Divide the total amount ($54) by the number of ways the money is to be split (3). Work from left to right. How many times does 3 divide 5? Write the answer, 1, directly above the 5 in the dividend, since both the 5 and the 1 represent a number of tens. Now multiply: since $1(\text{ten}) \times 3(\text{ones}) = 3(\text{tens})$, write the 3 under the 5, and subtract; $5(\text{tens}) - 3(\text{tens}) = 2(\text{tens})$.

$$
\begin{array}{r}
1 \\
3{\overline{)54}} \\
-3 \\
\hline
2
\end{array}
$$

2. Continue dividing. Bring down the 4 from the ones place in the dividend. How many times does 3 divide 24? Write the answer, 8, directly above the 4 in the dividend. Since $3 \times 8 = 24$, write 24 below the other 24 and subtract $24 - 24 = 0$.

$$
\begin{array}{r}
18 \\
3\overline{)54} \\
\underline{-3}\downarrow \\
24 \\
\underline{-24} \\
0
\end{array}
$$

REMAINDERS

If you get a number other than zero after your last subtraction, this number is your remainder.

Example

9 divided by 4.

$$
\begin{array}{r}
2 \\
4\overline{)9} \\
\underline{-8} \\
1
\end{array}
$$

1 is the remainder.

The answer is 2 r1. This answer can also be written as $2\frac{1}{4}$ since there was one part left over out of the four parts needed to make a whole.

Working with Integers

Remember, an integer is a whole number or its opposite. Here are some rules for working with integers:

ADDING

Adding numbers with the same sign results in a sum of the same sign:

(positive) + (positive) = positive   and   (negative) + (negative) = negative

When adding numbers of different signs, follow this two-step process:

1. Subtract the positive values of the numbers. Positive values are the values of the numbers without any signs.

2. Keep the sign of the number with the larger positive value.

Example

$-2 + 3 =$

1. Subtract the positive values of the numbers: $3 - 2 = 1$.
2. The number 3 is the larger of the two positive values. Its sign in the original example was positive, so the sign of the answer is positive. The answer is positive 1.

Example

$8 + -11 =$

1. Subtract the positive values of the numbers: $11 - 8 = 3$.
2. The number 11 is the larger of the two positive values. Its sign in the original example was negative, so the sign of the answer is negative. The answer is negative 3.

SUBTRACTING

When subtracting integers, change all subtraction signs to addition signs and change the sign of the number being subtracted to its opposite. Then follow the rules for addition.

Examples

$(+10) - (+12) = (+10) + (-12) = -2$
$(-5) - (-7) = (-5) + (+7) = +2$

MULTIPLYING AND DIVIDING

A simple method for remembering the rules of multiplying and dividing is that if the signs are the same when multiplying or dividing two quantities, the answer will be positive. If the signs are different, the answer will be negative.

$(\text{positive}) \times (\text{positive}) = \text{positive}$ $\qquad \dfrac{(\text{positive})}{(\text{positive})} = \text{positive}$

$(\text{positive}) \times (\text{negative}) = \text{negative}$ $\qquad \dfrac{(\text{positive})}{(\text{negative})} = \text{negative}$

$(\text{negative}) \times (\text{negative}) = \text{positive}$ $\qquad \dfrac{(\text{negative})}{(\text{negative})} = \text{positive}$

Examples

$(10)(-12) = -120$

$-5 \times -7 = 35$

$-\dfrac{12}{3} = -4$

$\dfrac{15}{3} = 5$

Sequence of Mathematical Operations

There is an order in which a sequence of mathematical operations must be performed:

> **P**: Parentheses/Grouping Symbols. Perform all operations within parentheses first. If there is more than one set of parentheses, begin to work with the innermost set and work toward the outside. If more than one operation is present within the parentheses, use the remaining rules of order to determine which operation to perform first.
>
> **E**: Exponents. Evaluate exponents.
>
> **M/D**: Multiply/Divide. Work from left to right in the expression.
>
> **A/S**: Add/Subtract. Work from left to right in the expression.

This order is illustrated by the following acronym PEMDAS, which can be remembered by using the first letter of each of the words in the phrase: **P**lease **E**xcuse **M**y **D**ear **A**unt **S**ally.

> *Example*
>
> $$\frac{(5+3)^2}{4} + 27$$
> $$= \frac{(8)^2}{4} + 27$$
> $$= \frac{64}{4} + 27$$
> $$= 16 + 27$$
> $$= 43$$

Properties of Arithmetic

Listed below are several properties of mathematics:

- **Commutative Property:** This property states that the result of an arithmetic operation is not affected by reversing the order of the numbers. Multiplication and addition are operations that satisfy the commutative property.

  > *Examples*
  >
  > $5 \times 2 = 2 \times 5$
  > $5a = a5$
  > $b + 3 = 3 + b$

However, neither subtraction nor division is commutative, because reversing the order of the numbers does not yield the same result.

> *Examples*
>
> $5 - 2 \neq 2 - 5$
> $6 \div 3 \neq 3 \div 6$

- **Associative Property:** If parentheses can be moved to group different numbers in an arithmetic problem without changing the result, then the operation is associative. Addition and multiplication are associative.

    ### Examples
    $2 + (3 + 4) = (2 + 3) + 4$
    $2(ab) = (2a)b$

- **Distributive Property:** When a value is being multiplied by a sum or difference, multiply that value by each quantity within the parentheses. Then, take the sum or difference to yield an equivalent result.

    ### Examples
    $5(a + b) = 5a + 5b$
    $5(100 - 6) = (5 \times 100) - (5 \times 6)$

This second example can be proved by performing the calculations:

$$5(94) = 5(100 - 6)$$
$$= 500 - 30$$
$$470 = 470$$

ADDITIVE AND MULTIPLICATIVE IDENTITIES AND INVERSES

- The **additive identity** is the value which, when added to a number, does not change the number. For all of the sets of numbers defined above (counting numbers, integers, rational numbers, etc.), the additive identity is 0.

    ### Examples
    $5 + 0 = 5$
    $-3 + 0 = -3$

Adding 0 does not change the values of 5 and −3, so 0 is the additive identity.

- The **additive inverse** of a number is the number which, when added to the number, gives you the additive identity.

    ### Example
    What is the additive inverse of −3?

This means, "what number can I add to –3 to give me the additive identity (0)?"

–3 + ___ = 0

–3 + 3 = 0

The answer is 3.

■ The **multiplicative identity** is the value which, when multiplied by a number, does not change the number. For all of the sets of numbers defined previously (counting numbers, integers, rational numbers, etc.) the multiplicative identity is 1.

Examples

$5 \times 1 = 5$

$-3 \times 1 = -3$

Multiplying by 1 does not change the values of 5 and –3, so 1 is the multiplicative identity.

■ The **multiplicative inverse** of a number is the number which, when multiplied by the number, gives you the multiplicative identity.

Example

What is the multiplicative inverse of 5?

This means, "what number can I multiply 5 by to give me the multiplicative identity (1)?"

$5 \times$ ___ $= 1$

$5 \times \frac{1}{5} = 1$

The answer is $\frac{1}{5}$.

There is an easy way to find the multiplicative inverse. It is the **reciprocal**, which is obtained by reversing the numerator and denominator of a fraction. In the above example, the answer is the reciprocal of 5; 5 can be written as $\frac{5}{1}$, so the reciprocal is $\frac{1}{5}$.

Some numbers and their reciprocals:

4	$\frac{1}{4}$
$\frac{2}{3}$	$\frac{3}{2}$
$-\frac{6}{5}$	$-\frac{5}{6}$
$\frac{1}{6}$	6

Note: Reciprocals do not change sign.

Note: The additive inverse of a number is the opposite of the number; the multiplicative inverse is the reciprocal.

Factors and Multiples

FACTORS

Factors are numbers that can be divided into a larger number without a remainder.

Example

$12 \div 3 = 4$

The number 3 is, therefore, a factor of the number 12. Other factors of 12 are 1, 2, 4, 6, and 12. The common factors of two numbers are the factors that both numbers have in common.

Examples

The factors of 24 = 1, 2, 3, 4, 6, 8, 12, and 24.
The factors of 18 = 1, 2, 3, 6, 9, and 18.

From the examples above, you can see that the common factors of 24 and 18 are 1, 2, 3, and 6. From this list it can also be determined that the *greatest* common factor of 24 and 18 is 6. Determining the **greatest common factor** (GCF) is useful for simplifying fractions.

Example

Simplify $\frac{16}{20}$.

The factors of 16 are 1, 2, 4, 8, and 16. The factors of 20 are 1, 2, 4, 5, and 20. The common factors of 16 and 20 are 1, 2, and 4. The greatest of these, the GCF, is 4. Therefore, to simplify the fraction, both numerator and denominator should be divided by 4.

$$\frac{16 \div 4}{20 \div 4} = \frac{4}{5}$$

MULTIPLES

Multiples are numbers that can be obtained by multiplying a number x by a positive integer.

Example

$5 \times 7 = 35$

The number 35 is, therefore, a multiple of the number 5 and of the number 7. Other multiples of 5 are 5, 10, 15, 20, etc. Other multiples of 7 are 7, 14, 21, 28, etc.

The common multiples of two numbers are the multiples that both numbers share.

Example

Some multiples of 4 are: 4, 8, 12, 16, 20, 24, 28, 32, 36 . . .

Some multiples of 6 are: 6, 12, 18, 24, 30, 36, 42, 48 . . .

Some common multiples are 12, 24, and 36. From the above it can also be determined that the *least* common multiple of the numbers 4 and 6 is 12, since this number is the smallest number that appeared in both lists. The **least common multiple**, or LCM, is used when performing addition and subtraction of fractions to find the least common denominator.

Example (using denominators 4 and 6 and LCM of 12)

$$\frac{1}{4} + \frac{5}{6} = \frac{1(3)}{4(3)} + \frac{5(2)}{6(2)}$$
$$= \frac{3}{12} + \frac{10}{12}$$
$$= \frac{13}{12}$$
$$= 1\frac{1}{12}$$

Decimals

The most important thing to remember about decimals is that the first place value to the right of the decimal point is the tenths place. The place values are as follows:

1	2	6	8	.	3	4	5	7
THOUSANDS	HUNDREDS	TENS	ONES	DECIMAL POINT	TENTHS	HUNDREDTHS	THOUSANDTHS	TEN THOUSANDTHS

In expanded form, this number can also be expressed as:

$1{,}268.3457 = (1 \times 1{,}000) + (2 \times 100) + (6 \times 10) + (8 \times 1) + (3 \times .1) + (4 \times .01) + (5 \times .001) + (7 \times .0001)$

ADDING AND SUBTRACTING DECIMALS

Adding and subtracting decimals is very similar to adding and subtracting whole numbers. The most important thing to remember is to line up the decimal points. Zeros may be filled in as placeholders when all numbers do not have the same number of decimal places.

Example

What is the sum of 0.45, 0.8, and 1.36?

$$
\begin{array}{r}
^{1\ 1} \\
0.45 \\
0.80 \\
+\ 1.36 \\
\hline
2.61
\end{array}
$$

Take away 0.35 from 1.06.

$$
\begin{array}{r}
^{0\ 1} \\
1.06 \\
-0.35 \\
\hline
0.71
\end{array}
$$

MULTIPLICATION OF DECIMALS

Multiplication of decimals is exactly the same as multiplication of integers, except one must make note of the total number of decimal places in the factors.

Example

What is the product of 0.14 and 4.3?

First, multiply as usual (do not line up the decimal points):

$$
\begin{array}{r}
4.3 \\
\times .14 \\
\hline
172 \\
+\ 430 \\
\hline
602
\end{array}
$$

Now, to figure out the answer, 4.3 has one decimal place and .14 has two decimal places. Add in order to determine the total number of decimal places the answer must have to the right of the decimal point. In this problem, there are a total of 3 (1 + 2) decimal places. When finished multiplying, start from the right side of the answer, and move to the left the number of decimal places previously calculated.

.602

In this example, 602 turns into .602 since there have to be 3 decimal places in the answer. If there are not enough digits in the answer, add zeros in front of the answer until there are enough.

Example
Multiply 0.03 × 0.2.

$$
\begin{array}{r}
.03 \\
\times\ .2 \\
\hline
6
\end{array}
$$

There are three total decimal places in the problem; therefore, the answer must contain three decimal places. Starting to the right of 6, move left three places. The answer becomes 0.006.

DIVIDING DECIMALS

Dividing decimals is a little different from integers for the set-up, and then the regular rules of division apply. It is easier to divide if the divisor does not have any decimals. In order to accomplish that, simply move the decimal place to the right as many places as necessary to make the divisor a whole number. If the decimal point is moved in the divisor, it must also be moved in the dividend in order to keep the answer the same as the original problem; 4 ÷ 2 has the same solution as its multiples 8 ÷ 4 and 28 ÷ 14, etc. Moving a decimal point in a division problem is equivalent to multiplying a numerator and denominator of a fraction by the same quantity, which is the reason the answer will remain the same.

If there are not enough decimal places in the answer to accommodate the required move, simply add zeros until the desired placement is achieved. Add zeros after the decimal point to continue the division until the decimal terminates, or until a repeating pattern is recognized. The decimal point in the quotient belongs directly above the decimal point in the dividend.

Example
What is $.425\overline{)1.53}$?

First, to make .425 a whole number, move the decimal point 3 places to the right: 425.
Now move the decimal point 3 places to the right for 1.53: 1,530.
The problem is now a simple long division problem.

$$
\begin{array}{r}
3.6 \\
425.\overline{)1,530.0} \\
-1,275\downarrow \\
\hline
2,550 \\
-2,550 \\
\hline
0
\end{array}
$$

COMPARING DECIMALS

Comparing decimals is actually quite simple. Just line up the decimal points and then fill in zeros at the end of the numbers until each one has an equal number of digits.

Example

Compare .5 and .005.

Line up decimal points.   .5
                                     .005

Add zeros.   .500
                                     .005

Now, ignore the decimal point and consider, which is bigger: 500 or 5?
500 is definitely bigger than 5, so .5 is larger than .005.

ROUNDING DECIMALS

It is often inconvenient to work with very long decimals. Often it is much more convenient to have an approximation for a decimal that contains fewer digits than the entire decimal. In this case, we **round** decimals to a certain number of decimal places. There are numerous options for rounding:

To the nearest integer:	zero digits to the right of the decimal point
To the nearest tenth:	one digit to the right of the decimal point (tenths unit)
To the nearest hundredth:	two digits to the right of the decimal point (hundredths unit)

In order to round, we look at two digits of the decimal: the digit we are rounding to, and the digit to the immediate right. If the digit to the immediate right is less than 5, we leave the digit we are rounding to alone, and omit all the digits to the right of it. If the digit to the immediate right is five or greater, we increase the digit we are rounding by one, and omit all the digits to the right of it.

Example

Round $\frac{3}{7}$ to the nearest tenth and the nearest hundredth.

Dividing 3 by 7 gives us the repeating decimal .428571428571... If we are rounding to the nearest tenth, we need to look at the digit in the tenths position (4) and the digit to the immediate right (2). Since 2 is less than 5, we leave the digit in the tenths position alone, and drop everything to the right of it. So, $\frac{3}{7}$ to the nearest tenth is .4.

To round to the nearest hundredth, we need to look at the digit in the hundredths position (2) and the digit to the immediate right (8). Since 8 is more than 5, we increase the digit in the hundredths position by 1, giving us 3, and drop everything to the right of it. So, $\frac{3}{7}$ to the nearest hundredth is .43.

Fractions

To work well with fractions, it is necessary to understand some basic concepts.

SIMPLIFYING FRACTIONS

Rule:

$$\frac{ac}{bc} = \frac{a}{b}$$

- To simplify fractions, identify the Greatest Common Factor (GCF) of the numerator and denominator and divide both the numerator and denominator by this number.

Example

Simplify $\frac{63}{72}$.

The GCF of 63 and 72 is 9 so divide 63 and 72 each by 9 to simplify the fraction:

$$\frac{63 \div 9 = 7}{72 \div 9 = 8}$$

$$\frac{63}{72} = \frac{7}{8}$$

ADDING AND SUBTRACTING FRACTIONS

Rules:

To add or subtract fractions with the same denominator:

$$\frac{a}{b} \pm \frac{c}{b} = \frac{a \pm c}{b}$$

To add or subtract fractions with different denominators:

$$\frac{a}{b} \pm \frac{c}{d} = \frac{ad \pm cb}{bd}$$

- To add or subtract fractions with like denominators, just add or subtract the numerators and keep the denominator.

Examples

$\frac{1}{7} + \frac{5}{7} = \frac{6}{7}$ and $\frac{5}{8} - \frac{2}{8} = \frac{3}{8}$

- To add or subtract fractions with unlike denominators, first find the Least Common Denominator or LCD. The LCD is the smallest number divisible by each of the denominators.

For example, for the denominators 8 and 12, 24 would be the LCD because 24 is the smallest number that is divisible by both 8 and 12: $8 \times 3 = 24$, and $12 \times 2 = 24$.

Using the LCD, convert each fraction to its new form by multiplying both the numerator and denominator by the appropriate factor to get the LCD, and then follow the directions for adding/subtracting fractions with like denominators.

Example

$$\frac{1}{3} + \frac{2}{5} = \frac{1(5)}{3(5)} + \frac{2(3)}{5(3)}$$
$$= \frac{5}{15} + \frac{6}{15}$$
$$= \frac{11}{15}$$

MULTIPLICATION OF FRACTIONS

Rule:

$$\frac{a}{b} \times \frac{c}{d} = \frac{a \times c}{b \times d}$$

- Multiplying fractions is one of the easiest operations to perform. To multiply fractions, simply multiply the numerators and the denominators.

Example

$$\frac{4}{5} \times \frac{6}{7} = \frac{24}{35}$$

If any numerator and denominator have common factors, these may be simplified before multiplying. Divide the common multiples by a common factor. In the example below, 3 and 6 are both divided by 3 before multiplying.

Example

$$\frac{\overset{1}{\cancel{3}}}{5} \times \frac{1}{\underset{2}{\cancel{6}}} = \frac{1}{10}$$

DIVIDING FRACTIONS

Rule:

$$\frac{a}{b} \div \frac{c}{d} = \frac{a}{b} \times \frac{d}{c} = \frac{a \times d}{b \times c}$$

- Dividing fractions is equivalent to multiplying the dividend by the reciprocal of the divisor. When dividing fractions, simply multiply the dividend by the divisor's reciprocal to get the answer.

Example

(dividend) ÷ (divisor)

$$\frac{1}{4} \div \frac{1}{2}$$

Determine the reciprocal of the divisor:

$$\frac{1}{2} \to \frac{2}{1}$$

Multiply the dividend ($\frac{1}{4}$) by the reciprocal of the divisor ($\frac{2}{1}$) and simplify if necessary.

$$\frac{1}{4} \div \frac{1}{2} = \frac{1}{4} \times \frac{2}{1}$$
$$= \frac{2}{4}$$
$$= \frac{1}{2}$$

COMPARING FRACTIONS

Rules:

If $\frac{a}{b} = \frac{c}{d}$, then $ad = bc$

If $\frac{a}{b} < \frac{c}{d}$, then $ad < bc$

If $\frac{a}{b} > \frac{c}{d}$, then $ad > bc$

Sometimes it is necessary to compare the size of fractions. This is very simple when the fractions are familiar or when they have a common denominator.

Examples

$\frac{1}{2} < \frac{3}{4}$ and $\frac{11}{18} > \frac{5}{18}$

- If the fractions are not familiar and/or do not have a common denominator, there is a simple trick to remember. Multiply the numerator of the first fraction by the denominator of the second fraction. Write this answer under the first fraction. Then multiply the numerator of the second fraction by the denominator of the first one. Write this answer under the second fraction. Compare the two numbers. The larger number represents the larger fraction.

Examples

Which is larger: $\frac{7}{11}$ or $\frac{4}{9}$?

Cross-multiply.

$7 \times 9 = 63 \qquad 4 \times 11 = 44$

$\qquad 63 > 44$, therefore,

$$\frac{7}{11} > \frac{4}{9}$$

Compare $\frac{6}{18}$ and $\frac{2}{6}$.
Cross-multiply.

$6 \times 6 = 36 \qquad 2 \times 18 = 36$

$\qquad 36 = 36$, therefore,

$$\frac{6}{18} = \frac{2}{6}$$

CONVERTING DECIMALS TO FRACTIONS

- To convert a non-repeating decimal to a fraction, the digits of the decimal become the numerator of the fraction, and the denominator of the fraction is a power of 10 that contains that number of digits as zeros.

Example

Convert .125 to a fraction.

The decimal .125 means 125 *thousandths*, so it is 125 parts of 1,000. An easy way to do this is to make 125 the numerator, and since there are three digits in the number 125, the denominator is 1 with three zeros, or 1,000.

$$.125 = \frac{125}{1,000}$$

Then we just need to reduce the fraction.

$$\frac{125}{1,000} = \frac{125 \div 125}{1,000 \div 125} = \frac{1}{8}$$

- When converting a repeating decimal to a fraction, the digits of the repeating pattern of the decimal become the numerator of the fraction, and the denominator of the fraction is the same number of 9s as digits.

Example

Convert $.\overline{3}$ to a fraction.

You may already recognize $.\overline{3}$ as $\frac{1}{3}$. The repeating pattern, in this case 3, becomes our numerator. There is one digit in the pattern, so 9 is our denominator.

$$.\overline{3} = \frac{3}{9} = \frac{3 \div 3}{9 \div 3} = \frac{1}{3}$$

Example
Convert $.\overline{36}$ to a fraction.

The repeating pattern, in this case 36, becomes our numerator. There are two digits in the pattern, so 99 is our denominator.

$$.\overline{36} = \frac{36}{99} = \frac{36 \div 9}{99 \div 9} = \frac{4}{11}$$

CONVERTING FRACTIONS TO DECIMALS

■ To convert a fraction to a decimal, simply treat the fraction as a division problem.

Example
Convert $\frac{3}{4}$ to a decimal.

$$\begin{array}{r} .75 \\ 4\overline{)3.00} \end{array}$$

So, $\frac{3}{4}$ is equal to .75.

CONVERTING MIXED NUMBERS TO AND FROM IMPROPER FRACTIONS
Rule:

$$a\frac{b}{c} = \frac{ac + b}{c}$$

■ A mixed number is number greater than 1 which is expressed as a whole number joined to a proper fraction. Examples of mixed numbers are $5\frac{3}{8}$, $2\frac{1}{3}$, and $-4\frac{5}{6}$. To convert from a mixed number to an improper fraction (a fraction where the numerator is greater than the denominator), multiply the whole number and the denominator and add the numerator. This becomes the new numerator. The new denominator is the same as the original.

Note: If the mixed number is negative, temporarily ignore the negative sign while performing the conversion, and just make sure you replace the negative sign when you're done.

Example
Convert $5\frac{3}{8}$ to an improper fraction.

Using the formula above, $5\frac{3}{8} = \frac{5 \times 8 + 3}{8} = \frac{43}{8}$.

Example

Convert $-4\frac{5}{6}$ to an improper fraction.

Temporarily ignore the negative sign and perform the conversion: $4\frac{5}{6} = \frac{4 \times 6 + 5}{6} = \frac{29}{6}$.
The final answer includes the negative sign: $-\frac{29}{6}$.

■ To convert from an improper fraction to a mixed number, simply treat the fraction like a division problem, and express the answer as a fraction rather than a decimal.

Example

Convert $\frac{23}{7}$ to a mixed number.

Perform the division: $23 \div 7 = 3\frac{2}{7}$.

Percents

Percents are always "out of 100." 45% means 45 out of 100. Therefore, to write percents as decimals, move the decimal point two places to the left (to the hundredths place).

$45\% = \frac{45}{100} = 0.45$

$3\% = \frac{3}{100} = 0.03$

$124\% = \frac{124}{100} = 1.24$

$0.9\% = \frac{.9}{100} = \frac{9}{1,000} = 0.009$

Here are some conversions you should be familiar with:

Fraction	Decimal	Percentage
$\frac{1}{2}$	.5	50%
$\frac{1}{4}$	.25	25%
$\frac{1}{3}$	.333 . . .	$33.\overline{3}\%$
$\frac{2}{3}$	.666 . . .	$66.\overline{6}\%$
$\frac{1}{10}$	.1	10%
$\frac{1}{8}$	.125	12.5%
$\frac{1}{6}$	.1666 . . .	$16.\overline{6}\%$
$\frac{1}{5}$	.2	20%

Absolute Value

The absolute value of a number is the distance of that number from zero. Distances are always represented by positive numbers, so the absolute value of any number is positive. Absolute value is represented by placing small vertical lines around the value: $|x|$.

Examples

The absolute value of seven: $|7|$.

The distance from seven to zero is seven, so $|7| = 7$.

The absolute value of negative three: $|-3|$.

The distance from negative three to zero is three, so $|-3| = 3$.

Exponents

POSITIVE EXPONENTS

A positive exponent indicates the number of times a base is used as a factor to attain a product.

Example

Evaluate 2^5.

2 is the base and 5 is the exponent. Therefore, 2 should be used as a factor 5 times to attain a product:

$$2^5 = 2 \times 2 \times 2 \times 2 \times 2 = 32$$

ZERO EXPONENT

Any non-zero number raised to the zero power equals 1.

Examples

$5^0 = 1$ $70^0 = 1$ $29,874^0 = 1$

NEGATIVE EXPONENTS

A base raised to a negative exponent is equivalent to the reciprocal of the base raised to the positive exponent (absolute value of the exponent).

Examples

$$5^{-1} = \frac{1}{5}$$
$$7^{-2} = \left(\frac{1}{7}\right)^2 = \frac{1}{49}$$
$$\left(\frac{2}{3}\right)^{-2} = \left(\frac{3}{2}\right)^2 = \frac{9}{4}$$

EXPONENT RULES

- When multiplying identical bases, you add the exponents.

Examples

$$2^2 \times 2^4 \times 2^6 = 2^{12}$$
$$a^2 \times a^3 \times a^5 = a^{10}$$

- When dividing identical bases, you subtract the exponents.

Examples

$$\frac{2^7}{2^3} = 2^4 \qquad\qquad \frac{a^9}{a^4} = a^5$$

- If a base raised to a power (in parentheses) is raised to another power, you multiply the exponents together.

Examples

$$(3^2)^7 = 3^{14} \qquad\qquad (g^4)^3 = g^{12}$$

PERFECT SQUARES

5^2 is read "5 to the second power," or, more commonly, "5 squared." Perfect squares are numbers that are second powers of other numbers. Perfect squares are always zero or positive, because when you multiply a positive or a negative by itself, the result is always positive. The perfect squares are $0^2, 1^2, 2^2, 3^2 \ldots$

Perfect squares: 0, 1, 4, 9, 16, 25, 36, 49, 64, 81, 100 . . .

PERFECT CUBES

5^3 is read "5 to the third power," or, more commonly, "5 cubed." (Powers higher than three have no special name.) Perfect cubes are numbers that are third powers of other numbers. Perfect cubes, unlike perfect squares, can be both positive or negative. This is because when a negative is multiplied by itself three times, the result is negative. The perfect cubes are $0^3, 1^3, 2^3, 3^3 \ldots$

Perfect cubes: 0, 1, 8, 27, 64, 125 . . .

- Note that 64 is both a perfect square and a perfect cube.

SQUARE ROOTS

The square of a number is the product of the number and itself. For example, in the statement $3^2 = 3 \times 3 = 9$, the number 9 is the square of the number 3. If the process is reversed, the number 3 is the square root of the number 9. The symbol for square root is $\sqrt{}$ and is called a **radical**. The number inside of the radical is called the **radicand**.

Example
$5^2 = 25$, therefore $\sqrt{25} = 5$

Since 25 is the square of 5, it is also true that 5 is the square root of 25.

The square root of a number might not be a whole number. For example, the square root of 7 is 2.645751311.... It is not possible to find a whole number that can be multiplied by itself to equal 7. Square roots of non-perfect squares are irrational.

CUBE ROOTS

The cube of a number is the product of the number and itself for a total of three times. For example, in the statement $2^3 = 2 \times 2 \times 2 = 8$, the number 8 is the cube of the number 2. If the process is reversed, the number 2 is the cube root of the number 8. The symbol for cube root is the same as the square root symbol, except for a small three $\sqrt[3]{}$. It is read as "cube root." The number inside of the radical is still called the radicand, and the three is called the index. (In a square root, the index is not written, but it has an index of 2.)

Example
$5^3 = 125$, therefore $\sqrt[3]{125} = 5$.

Like square roots, the cube root of a number might be not be a whole number. Cube roots of non-perfect cubes are irrational.

Probability

Probability is the numerical representation of the likelihood of an event occurring. Probability is always represented by a decimal or fraction between 0 and 1; 0 meaning that the event will never occur, and 1 meaning that the event will always occur. The higher the probability, the more likely the event is to occur.

A **simple event** is one action. Examples of simple events are: drawing one card from a deck, rolling one die, flipping one coin, or spinning a hand on a spinner once.

SIMPLE PROBABILITY

The probability of an event occurring is defined as the number of desired outcomes divided by the total number of outcomes. The list of all outcomes is often called the **sample space**.

$$P(\text{event}) = \frac{\text{\# of desired outcomes}}{\text{total number of outcomes}}$$

Example

What is the probability of drawing a king from a standard deck of cards?

There are 4 kings in a standard deck of cards. So, the number of desired outcomes is 4. There are a total of 52 ways to pick a card from a standard deck of cards, so the total number of outcomes is 52. The probability of drawing a king from a standard deck of cards is $\frac{4}{52}$. So, $P(\text{king}) = \frac{4}{52}$.

Example

What is the probability of getting an odd number on the roll of one die?

There are 3 odd numbers on a standard die: 1, 3, and 5. So, the number of desired outcomes is 3. There are 6 sides on a standard die, so there are a total of 6 possible outcomes. The probability of rolling an odd number on a standard die is $\frac{3}{6}$. So, $P(\text{odd}) = \frac{3}{6}$.

Note: It is not necessary to reduce fractions when working with probability.

PROBABILITY OF AN EVENT NOT OCCURRING

The sum of the probability of an event occurring and the probability of the event *not* occurring = 1. Therefore, if we know the probability of the event occurring, we can determine the probability of the event *not* occurring by subtracting from 1.

Example

If the probability of rain tomorrow is 45%, what is the probability that it will *not* rain tomorrow?

45% = .45, and 1 − .45 = .55 or 55%. The probability that it will not rain is 55%.

PROBABILITY INVOLVING THE WORD "OR"

Rule:

P(event A *or* event B) = P(event A) + P(event B) − P(overlap of event A and B)

When the word *or* appears in a simple probability problem, it signifies that you will be adding outcomes. For example, if we are interested in the probability of obtaining a king or a queen on a draw of a card, the number of desired outcomes is 8, because there are 4 kings and 4 queens in the deck. The probability of event A (drawing a king) is $\frac{4}{52}$, and the probability of drawing a queen is $\frac{4}{52}$. The overlap of event A and B would be any cards that are both a king and a queen at the same time, but there are no cards that are both a king and a queen at the same time. So the probability of obtaining a king or a queen is $\frac{4}{52} + \frac{4}{52} - \frac{0}{52} = \frac{8}{52}$.

Example

What is the probability of getting an even number or a multiple of 3 on the roll of a die?

The probability of getting an even number on the roll of a die is $\frac{3}{6}$, because there are three even numbers (2, 4, 6) on a die and a total of 6 possible outcomes. The probability of getting a multiple of 3 is $\frac{2}{6}$, because there are 2 multiples of three (3, 6) on a die. But because the outcome of rolling a 6 on the die is an overlap of both events, we must subtract $\frac{1}{6}$ from the result so we don't count it twice.

$$P(\text{even } or \text{ multiple of 3}) = P(\text{even}) + P(\text{multiple of 3}) - P(\text{overlap})$$
$$= \frac{3}{6} + \frac{2}{6} - \frac{1}{6} = \frac{4}{6}$$

COMPOUND PROBABILITY

A **compound event** is performing two or more simple events in succession. Drawing two cards from a deck, rolling three dice, flipping five coins, having four babies, are all examples of compound events.

This can be done "with replacement" (probabilities do not change for each event) or "without replacement" (probabilities change for each event).

The probability of event A followed by event B occurring is $P(A) \times P(B)$. This is called the **counting principle** for probability.

Note: In mathematics, the word *and* usually signifies addition. In probability, however, *and* signifies multiplication and *or* signifies addition.

Example

You have a jar filled with 3 red marbles, 5 green marbles, and 2 blue marbles. What is the probability of getting a red marble followed by a blue marble, with replacement?

"With replacement" in this case means that you will draw a marble, note its color, and then replace it back into the jar. This means that the probability of drawing a red marble does not change from one simple event to the next.

Note that there are a total of 10 marbles in the jar, so the total number of outcomes is 10.

$P(\text{red}) = \frac{3}{10}$ and $P(\text{blue}) = \frac{2}{10}$ so $P(\text{red followed by blue})$ is $\frac{3}{10} \times \frac{2}{10} = \frac{6}{100}$.

If the problem was changed to say "without replacement," that would mean you are drawing a marble, noting its color, but not returning it to the jar. This means that for the second event, you no longer have a total number of 10 outcomes, you only have 9 because you have taken one red marble out of the jar. In this case,

$P(\text{red}) = \frac{3}{10}$ and $P(\text{blue}) = \frac{2}{9}$ so $P(\text{red followed by blue})$ is $\frac{3}{10} \times \frac{2}{9} = \frac{6}{90}$.

Statistics

Statistics is the field of mathematics that deals with describing sets of data. Often, we want to understand trends in data by looking at where the center of the data lies. There are a number of ways to find the center of a set of data.

MEAN

When we talk about average, we usually are referring to the **arithmetic mean** (usually just called the **mean**). To find the mean of a set of numbers, add all of the numbers together and divide by the quantity of numbers in the set.

Average = (sum of set) ÷ (quantity of set)

Example

Find the average of 9, 4, 7, 6, and 4.

$$\frac{9+4+7+6+4}{5} = \frac{30}{5} = 6$$

The mean, or average, of the set is 6.
(Divide by 5 because there are 5 numbers in the set.)

MEDIAN

Another center of data is the median. It is literally the "center" number if you arrange all the data in ascending or descending order. To find the median of a set of numbers, arrange the numbers in ascending or descending order and find the middle value.

- If the set contains an odd number of elements, then simply choose the middle value.

Example

Find the median of the number set: 1, 5, 4, 7, 2.

First arrange the set in order—1, 2, 4, 5, 7—and then find the middle value. Since there are 5 values, the middle value is the third one: 4. The median is 4.

- If the set contains an even number of elements, simply average the two middle values.

Example

Find the median of the number set: 1, 6, 3, 7, 2, 8.

First arrange the set in order—1, 2, 3, 6, 7, 8—and then find the middle values, 3 and 6.
Find the average of the numbers 3 and 6: $\frac{3+6}{2} = \frac{9}{2} = 4.5$. The median is 4.5.

MODE

Sometimes when we want to know the average, we just want to know what occurs most often. The **mode** of a set of numbers is the number that appears the greatest number of times.

Example

For the number set 1, 2, 5, 9, 4, 2, 9, 6, 9, 7, the number 9 is the mode because it appears the most frequently.

► Measurement

This section will review the basics of measurement systems used in the United States (sometimes called customary measurement) and other countries, methods of performing mathematical operations with units of measurement, and the process of converting between different units.

The use of measurement enables a connection to be made between mathematics and the real world. To measure any object, assign a number and a unit of measure. For instance, when a fish is caught, it is often weighed in ounces and its length measured in inches. The following lesson will help you become more familiar with the types, conversions, and units of measurement.

Types of Measurements

The types of measurements used most frequently in the United States are listed below:

Units of Length

12 inches (in) = 1 foot (ft)
3 feet = 36 inches = 1 yard (yd)
5,280 feet = 1,760 yards = 1 mile (mi)

Units of Volume

8 ounces* (oz) = 1 cup (c)
2 cups = 16 ounces = 1 pint (pt)
2 pints = 4 cups = 32 ounces = 1 quart (qt)
4 quarts = 8 pints = 16 cups = 128 ounces = 1 gallon (gal)

Units of Weight

16 ounces* (oz) = 1 pound (lb)
2,000 pounds = 1 ton (T)

Units of Time

    60 seconds (sec) = 1 minute (min)

    60 minute = 1 hour (hr)

    24 hours = 1 day

    7 days = 1 week

    52 weeks = 1 year (yr)

    12 months = 1 year

    365 days = 1 year

*Notice that ounces are used to measure the dimensions of both volume and weight.

Converting Units

When performing mathematical operations, it may be necessary to convert units of measure to simplify a problem. Units of measure are converted by using either multiplication or division.

- To convert from a larger unit into a smaller unit, *multiply* the given number of larger units by the number of smaller units in only one of the larger units:

(given number of the larger units) × (the number of smaller units per larger unit) = answer in smaller units

For example, to find the number of inches in 5 feet, multiply 5, the number of larger units, by 12, the number of inches in one foot:

5 feet = _?_ inches

5 feet × 12 (the number of inches in a single foot) = 60 inches: $5 \text{ ft} \times \frac{12 \text{ in}}{1 \text{ ft}} = 60 \text{ in}$

Therefore, there are 60 inches in 5 feet.

Example

Change 3.5 tons to pounds.

3.5 tons = _?_ pounds

$3.5 \text{ tons} \times \frac{2{,}000 \text{ pounds}}{1 \text{ ton}} = 7{,}000 \text{ pounds}$

Therefore, there are 7,000 pounds in 3.5 tons.

- To change a smaller unit to a larger unit, *divide* the given number of smaller units by the number of smaller units in only one of the larger units:

$$\frac{\text{given number of smaller units}}{\text{the number of smaller units per larger unit}} = \text{answer in larger units}$$

For example, to find the number of pints in 64 ounces, divide 64, the number of smaller units, by 16, the number of ounces in one pint.

64 ounces = _?_ pints

$$\frac{64 \text{ ounces}}{16 \text{ ounces per pint}} = 4 \text{ pints}$$

Therefore, 64 ounces equals four pints.

Example

Change 32 ounces to pounds.

32 ounces = _?_ pounds

$$\frac{32 \text{ ounces}}{16 \text{ ounces per pound}} = 2 \text{ pounds}$$

Therefore, 32 ounces equals two pounds.

Basic Operations with Measurement

You may need to add, subtract, multiply, and divide with measurement. The mathematical rules needed for each of these operations with measurement follow.

ADDITION WITH MEASUREMENTS

To add measurements, follow these two steps:

1. Add like units.
2. Simplify the answer by converting smaller units into larger units when possible.

Example

Add 4 pounds 5 ounces to 20 ounces.

```
    4 lb 5 oz        Be sure to add ounces to ounces.
  +    20 oz
    4 lb 25 oz
```

Because 25 ounces is more than 16 ounces (1 pound), simplify by dividing by 16:

```
          1 lb r 9 oz
   16 oz)25 oz
         −16 oz
            9 oz
```

Then add the 1 pound to the 4 pounds:

4 pounds 25 ounces = 4 pounds + 1 pound 9 ounces = 5 pounds 9 ounces

SUBTRACTION WITH MEASUREMENTS

1. Subtract like units if possible.
2. If not, regroup units to allow for subtraction.
3. Write the answer in simplest form.

For example, 6 pounds 2 ounces subtracted from 9 pounds 10 ounces.

$$\begin{array}{r} 9 \text{ lb } 10 \text{ oz} \\ - 6 \text{ lb } 2 \text{ oz} \\ \hline 3 \text{ lb } 8 \text{ oz} \end{array}$$

Subtract ounces from ounces.

Then subtract pounds from pounds.

Sometimes, it is necessary to regroup units when subtracting.

Example

Subtract 3 yards 2 feet from 5 yards 1 foot.

Because 2 feet cannot be taken from 1 foot, regroup 1 yard from the 5 yards and convert the 1 yard to 3 feet. Add 3 feet to 1 foot. Then subtract feet from feet and yards from yards:

$$\begin{array}{r} \overset{4}{\cancel{5}} \text{ yd } \overset{4}{\cancel{1}} \text{ ft} \\ - \quad 3 \text{ yd } 2 \text{ ft} \\ \hline 1 \text{ yd } 2 \text{ft} \end{array}$$

5 yards 1 foot − 3 yards 2 feet = 1 yard 2 feet

MULTIPLICATION WITH MEASUREMENTS

1. Multiply like units if units are involved.
2. Simplify the answer.

Example

Multiply 5 feet 7 inches by 3.

$$\begin{array}{r} 5 \text{ ft } 7 \text{ in} \\ \times \quad 3 \\ \hline 15 \text{ ft } 21 \text{ in} \end{array}$$

Multiply 7 inches by 3, then multiply 5 feet by 3. Keep the units separate.

Since 12 inches = 1 foot, simplify 21 inches.

15 ft 21 in = 15 ft + 1 ft 9 in = 16 ft 9 in

Example
Multiply 9 feet by 4 yards.

First, decide on a common unit: either change the 9 feet to yards, or change the 4 yards to feet. Both options are explained below:

Option 1:
To change yards to feet, multiply the number of feet in a yard (3) by the number of yards in this problem (4).

   3 feet in a yard $\times$ 4 yards = 12 feet

Then multiply: 9 feet $\times$ 12 feet = 108 square feet.

(Note: feet $\times$ feet = square feet = ft^2)

Option 2:
To change feet to yards, divide the number of feet given (9), by the number of feet in a yard (3).

   9 feet $\div$ 3 feet in a yard = 3 yards

Then multiply 3 yards by 4 yards = 12 square yards.

(Note: yards $\cdot$ yards = square yards = yd^2)

DIVISION WITH MEASUREMENTS

1. Divide into the larger units first.
2. Convert the remainder to the smaller unit.
3. Add the converted remainder to the existing smaller unit if any.
4. Divide into smaller units.
5. Write the answer in simplest form.

Example
Divide 5 quarts 4 ounces by 4.

1. Divide into the larger unit:

$$
\begin{array}{r}
1 \text{ qt r } 1 \text{ qt} \\
4\overline{)5 \text{ qt}} \\
\underline{-4 \text{ qt}} \\
1 \text{ qt}
\end{array}
$$

2. Convert the remainder:

   1 qt = 32 oz

3. Add remainder to original smaller unit:

   32 oz + 4 oz = 36 oz

4. Divide into smaller units:

$36 \text{ oz} \div 4 = 9 \text{ oz}$

5. Write the answer in simplest form:

1 qt 9 oz

Metric Measurements

The metric system is an international system of measurement also called the **decimal system**. Converting units in the metric system is much easier than converting units in the customary system of measurement. However, making conversions between the two systems is much more difficult. The basic units of the metric system are the meter, gram, and liter. Here is a general idea of how the two systems compare:

Metric System	Customary System
1 meter	A meter is a little more than a yard; it is equal to about 39 inches
1 gram	A gram is a very small unit of weight; there are about 30 grams in one ounce.
1 liter	A liter is a little more than a quart.

Prefixes are attached to the basic metric units listed above to indicate the amount of each unit. For example, the prefix *deci* means one-tenth ($\frac{1}{10}$); therefore, one decigram is one-tenth of a gram, and one decimeter is one-tenth of a meter. The following six prefixes can be used with every metric unit:

Kilo	Hecto	Deka	Deci	Centi	Milli
(k)	(h)	(dk)	(d)	(c)	(m)
1,000	100	10	$\frac{1}{10}$	$\frac{1}{100}$	$\frac{1}{1,000}$

Examples
- 1 hectometer = 1 hm = 100 meters
- 1 millimeter = 1 mm = $\frac{1}{1,000}$ meter = .001 meter
- 1 dekagram = 1 dkg = 10 grams
- 1 centiliter = 1 cL* = $\frac{1}{100}$ liter = .01 liter
- 1 kilogram = 1 kg = 1,000 grams
- 1 deciliter = 1 dL* = $\frac{1}{10}$ liter = .1 liter

*Notice that liter is abbreviated with a capital letter—*L*.

An easy way to remember the metric prefixes is to remember the mnemonic: "King Henry Died of Drinking Chocolate Milk". The first letter of each word represents a corresponding metric heading from Kilo down to Milli: 'King'—Kilo, 'Henry'—Hecto, 'Died'—Deka, 'of'—original unit, 'Drinking'—Deci, 'Chocolate'—Centi, and 'Milk'—Milli.

The chart below illustrates some common relationships used in the metric system:

Length	Weight	Volume
1 km = 1,000 m	1 kg = 1,000 g	1 kL = 1,000 L
1 m = .001 km	1 g = .001 kg	1 L = .001 kL
1 m = 100 cm	1 g = 100 cg	1 L = 100 cL
1 cm = .01 m	1 cg = .01 g	1 cL = .01 L
1 m = 1,000 mm	1 g = 1,000 mg	1 L = 1,000 mL
1 mm = .001 m	1 mg = .001 g	1 mL = .001 L

Conversions within the Metric System

An easy way to do conversions with the metric system is to move the decimal point either to the right or left because the conversion factor is always ten or a power of ten. Remember, when changing from a large unit to a smaller unit, multiply. When changing from a small unit to a larger unit, divide.

Making Easy Conversions within the Metric System

When multiplying by a power of ten, move the decimal point to the right, since the number becomes larger. When dividing by a power of ten, move the decimal point to the left, since the number becomes smaller. (See below.)

To change from a larger unit to a smaller unit, move the decimal point to the right.

$$\rightarrow$$

kilo hecto deka UNIT deci centi milli

$$\leftarrow$$

To change from a smaller unit to a larger unit, move the decimal point to the left.

Example
Change 520 grams to kilograms.

1. Be aware that changing meters to kilometers is going from small units to larger units and, thus, requires that the decimal point move to the left.

2. Beginning at the UNIT (for grams), note that the kilo heading is three places away. Therefore, the decimal point will move three places to the left.

k h dk UNIT d c m

3. Move the decimal point from the end of 520 to the left three places.
520
←
.520
Place the decimal point before the 5: .520
The answer is 520 grams = .520 kilograms.

Example

Ron's supply truck can hold a total of 20,000 kilograms. If he exceeds that limit, he must buy stabilizers for the truck that cost $12.80 each. Each stabilizer can hold 100 additional kilograms. If he wants to pack 22,300,000 grams of supplies, how much money will he have to spend on the stabilizers?

1. First, change 2,300,000 grams to kilograms.

kg hg dkg g dg cg mg

2. Move the decimal point 3 places to the left: 22,300,000 g = 22,300.000 kg = 22,300 kg.
3. Subtract to find the amount over the limit: 22,300 kg − 20,000 kg = 2,300 kg.
4. Because each stabilizer holds 100 kilograms and the supplies exceed the weight limit of the truck by 2,300 kilograms, Ron must purchase 23 stabilizers: 2,300 kg ÷ 100 kg per stabilizer = 23 stabilizers.
5. Each stabilizer costs $12.80, so multiply $12.80 by 23: $12.80 × 23 = $294.40.

► Algebra

This section will help in mastering algebraic equations by reviewing variables, cross multiplication, algebraic fractions, reciprocal rules, and exponents. Algebra is arithmetic using letters, called **variables**, in place of numbers. By using variables, the general relationships among numbers can be easier to see and understand.

Algebra Terminology

A **term** of a polynomial is an expression that is composed of variables and their exponents, and coefficients. A **variable** is a letter that represents an unknown number. Variables are frequently used in equations, formulas, and in mathematical rules to help illustrate numerical relationships. When a number is placed next to a variable, indicating multiplication, the number is said to be the **coefficient** of the variable.

Examples

8*c*   8 is the coefficient to the variable *c*.

6*ab*   6 is the coefficient to both variables, *a* and *b*.

THREE KINDS OF POLYNOMIALS

- **Monomials** are single terms that are composed of variables and their exponents and a positive or negative coefficient. The following are examples of monomials: x, $5x$, $-6y^3$, $10x^2y$, 7, 0.
- **Binomials** are two non-like monomial terms separated by + or − signs. The following are examples of binomials: $x + 2$, $3x^2 - 5x$, $-3xy^2 + 2xy$.
- **Trinomials** are three non-like monomial terms separated by + or − signs. The following are examples of trinomials: $x^2 + 2x - 1$, $3x^2 - 5x + 4$, $-3xy^2 + 2xy - 6x$.
- Monomials, binomials, and trinomials are all examples of **polynomials**, but we usually reserve the word polynomial for expressions formed by more three terms.
- The **degree** of a polynomial is the largest sum of the terms' exponents.

Examples

- The degree of the trinomial $x^2 + 2x - 1$ is 2, because the x^2 term has the highest exponent of 2.
- The degree of the binomial $x + 2$ is 1, because the x term has the highest exponent of 1.
- The degree of the binomial $-3x^4y^2 + 2xy$ is 6, because the x^4y^2 term has the highest exponent sum of 6.

LIKE TERMS

If two or more terms have exactly the same variable(s), and these variables are raised to exactly the same exponents, they are said to be **like terms**. Like terms can be simplified when added and subtracted.

Examples

$7x + 3x = 10x$

$6y^2 - 4y^2 = 2y^2$

$3cd^2 + 5c^2d$ cannot be simplified. Since the exponent of 2 is on d in $3cd^2$ and on c in $5c^2d$, they are not like terms.

The process of adding and subtracting like terms is called **combining** like terms. It is important to combine like terms carefully, making sure that *the variables are exactly the same.*

Algebraic Expressions

An algebraic expression is a combination of monomials and operations. The difference between algebraic expressions and algebraic equations is that algebraic expressions are evaluated at different given values for variables, while algebraic equations are solved to determine the value of the variable that makes the equation a true statement.

There is very little difference between expressions and equations, because equations are nothing more than two expressions set equal to each other. Their usage is subtly different.

Example

A mobile phone company charges a $39.99 a month flat fee for the first 600 minutes of calls, with a charge of $.55 for each minute thereafter.

Write an algebraic expression for the cost of a month's mobile phone bill:
$39.99 + $.55$x$, where x represents the number of additional minutes used.

Write an equation for the cost (C) of a month's mobile phone bill:
C = $39.99 + $.55$x$, where x represents the number of additional minutes used.

In the above example, you might use the expression $39.99 + $.55$x$ to determine the cost if you are given the value of x by substituting the value for x. You could also use the equation C = $39.99 + $.55$x$ in the same way, but you can also use the equation to determine the value of x if you were given the cost.

SIMPLIFYING AND EVALUATING ALGEBRAIC EXPRESSIONS

We can use the mobile phone company example above to illustrate how to simplify algebraic expressions. Algebraic expressions are evaluated by a two-step process; substituting the given value(s) into the expression, and then simplifying the expression by following the order of operations (PEMDAS).

Example

Using the cost expression $39.99 + $.55$x$, determine the total cost of a month's mobile phone bill if the owner made 700 minutes of calls.
Let x represent the number of minutes over 600 used, so in order to find out the difference, subtract 700 − 600; x = 100 minutes over 600 used.

Substitution: Replace x with its value, using parentheses around the value.
$39.99 + $.55$x$
$39.99 + $.55(100)

Evaluation: PEMDAS tells us to evaluate Parentheses and Exponents first. There is no operation to perform in the parentheses, and there are no exponents, so the next step is to multiply, and then add.

$39.99 + $.55(100)
$39.99 + $55 = $94.99
The cost of the mobile phone bill for the month is $94.99.

You can evaluate algebraic expressions that contain any number of variables, as long as you are given all of the values for all of the variables.

Simple Rules for Working with Linear Equations

A linear equation is an equation whose variables' highest exponent is 1. It is also called a **first-degree equation**. An equation is solved by finding the value of an unknown variable.

1. The equal sign separates an equation into two sides.
2. Whenever an operation is performed on one side, the same operation must be performed on the other side.
3. The first goal is to get all of the variable terms on one side and all of the numbers (called **constants**) on the other side. This is accomplished by *undoing* the operations that are attaching numbers to the variable, thereby isolating the variable. The operations are always done in reverse "PEMDAS" order: start by adding/subtracting, then multiply/divide.
4. The final step often will be to divide each side by the coefficient, the number in front of the variable, leaving the variable alone and equal to a number.

Example

$$5m + 8 = 48$$
$$-8 = -8$$
$$\frac{5m}{5} = \frac{40}{5}$$
$$m = 8$$

Undo the addition of 8 by subtracting 8 from both sides of the equation. Then undo the multiplication by 5 by dividing by 5 on both sides of the equation. The variable, m, is now isolated on the left side of the equation, and its value is 8.

Checking Solutions to Equations

To check an equation, substitute the value of the variable into the original equation.

Example

To check the solution of the previous equation, substitute the number 8 for the variable m in $5m + 8 = 48$.

$$5(8) + 8 = 48$$
$$40 + 8 = 48$$
$$48 = 48$$

Because this statement is true, the answer $m = 8$ must be correct.

ISOLATING VARIABLES USING FRACTIONS

Working with equations that contain fractions is almost exactly the same as working with equations that do not contain variables, except for the final step. The final step when an equation has no fractions is to divide each side by the coefficient. When the coefficient of the variable is a fraction, you will instead multiply both sides by the reciprocal of the coefficient. Technically, you could still divide both sides by the coefficient, but that involves division of fractions which can be trickier.

Example

$$\frac{2}{3}m + \frac{1}{2} = 12$$
$$-\frac{1}{2} = -\frac{1}{2}$$
$$\frac{2}{3}m = 11\frac{1}{2}$$
$$\frac{3}{2} \cdot \frac{2}{3}m = 11\frac{1}{2} \cdot \frac{3}{2}$$
$$\frac{3}{2} \cdot \frac{2}{3}m = \frac{23}{2} \cdot \frac{3}{2}$$
$$m = \frac{69}{4}$$

Undo the addition of $\frac{1}{2}$ by subtracting $\frac{1}{2}$ from both sides of the equation. Multiply both sides by the reciprocal of the coefficient. Convert the $11\frac{1}{2}$ to an improper fraction to facilitate multiplication. The variable m is now isolated on the left side of the equation, and its value is $\frac{69}{4}$.

Equations with More than One Variable

Equations can have more than one variable. Each variable represents a different value, although it is possible that the variables have the same value.

Remember that like terms have the same variable and exponent. All of the rules for working with variables apply in equations that contain more than one variable, but you must remember not to combine terms that are not alike.

Equations with more than one variable cannot be "solved," because if there is more than one variable in an equation there is usually an infinite number of values for the variables that would make the equation true. Instead, we are often required to "solve for a variable," which instead means to isolate that variable on one side of the equation.

Example

Solve for y in the equation $2x + 3y = 5$.

There are an infinite number of values for x and y that that satisfy the equation. Instead, we are asked to isolate y on one side of the equation.

$$2x + 3y = 5$$
$$-2x = -2x$$
$$\frac{3y}{3} = \frac{-2x + 5}{3}$$
$$y = \frac{-2x + 5}{3}$$

Cross Multiplying

Since algebra uses percents and proportions, it is necessary to learn how to cross multiply. You can solve an equation that sets one fraction equal to another by **cross multiplication**. Cross multiplication involves setting the cross products of opposite pairs of terms equal to each other.

> ### Example
>
> $$\frac{x}{10} = \frac{70}{100}$$
>
> $$100x = 700$$
>
> $$\frac{100x}{100} = \frac{700}{100}$$
>
> $$x = 7$$

Algebraic Fractions

Working with algebraic fractions is very similar to working with fractions in arithmetic. The difference is that algebraic fractions contain algebraic expressions in the numerator and/or denominator.

> ### Example
>
> A hotel currently has only one-fifth of their rooms available. If x represents the total number of rooms in the hotel, find an expression for the number of rooms that will be available if another tenth of the total rooms are reserved.

Since x represents the total number of rooms, $\frac{x}{5}$ (or $\frac{1}{5}x$) represents the number of available rooms. One tenth of the total rooms in the hotel would be represented by the fraction $\frac{x}{10}$. To find the new number of available rooms, find the difference: $\frac{x}{5} - \frac{x}{10}$.

Write $\frac{x}{5} - \frac{x}{10}$ as a single fraction.

Just like in arithmetic, the first step is to find the LCD of 5 and 10, which is 10. Then change each fraction into an equivalent fraction that has 10 as a denominator.

$$\frac{x}{5} - \frac{x}{10} = \frac{x(2)}{5(2)} - \frac{x}{10}$$

$$= \frac{2x}{10} - \frac{x}{10}$$

$$= \frac{x}{10}$$

Therefore, $\frac{x}{10}$ rooms will be available after another tenth of the rooms are reserved.

Reciprocal Rules

There are special rules for the sum and difference of reciprocals. The reciprocal of 3 is $\frac{1}{3}$ and the reciprocal of x is $\frac{1}{x}$.

- If x and y are not 0, then $\frac{1}{x} + \frac{1}{y} = \frac{y}{xy} + \frac{x}{xy} = \frac{y+x}{xy}$.
- If x and y are not 0, then $\frac{1}{x} - \frac{1}{y} = \frac{y}{xy} - \frac{x}{xy} = \frac{y-x}{xy}$.

Translating Words into Numbers

The most important skill needed for word problems is being able to translate words into mathematical operations. The following will be helpful in achieving this goal by providing common examples of English phrases and their mathematical equivalents.

Phrases meaning addition: *increased by; sum of; more than; exceeds by.*

Examples

A number increased by five: $x + 5$.

The sum of two numbers: $x + y$.

Ten more than a number: $x + 10$.

Phrases meaning subtraction: *decreased by; difference of; less than; diminished by.*

Examples

10 less than a number: $x - 10$.

The difference of two numbers: $x - y$.

Phrases meaning multiplication: *times; times the sum/difference; product; of.*

Examples

Three times a number: $3x$.

Twenty percent of 50: $20\% \times 50$.

Five times the sum of a number and three: $5(x + 3)$.

Phrases meaning "equals": *is; result is.*

Examples

15 is 14 plus 1: $15 = 14 + 1$.

10 more than 2 times a number is 15: $2x + 10 = 15$.

Assigning Variables in Word Problems

It may be necessary to create and assign variables in a word problem. To do this, first identify any knowns and unknowns. The known may not be a specific numerical value, but the problem should indicate something about its value. Then let x represent the unknown you know the least about.

Examples

Max has worked for three more years than Ricky.
Unknown: Ricky's work experience $= x$
Known: Max's experience is three more years $= x + 3$

Heidi made twice as many sales as Rebecca.
Unknown: number of sales Rebecca made $= x$
Known: number of sales Heidi made is twice Rebecca's amount $= 2x$

There are six less than four times the number of pens than pencils.
Unknown: the number of pencils $= x$
Known: the number of pens $= 4x - 6$

Todd has assembled five more than three times the number of cabinets that Andrew has.
Unknown: the number of cabinets Andrew has assembled $= x$
Known: the number of cabinets Todd has assembled is five more than 3 times the number Andrew has assembled $= 3x + 5$

Percentage Problems

To solve percentage problems, determine what information has been given in the problem and fill this information into the following template:

_____ is _____% of _____

Then translate this information into a one-step equation and solve. In translating, remember that *is* translates to "=" and *of* translates to "×". Use a variable to represent the unknown quantity.

Examples

A) Finding a percentage of a given number:
In a new housing development there will be 50 houses; 40% of the houses must be completed in the first stage. How many houses are in the first stage?

1. Translate.

_____ is 40% of 50.

x is $.40 \times 50$.

2. Solve.

$x = .40 \times 50$

$x = 20$

20 is 40% of 50. There are 20 houses in the first stage.

B) Finding a number when a percentage is given:

40% of the cars on the lot have been sold. If 24 were sold, how many total cars are there on the lot?

1. Translate.

24 is 40% of _____.

$24 = .40 \times x$.

2. Solve.

$\frac{24}{.40} = \frac{.40x}{.40}$

$60 = x$

24 is 40% of 60. There were 60 total cars on the lot.

C) Finding what percentage one number is of another:

Matt has 75 employees. He is going to give 15 of them raises. What percentage of the employees will receive raises?

1. Translate.

15 is _____% of 75.

$15 = x \times 75$.

2. Solve.

$\frac{15}{75} = \frac{75x}{75}$

$.20 = x$

$20\% = x$

15 is 20% of 75. Therefore, 20% of the employees will receive raises.

Problems Involving Ratio

A **ratio** is a comparison of two quantities measured in the same units. It is symbolized by the use of a colon—$x:y$. Ratios can also be expressed as fractions $(\frac{x}{y})$ or using words (x to y).

Ratio problems are solved using the concept of multiples.

Example

A bag contains 60 screws and nails. The ratio of the number of screws to nails is 7:8. How many of each kind are there in the bag?

From the problem, it is known that 7 and 8 share a multiple and that the sum of their product is 60. Whenever you see the word *ratio* in a problem, place an "x" next to each of the numbers in the ratio, and those are your unknowns.

Let $7x$ = the number of screws.

Let $8x$ = the number of nails.

Write and solve the following equation:

$$7x + 8x = 60$$
$$\frac{15x}{15} = \frac{60}{15}$$
$$x = 4$$

Therefore, there are $(7)(4) = 28$ screws and $(8)(4) = 32$ nails.

Check: $28 + 32 = 60$ screws, $\frac{28}{32} = \frac{7}{8}$.

Problems Involving Variation

Variation is a term referring to a constant ratio in the change of a quantity.

- Two quantities are said to vary directly if their ratios are constant. Both variables change in an equal direction. In other words, two quantities vary directly if an increase in one causes an increase in the other. This is also true if a decrease in one causes a decrease in the other.

Example

If it takes 300 new employees a total of 58.5 hours to train, how many hours of training will it take for 800 employees?

Since each employee needs about the same amount of training, you know that they vary directly. Therefore, you can set the problem up the following way:

$$\frac{\text{employees}}{\text{hours}} \rightarrow \frac{300}{58.5} = \frac{800}{x}$$

Cross-multiply to solve:

$(800)(58.5) = 300x$

$$\frac{46,800}{300} = \frac{300x}{300}$$

$$156 = x$$

Therefore, it would take 156 hours to train 800 employees.

■ Two quantities are said to vary inversely if their products are constant. The variables change in opposite directions. This means that as one quantity increases, the other decreases, or as one decreases, the other increases.

Example

If two people plant a field in six days, how many days will it take six people to plant the same field? (Assume each person is working at the same rate.)

As the number of people planting increases, the days needed to plant decreases. Therefore, the relationship between the number of people and days varies inversely. Because the field remains constant, the two products can be set equal to each other.

2 people $\times$ 6 days = 6 people $\times$ x days

$$2 \times 6 = 6x$$

$$\frac{12}{6} = \frac{6x}{6}$$

$$2 = x$$

Thus, it would take 6 people 2 days to plant the same field.

Rate Problems

In general, there are three different types of rate problems likely to be encountered in the workplace: cost per unit, movement, and work-output. **Rate** is defined as a comparison of two quantities with different units of measure.

$$\text{Rate} = \frac{x \text{ units}}{y \text{ units}}$$

Examples

$$\frac{\text{dollars}}{\text{hour}}, \frac{\text{cost}}{\text{pound}}, \frac{\text{miles}}{\text{hour}}$$

Cost Per Unit

Some problems will require the calculation of unit cost.

Example

If 100 square feet cost $1,000, how much does 1 square foot cost?

$$\frac{\text{Total cost}}{\text{\# of square feet}} = \frac{\$1,000}{100 \text{ ft}^2}$$

$$= \$10 \text{ per square foot}$$

Movement

In working with movement problems, it is important to use the following formula:

$$(\text{Rate})(\text{Time}) = \text{Distance}$$

Example

A courier traveling at 15 mph traveled from his base to a company in $\frac{1}{4}$ of an hour less than it took when the courier traveled 12 mph. How far away was his drop off?

First, write what is known and unknown.
Unknown: time for courier traveling 12 mph = x.
Known: time for courier traveling 15 mph = $x - \frac{1}{4}$.
Then, use the formula (Rate)(Time) = Distance to find expressions for the distance traveled at each rate:
12 mph for x hours = a distance of $12x$ miles.
15 miles per hour for $x - \frac{1}{4}$ hours = a distance of $15x - \frac{15}{4}$ miles.
The distance traveled is the same, therefore, make the two expressions equal to each other:

$$12x = 15x - 3.75$$
$$-15x = -15x$$
$$\frac{-3x}{-3} = \frac{-3.75}{-3}$$
$$x = 1.25$$

Be careful, 1.25 is not the distance; it is the time. Now you must plug the time into the formula (Rate)(Time) = Distance. Either rate can be used.
$12x = \text{distance}$
$12(1.25) = \text{distance}$
$15 \text{ miles} = \text{distance}$

WORK-OUTPUT

Work-output problems are word problems that deal with the rate of work. The following formula can be used on these problems:

(Rate of Work)(Time Worked) = Job or Part of Job Completed

Example

Danette can wash and wax 2 cars in 6 hours, and Judy can wash and wax the same two cars in 4 hours. If Danette and Judy work together, how long will it take to wash and wax one car?

Since Danette can wash and wax 2 cars in 6 hours, her rate of work is $\frac{2 \text{ cars}}{6 \text{ hours}}$, or one car every three hours. Judy's rate of work is therefore, $\frac{2 \text{ cars}}{4 \text{ hours}}$, or one car every two hours. In this problem, making a chart will help:

	Rate	Time	=	Part of job completed
Danette	$\frac{1}{3}$	x	=	$\frac{1}{3}x$
Judy	$\frac{1}{2}$	x	=	$\frac{1}{2}x$

Since they are both working on only one car, you can set the equation equal to one:

Danette's part + Judy's part = 1 car:

$$\frac{1}{3}x + \frac{1}{2}x = 1$$

Solve by using 6 as the LCD for 3 and 2 and clear the fractions by multiplying by the LCD:

$$6\left(\frac{1}{3}x\right) + 6\left(\frac{1}{2}x\right) = 6(1)$$
$$2x + 3x = 6$$
$$\frac{5x}{5} = \frac{6}{5}$$
$$x = 1\frac{1}{5}$$

Thus, it will take Judy and Danette $1\frac{1}{5}$ hours to wash and wax one car.

Patterns and Functions

The ability to detect patterns in numbers is a very important mathematical skill. Patterns exist everywhere in nature, business, and finance.

When you are asked to find a pattern in a series of numbers, look to see if there is some common number you can add, subtract, multiply, or divide each number in the pattern by to give you the next number in the series.

For example, in the sequence 5, 8, 11, 14 . . . you can add three to each number in the sequence to get the next number in the sequence. The next number in the sequence is 17.

Example

What is the next number in the sequence $\frac{3}{4}$, 3, 12, 48?

Each number in the sequence can be multiplied by the number 4 to get the next number in the sequence: $\frac{3}{4} \times 4 = 3$, $3 \times 4 = 12$, $12 \times 4 = 48$, so the next number in the sequence is $48 \times 4 = 192$.

Sometimes it is not that simple. You may need to look for a combination of multiplying and adding, dividing and subtracting, or some combination of other operations.

Example

What is the next number in the sequence 0, 1, 2, 5, 26?

Keep trying various operations until you find one that works. In this case, the correct procedure is to square the term and add 1: $0^2 + 1 = 1$, $1^2 + 1 = 2$, $2^2 + 1 = 5$, $5^2 + 1 = 26$, so the next number in the sequence is $26^2 + 1 = 677$.

PROPERTIES OF FUNCTIONS

A **function** is a relationship between two variables x and y where for each value of x, there is one and only one value of y. Functions can be represented in four ways:

- a table or chart
- an equation
- a word problem
- a graph

For example, the following four representations are equivalent to the same function:

Word Problem
Javier has one more than two times the
number of books Susanna has.

Equation

$y = 2x + 1$

Graph

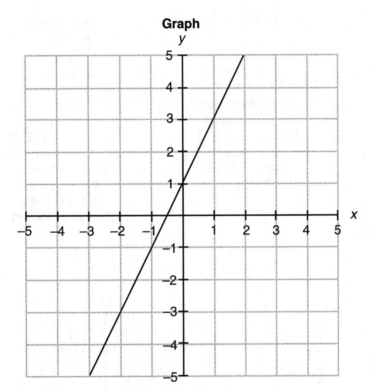

Table

x	y
−3	−5
−2	−3
−1	−1
0	1
1	3
2	5

Helpful hints for determining if a relation is a function:

- If you can isolate y in terms of x using only one equation, it **is** a function.
- If the equation contains y^2, it will **not** be a function.
- If you can draw a vertical line anywhere on a graph such that it touches the graph in more than one place, it is **not** a function.
- If there is a value for x that has more than one y-value assigned to it, it is **not** a function.

x	y
5	2
3	−1
2	0
6	1
5	4

x	y
−2	5
−1	6
0	7
1	8
2	9

x	y
−2	3
−1	3
0	3
1	3
2	3

In this table, the *x*-value of 5 has **two** corresponding *y*-values, 2 and 4. Therefore, it is **not** a function.

In this table, every *x*-value {−2, −1, 0, 1, 2, 3} has **one** corresponding *y*-value. This **is** a function.

In this table, every *x*-value {−2, −1, 0, 1, 2, 3} has **one** corresponding *y*-value, even though that value is 3 in every case. This **is** a function.

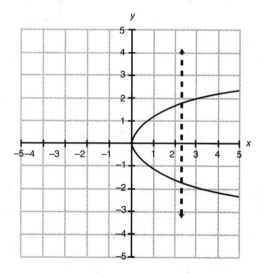

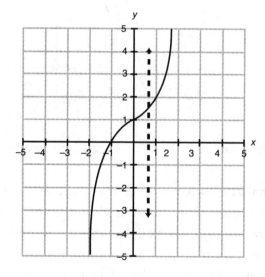

In this graph, there is at least one vertical line that can be drawn (the dotted line) that intersects the graph in more than one place. This is **not** a function.

In this graph, there is no vertical line that can be drawn that intersects the graph in more than one place. This **is** a function.

Examples

$x = 5$ Contains no variable y, so you cannot isolate y. This is **not** a function.

$2x + 3y = 5$ Isolate y:

$$2x + 3y = 5$$
$$-2x \qquad -2x$$
$$\frac{3y}{3} = \frac{-2x + 5}{3}$$
$$y = -\frac{2}{3x} + \frac{5}{3}$$

This is a **linear function**, of the form $y = mx + b$.

$x^2 + y^2 = 36$ Contains y^2, so it is **not** a function.

$|y| = 5$ There is no way to isolate y with a single equation, therefore it is **not** a function.

FUNCTION NOTATION

Instead of using the variable y, often you will see the variable $f(x)$. This is shorthand for "function of x" to automatically indicate that an equation is a function. This can be confusing; $f(x)$ does not indicate two variables f and x multiplied together, it is a notation that means the single variable y.

Although it may seem that $f(x)$ is not an efficient shorthand (it has more characters than y), it is very eloquent way to indicate that you are being given expressions to evaluate. For example, if you are given the equation $f(x) = 5x - 2$, and you are being asked to determine the value of the equation at $x = 2$, you need to write "evaluate the equation $f(x) = 5x - 2$ when $x = 2$." This is very wordy. With function notation, you only need to write "determine $f(2)$." The x in $f(x)$ is replaced with a 2, indicating that the value of x is 2. This means that $f(2) = 5(2) - 2 = 10 - 2 = 8$.

All you need to do when given an equation $f(x)$ and told to evaluate $f(value)$, replace the *value* for every occurrence of x in the equation.

Example

Given the equation $f(x) = 2x^2 + 3x + 1$, determine $f(0)$ and $f(-1)$.

$f(0)$ means replace the value 0 for every occurrence of x in the equation and evaluate.
$$f(0) = 2(0)^2 + 3(0) + 1$$
$$= 0 + 0 + 1$$
$$= 1$$

$f(-1)$ means replace the value -1 for every occurrence of x in the equation and evaluate.
$$f(0) = 2(-1)^2 + 3(-1) + 1$$
$$= 2(1) + -3 + 1$$
$$= 2 - 3 + 1$$
$$= 0$$

FAMILIES OF FUNCTIONS

There are a number of different types, or families, of functions. Each function family has a certain equation and its graph takes on a certain appearance. You can tell what type of function an equation is by just looking at the equation or its graph.

These are the shapes that various functions have. They can appear thinner or wider, higher or lower, or upside down.

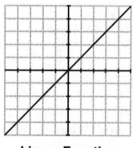

Linear Function
$f(x) = mx + b$
$y = mx + b$

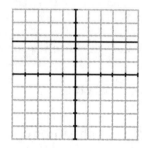

Constant Function
$f(x) = c$
$y = c$
The equation contains no variable x.

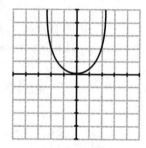

Quadratic Function
$f(x) = ax^2 + bx + c$
$y = ax^2 + bx + c$
This is the function name for a parabola.

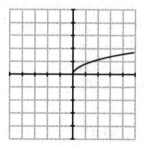

Square Root Function
The equation has to contain a square root symbol.

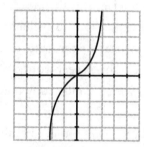

Cubic Function
$f(x) = ax^3 + bx^2 + cx + d$
$y = ax^3 + bx^2 + cx + d$

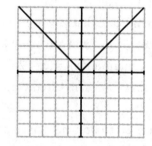

Absolute Value Function
The equation has to have an absolute value symbol in it.

Systems of Equations

A system of equations is a set of two or more equations with the same solution. Two methods for solving a system of equations are substitution and elimination.

SUBSTITUTION

Substitution involves solving for one variable in terms of another and then substituting that expression into the second equation.

Example

$2p + q = 11$ and $p + 2q = 13$

- First, choose an equation and rewrite it, isolating one variable in terms of the other. It does not matter which variable you choose.

  $2p + q = 11$ becomes $q = 11 - 2p$.

- Second, substitute $11 - 2p$ for q in the other equation and solve:

  $p + 2(11 - 2p) = 13$

  $p + 22 - 4p = 13$

  $22 - 3p = 13$

  $22 = 13 + 3p$

  $9 = 3p$

  $p = 3$

- Now substitute this answer into either original equation for p to find q.

  $2p + q = 11$

  $2(3) + q = 11$

  $6 + q = 11$

  $q = 5$

- Thus, $p = 3$ and $q = 5$.

ELIMINATION

The elimination method involves writing one equation over another and then adding or subtracting the like terms on the same sides of the equal sign so that one letter is eliminated.

Example

$x - 9 = 2y$ and $x - 3 = 5y$

- Rewrite each equation in the same form.

  $x - 9 = 2y$ becomes $x - 2y = 9$ and $x - 3 = 5y$ becomes $x - 5y = 3$.

- If you subtract the two equations, the x terms will be eliminated, leaving only one variable:

  Subtract:

  $x - 2y = 9$

  $-(x - 5y = 3)$

  $\frac{3y}{3} = \frac{6}{3}$

  $y = 2$ is the answer.

■ Substitute 2 for y in one of the original equations and solve for x.

$x - 9 = 2y$

$x - 9 = 2(2)$

$x - 9 = 4$

$x - 9 + 9 = 4 + 9$

$x = 13$

■ The answer to the system of equations is $y = 2$ and $x = 13$.

If the variables do not have the same or opposite coefficients as in the example above, adding or subtracting will not eliminate a variable. In this situation, it is first necessary to multiply one or both of the equations by some constant or constants so that the coefficients of one of the variables are the same or opposite. There are many different ways you can choose to do this.

Example

$3x + y = 13$

$x + 6y = -7$

We need to multiply one or both of the equations by some constant that will give equal or opposite coefficients of one of the variable. One way to do this is to multiply every term in the second equation by -3.

$3x + y = 13$

$-3(x + 6y = -7) \rightarrow -3x - 18y = 21$

Now if you add the two equations, the "x" terms will be eliminated, leaving only one variable. Continue as in the example above.

$3x + y = 13$

$-3x - 18y = 21$

$$\frac{-17y}{-17} = \frac{34}{-17}$$

$y = -2$ is the answer.

■ Substitute -2 for y in one of the original equations and solve for x.

$3x + y = 13$

$3x + (-2) = 13$

$3x + (-2) + -2 = 13 + -2$

$3x = 11$

$$x = \frac{11}{3}$$

■ The answer to the system of equations is $y = -2$ and $x = \frac{11}{3}$.

Inequalities

Linear inequalities are solved in much the same way as simple equations. The most important difference is that when an inequality is multiplied or divided by a negative number, the inequality symbol changes direction.

Example

$$10 > 5 \qquad \text{so} \qquad (10)(-3) < (5)(-3)$$
$$-30 < -15$$

SOLVING LINEAR INEQUALITIES

To solve a linear inequality, isolate the letter and solve the same way as you would in a linear equation. Remember to reverse the direction of the inequality sign if you divide or multiply both sides of the equation by a negative number.

Example

If $7 - 2x > 21$, find x.

- Isolate the variable.

$$7 - 2x > 21$$
$$\underline{-7 \qquad -7}$$
$$-2x > 14$$

- Because you are dividing by a negative number, the direction of the inequality symbol changes direction.

$$\frac{-2x}{-2} > \frac{14}{-2}$$
$$x < -7$$

- The answer consists of all real numbers less than -7.

SOLVING COMPOUND INEQUALITIES

To solve an inequality that has the form $c < ax + b < d$, isolate the letter by performing the same operation on each part of the equation.

Example

If $-10 < -5y - 5 < 15$, find y.

- Add five to each member of the inequality.

$$-10 + 5 < -5y - 5 + 5 < 15 + 5 - 5 < -5y < 20$$

- Divide each term by -5, changing the direction of both inequality symbols:

$$\frac{-5}{-5} < -\frac{5y}{-5} < \frac{20}{-5} = 1 > y > -4$$

The solution consists of all real numbers less than 1 and greater than -4.

▶ Geometry

This section will familiarize you with the properties of angles, lines, polygons, triangles, and circles, as well as the formulas for area, volume, and perimeter.

Geometry is the study of shapes and the relationships among them. Basic concepts in geometry will be detailed and applied in this section. The study of geometry always begins with a look at basic vocabulary and concepts. Therefore, a list of definitions and important formulas is provided below.

Geometry Terms

Area	the space inside a 2-dimensional figure
Circumference	the distance around a circle
Chord	a line segment that goes through a circle, with its endpoints on the circle
Congruent	lengths, measures of angles, or size of figures are equal
Diameter	a chord that goes directly through the center of a circle—the longest line segment that can be drawn in a circle
Hypotenuse	the longest side of a right triangle, always opposite the right angle
Leg	either of the two sides of a right triangle that make the right angle
Perimeter	the distance around a figure
π (pi)	The ratio of any circle's circumference to its diameter. Pi is an irrational number, but most of the time it is okay to approximate π with 3.14.
Radius	a line segment from the center of a circle to a point on the circle (half of the diameter)
Surface Area	the sum of the areas of all of a 3-dimensional figure's faces
Volume	the space inside a 3-dimensional figure

Coordinate Geometry

Coordinate geometry is a form of geometrical operations in relation to a coordinate plane. A **coordinate plane** is a grid of square boxes divided into four quadrants by both a horizontal (x) axis and a vertical (y) axis. These two axes intersect at one coordinate point, (0,0), the **origin**. A coordinate point, also called an **ordered pair**, is a specific point on the coordinate plane with the first number representing the horizontal placement and the second number representing the vertical placement. Coordinate points are given in the form of (x,y).

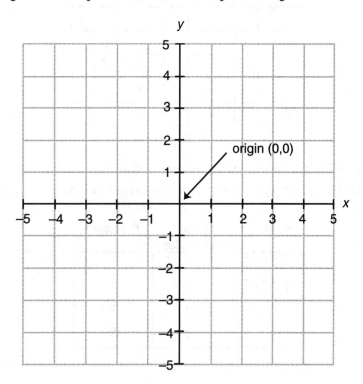

Graphing Ordered Pairs (Points)

- The x-coordinate is listed first in the ordered pair and tells you how many units to move to either the left or to the right. If the x-coordinate is positive, move to the right. If the x-coordinate is negative, move to the left.
- The y-coordinate is listed second and tells you how many units to move up or down. If the y-coordinate is positive, move up. If the y-coordinate is negative, move down.

Example
Graph the following points: (2,3), (3,–2), (–2,3), and (–3,–2).

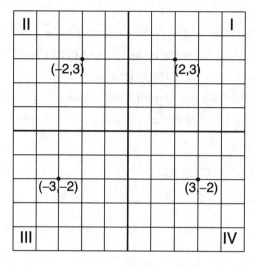

- Notice that the graph is broken up into four quadrants with one point plotted in each one. Here is a chart to indicate which quadrants contain which ordered pairs based on their signs:

Points	Sign of Coordinates	Quadrant
(2,3)	(+,+)	I
(−2,3)	(−,+)	II
(−3,−2)	(−,−)	III
(3,−2)	(+,−)	IV

Lines, Line Segments, and Rays

A **line** is a straight geometric object that goes on forever in both directions. It is infinite in length, and is represented by a straight line with an arrow at both ends. Lines can be labeled with one letter (usually in italics) or with two capital letters near the arrows. **Line segments** are portions of lines. They have two endpoints and a definitive length. Line segments are named by their endpoints. **Rays** have an endpoint and continue straight in one direction. Rays are named by their endpoint and one point on the ray.

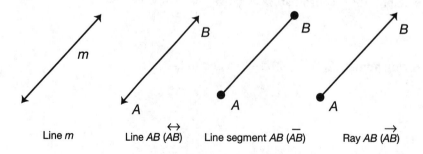

Line *m*   Line *AB* ($\overleftrightarrow{AB}$)   Line segment *AB* ($\overline{AB}$)   Ray *AB* ($\overrightarrow{AB}$)

PARALLEL AND PERPENDICULAR LINES

Parallel lines (or line segments) are a pair of lines, that if extended, would never intersect or meet. The symbol || is used to denote that two lines are parallel. **Perpendicular lines** (or line segments) are lines that intersect to form right angles, and are denoted with the symbol ⊥.

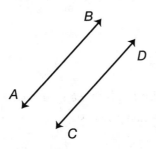

Parallel Lines *AB* and *CD*

$$\overset{\leftrightarrow}{AB} \parallel \overset{\leftrightarrow}{CD}$$

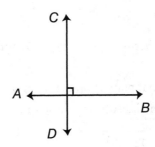

Parallel Lines *AB* and *CD*

$$\overset{\leftrightarrow}{AB} \perp \overset{\leftrightarrow}{CD}$$

LENGTHS OF HORIZONTAL AND VERTICAL SEGMENTS

Two points with the same *y*-coordinate lie on the same horizontal line and two points with the same *x*-coordinate lie on the same vertical line. The distance between a horizontal or vertical segment can be found by taking the absolute value of the difference of the two points.

Example

Find the lengths of line segments $\overline{AB}$ and $\overline{BC}$.

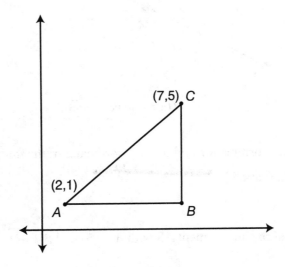

$$|\,2 - 7\,| = 5 = \overline{AB}$$
$$|\,1 - 5\,| = 4 = \overline{BC}$$

DISTANCE OF COORDINATE POINTS

The distance between any two points is given by the formula $d = \sqrt{(x_2 - x_1)^2 + (y_2 - y_1)^2}$, where (x_1, y_1) represents the coordinates of one point and (x_2, y_2) is the other. The subscripts are used to differentiate between the two different coordinate pairs.

Example

Find the distance between points $A(-3,5)$ and $B(1,-4)$.

Let (x_1, y_1) represent point A and let (x_2, y_2) represent point B. This means that $x_1 = -3$, $y_1 = 5$, $x_2 = 1$, and $y_2 = -4$. Substituting these values into the formula gives us:

$$d = \sqrt{(x_2 - x_1)^2 + (y_2 - y_1)^2}$$
$$d = \sqrt{(-3 - 1)^2 + (5 - (-4))^2}$$
$$d = \sqrt{(-4)^2 + (9)^2}$$
$$d = \sqrt{16 + 81}$$
$$d = \sqrt{97}$$

MIDPOINT

The midpoint of a line segment is a point located at an equal distance from each endpoint. This point is in the exact center of the line segment, and is said to be **equidistant** from the segment's endpoints.

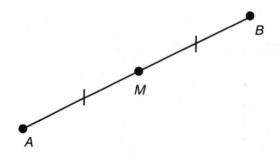

M is the midpoint of $\overline{AB}$

In coordinate geometry, the formula for finding the coordinates of the midpoint of a line segment whose endpoints are (x_1, y_1) and (x_2, y_2) is given by $M = (\frac{x_1 + x_2}{2}, \frac{y_1 + y_2}{2})$.

Example

Determine the midpoint of the line segment $\overline{AB}$ with $A(-3,5)$ and $B(1,-4)$.

Let (x_1, y_1) represent point A and let (x_2, y_2) represent point B. This means that $x_1 = -3$, $y_1 = 5$, $x_2 = 1$, and $y_2 = -4$. Substituting these values into the formula gives us:

$$M = (\frac{-3+1}{2}, \frac{5+(-4)}{2})$$

$$M = (-\frac{2}{2}, \frac{1}{2})$$

$$M = (-1, \frac{1}{2})$$

Note: There is no such thing as the midpoint of a line, as lines are infinite in length.

SLOPE

The **slope** of a line (or line segment) is a numerical value given to show how steep a line is. A line or segment can have one of four types of slope:

- A line with a **positive slope** increases from the bottom left to the upper right on a graph.
- A line with a **negative slope** decreases from the upper left to the bottom right on a graph.
- A horizontal line is said to have a **zero slope**.
- A vertical line is said to have **no slope** (undefined).
- Parallel lines have **equal slopes**.
- Perpendicular lines have slopes that are negative reciprocals of each other.

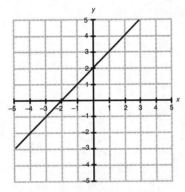

Positive slope

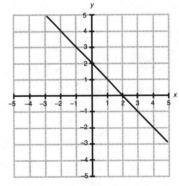

Negative slope

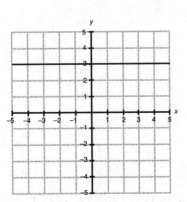

Zero slope

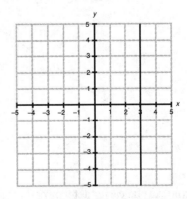

Undefined (no) slope

The slope of a line can be found if you know the coordinates of any two points that lie on the line. It does not matter which two points you use. It is found by writing the change in the y-coordinates of any two points on the line, over the change in the corresponding x-coordinates. (This is also known as the *rise* over the *run*.)

The formula for the slope of a line (or line segment) containing points (x_1, y_1) and (x_2, y_2): $m = \frac{y_2 - y_1}{x_2 - x_1}$.

Example

Determine the slope of the line joining points $A(-3,5)$ and $B(1,-4)$.

Let (x_1, y_1) represent point A and let (x_2, y_2) represent point B. This means that $x_1 = -3$, $y_1 = 5$, $x_2 = 1$, and $y_2 = -4$. Substituting these values into the formula gives us:

$$m = \frac{y_2 - y_1}{x_2 - x_1}$$

$$m = \frac{-4 - 5}{1 - (-3)}$$

$$m = \frac{-9}{4}$$

Example

Determine the slope of the line graphed below.

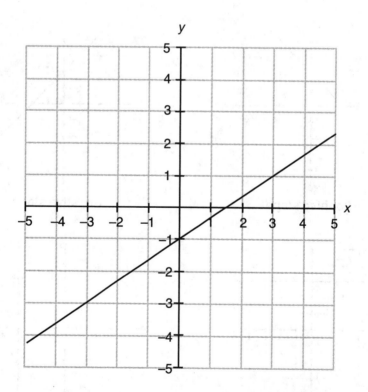

Two points that can be easily determined on the graph are $(3,1)$ and $(0,-1)$. Let $(3,1) = (x_1, y_1)$, and let $(0,-1) = (x_2, y_2)$. This means that $x_1 = 3$, $y_1 = 1$, $x_2 = 0$, and $y_2 = -1$. Substituting these values into the formula gives us:

$$m = \frac{-1-1}{0-3}$$

$$m = \frac{-2}{-3} = \frac{2}{3}$$

Note: If you know the slope and at least one point on a line, you can find the coordinate point of other points on the line. Simply move the required units determined by the slope. For example, from (8,9), given the slope $\frac{7}{5}$, move up seven units and to the right five units. Another point on the line, thus, is (13,16).

Determining the Equation of a Line

The equation of a line is given by $y = mx + b$ where:

- y and x are variables such that every coordinate pair (x,y) is on the line
- m is the **slope** of the line
- b is the **y-intercept**, the y-value at which the line intersects (or intercepts) the y-axis

In order to determine the equation of a line from a graph, determine the slope and y-intercept and substitute it in the appropriate place in the general form of the equation.

Example

Determine the equation of the line in the graph below.

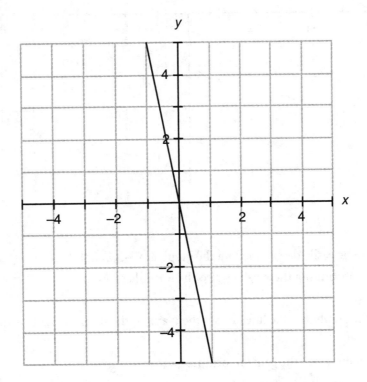

In order to determine the slope of the line, choose two points that can be easily determined on the graph. Two easy points are $(-1,4)$ and $(1,-4)$. Let $(-1,4) = (x_1, y_1)$, and let $(1,-4) = (x_2, y_2)$. This means that $x_1 = -1$, $y_1 = 4$, $x_2 = 1$, and $y_2 = -4$. Substituting these values into the formula gives us: $m = \frac{-4-4}{1-(-1)} = \frac{-8}{2} = -4$.

Looking at the graph, we can see that the line crosses the y-axis at the point $(0,0)$. The y-coordinate of this point is 0. This is the y-intercept.

Substituting these values into the general formula gives us $y = -4x + 0$, or just $y = -4x$.

Example

Determine the equation of the line in the graph below.

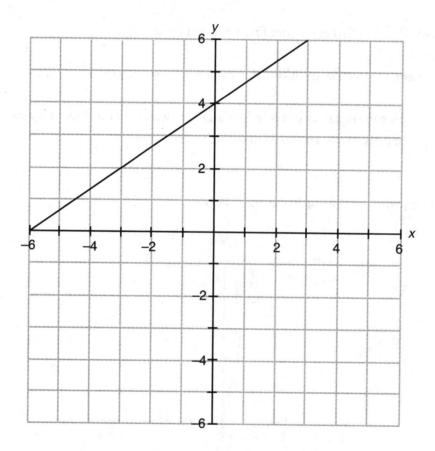

Two points that can be easily determined on the graph are $(-3,2)$ and $(3,6)$. Let $(-3,2) = (x_1, y_1)$, and let $(3,6) = (x_2, y_2)$. Substituting these values into the formula gives us: $m = \frac{6-2}{3-(-3)} = \frac{4}{6} = \frac{2}{3}$.

We can see from the graph that the line crosses the y-axis at the point $(0,4)$. This means the y-intercept is 4.

Substituting these values into the general formula gives us $y = \frac{2}{3}x + 4$.

Angles

NAMING ANGLES

An angle is a figure composed of two rays or line segments joined at their endpoints. The point at which the rays or line segments meet is called the **vertex** of the angle. Angles are usually named by three capital letters, where the first and last letter are points on the end of the rays, and the middle letter is the vertex.

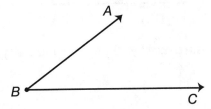

This angle can either be named either ∠ABC or ∠CBA, but because the vertex of the angle is point B, letter B must be in the middle.

We can sometimes name an angle by its vertex, as long as there is no ambiguity in the diagram. For example, in the angle above, we may call the angle ∠B, because there is only one angle in the diagram that has B as its vertex.

But, in the following diagram, there are a number of angles which have point B as their vertex, so we must name each angle in the diagram with three letters.

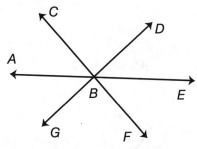

Angles may also be numbered (not measured) with numbers written between the sides of the angles, on the interior of the angle, near the vertex.

CLASSIFYING ANGLES

The unit of measure for angles is the degree.

Angles can be classified into the following categories: acute, right, obtuse, and straight.

- An **acute angle** is an angle that measures between 0 and 90 degrees.

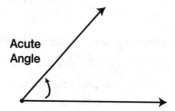

Acute
Angle

- A **right angle** is an angle that measures exactly 90°. A right angle is symbolized by a square at the vertex.

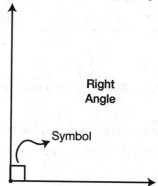

Right
Angle

Symbol

- An **obtuse angle** is an angle that measures more than 90°, but less than 180°.

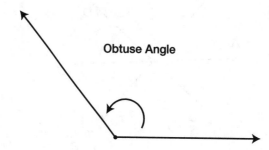

Obtuse Angle

- A **straight angle** is an angle that measures 180°. Thus, both of its sides form a line.

Straight Angle

180°

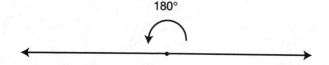

SPECIAL ANGLE PAIRS

- **Adjacent angles** are two angles that share a common vertex and a common side. There is no numerical relationship between the measures of the angles.

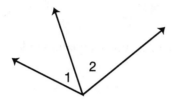
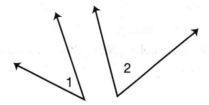

Adjacent angles ∠1 and ∠2   Non-adjacent angles ∠1 and ∠2

- A **linear pair** is a pair of adjacent angles whose measures add to 180°.
- **Supplementary angles** are any two angles whose sum is 180°. A linear pair is a special case of supplementary angles. A linear pair is always supplementary, but supplementary angles do not have to form a linear pair.

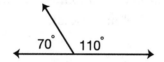
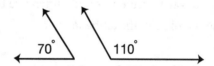

Linear pair (also supplementary)   Supplementary angles (but not a linear pair)

- **Complementary angles** are two angles whose sum measures 90 degrees. Complementary angles may or may not be adjacent.

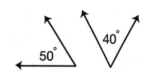

Adjacent complementary angles   Non-adjacent complementary angles

Example

Two complementary angles have measures $2x°$ and $3x + 20°$. What are the measures of the angles?

Since the angles are complementary, their sum is 90°. We can set up an equation to let us solve for x:

$2x + 3x + 20 = 90$

$5x + 20 = 90$

$5x = 70$

$x = 14$

Substituting $x = 14$ into the measures of the two angles, we get $2(14) = 28°$ and $3(14) + 20 = 62°$.

We can check our answers by observing that $28 + 62 = 90$, so the angles are indeed complementary.

Example

One angle is 40 more than 6 times its supplement. What are the measures of the angles?

Let x = one angle.

Let $6x + 40$ = its supplement.

Since the angles are supplementary, their sum is 180°. We can set up an equation to let us solve for x:

$x + 6x + 40 = 180$

$7x + 40 = 180$

$7x = 140$

$x = 20$

Substituting $x = 20$ into the measures of the two angles, we see that one of the angles is 20° and its supplement is $6(20) + 40 = 160°$. We can check our answers by observing that $20 + 160 = 180$, proving that the angles are supplementary.

Note: A good way to remember the difference between supplementary and complementary angles is that the letter c comes before s in the alphabet; likewise "90" comes before "180" numerically.

ANGLES OF INTERSECTING LINES

Important mathematical relationships between angles are formed when lines intersect. When two lines intersect, four smaller angles are formed.

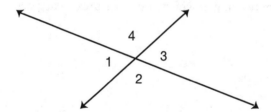

Any two adjacent angles formed when two lines intersect form a linear pair, therefore they are supplementary. In this diagram, $\angle 1$ and $\angle 2$, $\angle 2$ and $\angle 3$, $\angle 3$ and $\angle 4$, and $\angle 4$ and $\angle 1$ are all examples of linear pairs.

Also, the angles that are opposite each other are called **vertical angles**. Vertical angles are angles who share a vertex and whose sides are two pairs of opposite rays. Vertical angles are congruent. In this diagram, $\angle 1$ and $\angle 3$ are vertical angles, so $\angle 1 \cong \angle 3$; $\angle 2$ and $\angle 4$ are congruent vertical angles as well.

Note: Vertical angles is a name given to a special angle pair. Try not to confuse this with right angle or perpendicular angles, which often have vertical components.

Example

Determine the value of *y* in the diagram below:

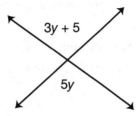

The angles marked $3y + 5$ and $5y$ are vertical angles, so they are congruent and their measures are equal. We can set up and solve the following equation for *y*:

$3y + 5 = 5y$

$\quad 5 = 2y$

$\quad 2.5 = y$

Replacing *y* with the value 2.5 gives us the $3(2.5) + 5 = 12.5$ and $5(2.5) = 12.5$. This proves that the two vertical angles are congruent, with each measuring 12.5°.

PARALLEL LINES AND TRANSVERSALS

Important mathematical relationships are formed when two parallel lines are intersected by a third, non-parallel line called a **transversal**.

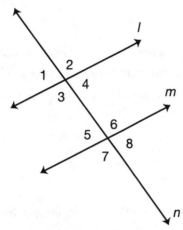

In the diagram above, parallel lines *l* and *m* are intersected by transversal *n*. Supplementary angle pairs and vertical angle pairs are formed in this diagram, too.

Supplementary Angle Pairs		Vertical Angle Pairs
∠1 and ∠2	∠2 and ∠4	∠1 and ∠4
∠4 and ∠3	∠3 and ∠1	∠2 and ∠3
∠5 and ∠6	∠6 and ∠8	∠5 and ∠8
∠8 and ∠7	∠7 and ∠5	∠6 and ∠7

Other congruent angle pairs are formed:

- Alternate interior angles are angles on the **interior** of the parallel lines, on **alternate** sides of the transversal: $\angle 3$ and $\angle 6$; $\angle 4$ and $\angle 5$.
- Corresponding angles are angles on **corresponding** sides of the parallel lines, on **corresponding** sides of the transversal: $\angle 1$ and $\angle 5$; $\angle 2$ and $\angle 6$; $\angle 3$ and $\angle 7$; $\angle 4$ and $\angle 8$.

Example

In the diagram below, line l is parallel to line m. Determine the value of x.

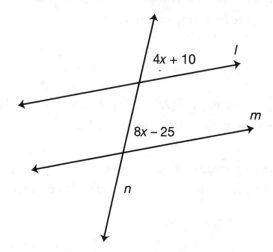

The two angles labeled are **corresponding** angle pairs, because they are located on top of the parallel lines and on the same side of the transversal (same relative location). This means that they are congruent, and we can determine the value of x by solving the equation:

$$4x + 10 = 8x - 25$$
$$10 = 4x - 25$$
$$35 = 4x$$
$$8.75 = x$$

We can check our answer by replacing the value 8.75 in for x in the expressions $4x + 10$ and $8x - 25$:
$$4(8.75) + 10 = 8(8.75) - 25$$
$$45 = 45$$

Note: If the diagram showed the two angles were a vertical angle pair or alternate interior angle pair, the problem would be solved in the same way.

Area, Circumference, and Volume Formulas

Here are the basic formulas for finding area, circumference, and volume. They will be discussed in detail in the following sections.

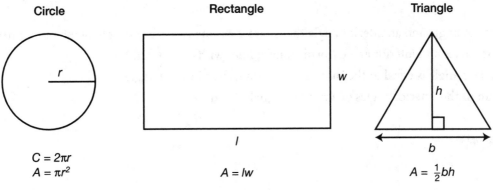

Circle

$C = 2\pi r$
$A = \pi r^2$

Rectangle

$A = lw$

Triangle

$A = \frac{1}{2}bh$

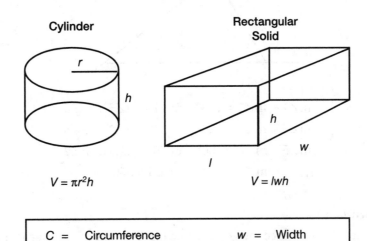

Cylinder

$V = \pi r^2 h$

Rectangular Solid

$V = lwh$

C	=	Circumference	w =	Width
A	=	Area	h =	Height
r	=	Radius	v =	Volume
l	=	Length	b =	Base

Triangles

The sum of the measures of the three angles in a triangle always equals 180 degrees.

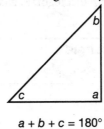

$a + b + c = 180°$

Exterior Angles

An **exterior angle** can be formed by extending a side from any of the three vertices of a triangle. Here are some rules for working with exterior angles:

- An exterior angle and an interior angle that share the same vertex are supplementary. In other words, exterior angles and interior angles form straight lines with each other.
- An exterior angle is equal to the sum of the non-adjacent interior angles.
- The sum of the exterior angles of a triangle equals 360 degrees.

Example

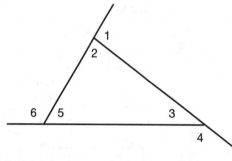

$$m\angle 1 + m\angle 2 = 180° \quad m\angle 1 = m\angle 3 + m\angle 5$$
$$m\angle 3 + m\angle 4 = 180° \quad m\angle 4 = m\angle 2 + m\angle 5$$
$$m\angle 5 + m\angle 6 = 180° \quad m\angle 6 = m\angle 3 + m\angle 2$$
$$m\angle 1 + m\angle 4 + m\angle 6 = 360°$$

CLASSIFYING TRIANGLES

It is possible to classify triangles into three categories based on the number of congruent (indicated by the symbol: ≅) sides. Sides are congruent when they have equal lengths.

Scalene Triangle	Isosceles Triangle	Equilateral Triangle
no sides congruent	more than 2 congruent sides	all sides congruent

It is also possible to classify triangles into three categories based on the measure of the greatest angle:

Acute Triangle	Right Triangle	Obtuse Triangle
greatest angle is acute	greatest angle is 90°	greatest angle is obtuse

ANGLE-SIDE RELATIONSHIPS

Knowing the angle-side relationships in isosceles, equilateral, and right triangles is helpful.

- In isosceles triangles, congruent angles are opposite congruent sides.

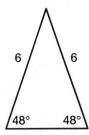

- In equilateral triangles, all sides are congruent and all angles are congruent. The measure of each angle in an equilateral triangle is always 60°.

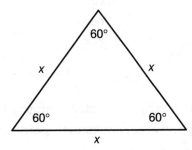

- In a right triangle, the side opposite the right angle is called the **hypotenuse** and the other sides are called **legs**. The box in the angle of the 90-degree angle symbolizes that the triangle is, in fact, a right triangle.

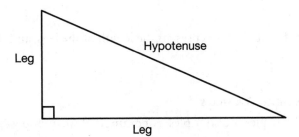

Pythagorean Theorem

The **Pythagorean theorem** is an important tool for working with right triangles. It states: $a^2 + b^2 = c^2$, where a and b represent the legs and c represents the hypotenuse.

This theorem makes it easy to find the length of any side as long as the measure of two sides is known. So, if leg $a = 1$ and leg $b = 2$ in the triangle below, it is possible to find the measure of the hypotenuse, c.

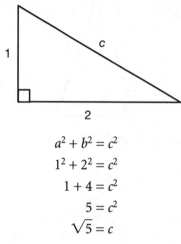

$$a^2 + b^2 = c^2$$
$$1^2 + 2^2 = c^2$$
$$1 + 4 = c^2$$
$$5 = c^2$$
$$\sqrt{5} = c$$

PYTHAGOREAN TRIPLES

Sometimes, the measures of all three sides of a right triangle are integers. If three integers are the lengths of a right triangle, we call them **Pythagorean triples**. Some popular Pythagorean triples are:

3, 4, 5
5, 12, 13
8, 15, 17
9, 40, 41

The smaller two numbers in each triple represent the length of the legs, and the largest number represents the length of the hypotenuse.

MULTIPLES OF PYTHAGOREAN TRIPLES

Whole-number multiples of each triple are also triples. For example, if we multiply each of the lengths of the triple 3, 4, 5 by 2, we get 6, 8, 10. This is also a triple.

Example

If given a right triangle with sides measuring 6, x, and a hypotenuse 10, what is the value of x?

3, 4, 5 is a Pythagorean triple, and a multiple of that is 6, 8, 10. Therefore, the missing side length is 8.

COMPARING TRIANGLES

Triangles are said to be congruent (indicated by the symbol: ≅) when they have exactly the same size and shape. Two triangles are congruent if their corresponding parts (their angles and sides) are congruent. Sometimes, it is easy to tell if two triangles are congruent by looking at them. However, in geometry, it must be able to be proven that the triangles are congruent.

There are a number of ways to prove that two triangles are congruent:

Side-Side-Side (SSS)   If the three sides of one triangle are congruent to the three corresponding sides of another triangle, the triangles are congruent.

Side-Angle-Side (SAS)   If two sides and the included angle of one triangle are congruent to the corresponding two sides and included angle of another triangle, the triangles are congruent.

Angle-Side-Angle (ASA)   If two angles and the included side of one triangle are congruent to the corresponding two angles and included side of another triangle, the triangles are congruent.

Used less often but also valid:

Angle-Angle-Side (AAS)   If two angles and the non-included side of one triangle are congruent to the corresponding two angles and non-included side of another triangle, the triangles are congruent.

Hypotenuse-Leg (Hy-Leg)   If the hypotenuse and a leg of one right triangle are congruent to the hypotenuse and leg of another right triangle, the triangles are congruent.

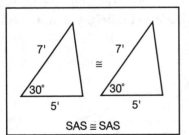

SAS ≅ SAS

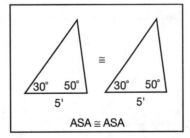

ASA ≅ ASA

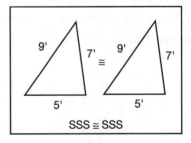

SSS ≅ SSS

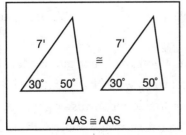

AAS ≅ AAS

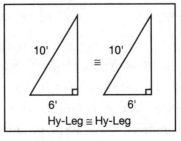

Hy-Leg ≅ Hy-Leg

Example

Determine if these two triangles are congruent.

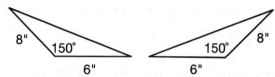

Although the triangles are not aligned the same, there are two congruent corresponding sides, and the angle between them (150°) is congruent. Therefore, the triangles are congruent by the SAS postulate.

Example

Determine if these two triangles are congruent.

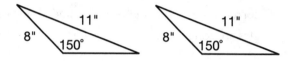

Although the triangles have two congruent corresponding sides, and a corresponding congruent angle, the 150° angle is not included between them. This would be "SSA," but SSA is not a way to prove that two triangles are congruent.

Area of a Triangle

Area is the amount of space inside a two-dimensional object. Area is measured in square units, often written as *unit²*. So, if the length of a triangle is measured in feet, the area of the triangle is measured in *feet²*.

A triangle has three sides, each of which can be considered a **base** of the triangle. A perpendicular line segment drawn from a vertex to the opposite base of the triangle is called the **altitude**, or the **height**. It measures how tall the triangle stands.

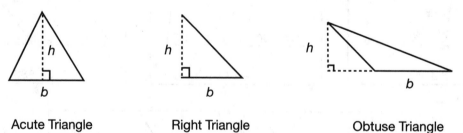

Acute Triangle   Right Triangle   Obtuse Triangle

It is important to note that the height of a triangle is not necessarily one of the sides of the triangle. The correct height for the following triangle is 8, not 10. The height will always be associated with a line segment (called an **altitude**) that comes from one vertex (angle) to the opposite side and forms a right angle (signified by the box). In other words, the height must always be perpendicular to (form a right angle with) the base. Note that in an obtuse triangle, the height is outside the triangle, and in a right triangle the height is one of the sides.

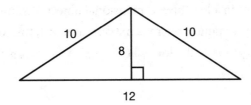

The formula for the area of a triangle is given by $A = \frac{1}{2}bh$, where b is the base of the triangle, and h is the height.

Example

Determine the area of the triangle below.

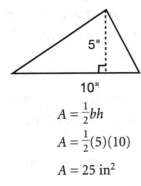

$$A = \frac{1}{2}bh$$

$$A = \frac{1}{2}(5)(10)$$

$$A = 25 \text{ in}^2$$

VOLUME FORMULAS

A **prism** is a three-dimensional object that has matching polygons as its top and bottom. The matching top and bottom are called the **bases** of the prism. The prism is named for the shape of the prism's base, so a **triangular prism** has congruent triangles as its bases.

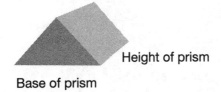

Height of prism

Base of prism

Note: This can be confusing. The **base** of the prism is the shape of the polygon that forms it; the **base** of a triangle is one of its sides.

Volume is the amount of space inside a three-dimensional object. Volume is measured in cubic units, often written as $unit^3$. So, if the edge of a triangular prism is measured in feet, the volume of it is measured in $feet^3$.

The volume of ANY prism is given by the formula $V = A_b h$, where A_b is the area of the prism's base, and h is the height of the prism.

Example

Determine the volume of the following triangular prism:

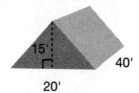

The area of the triangular base can be found by using the formula $A = \frac{1}{2}bh$, so the area of the base is $A = \frac{1}{2}(15)(20) = 150$. The volume of the prism can be found by using the formula $V = A_b h$, so the volume is $V = (150)(40) = 6,000$ cubic feet.

A **pyramid** is a three-dimensional object that has a polygon as one base, and instead of a matching polygon as the other, there is a point. Each of the sides of a pyramid is a triangle. Pyramids are also named for the shape of their (non-point) base.

The volume of a pyramid is determined by the formula $\frac{1}{3}A_b h$.

Example

Determine the volume of a pyramid whose base has an area of 20 square feet and stands 50 feet tall.

Since the area of the base is given to us, we only need to replace the appropriate values into the formula.

$V = \frac{1}{3}A_b h$

$V = \frac{1}{3}(20)(50)$

$V = 33\frac{1}{3}$

The pyramid has a volume of $33\frac{1}{3}$ cubic feet.

Polygons

A polygon is a closed figure with three or more sides, for example triangles, rectangles, pentagons, etc.

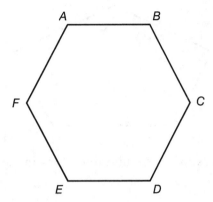

Shape	Number of Sides
Circle	0
Triangle	3
Quadrilateral (square/rectangle)	4
Pentagon	5
Hexagon	6
Heptagon	7
Octagon	8
Nonagon	9
Decagon	10

TERMS RELATED TO POLYGONS

- **Vertices** are corner points, also called **endpoints**, of a polygon. The vertices in the above polygon are: *A, B, C, D, E,* and *F* and they are always labeled with capital letters.
- A **regular polygon** has congruent sides and congruent angles.
- An **equiangular polygon** has congruent angles.

Interior Angles

To find the sum of the interior angles of any polygon, use this formula:

$S = 180(x - 2)°$, where $x =$ the number of sides of the polygon.

Example

Find the sum of the interior angles in the polygon below:

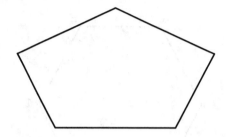

The polygon is a pentagon that has 5 sides, so substitute 5 for x in the formula:

$S = (5 - 2) \times 180°$

$S = 3 \times 180°$

$S = 540°$

EXTERIOR ANGLES

Similar to the exterior angles of a triangle, the sum of the exterior angles of any polygon equals 360 degrees.

SIMILAR POLYGONS

If two polygons are similar, their corresponding angles are congruent and the ratios of the corresponding sides are in proportion.

Example

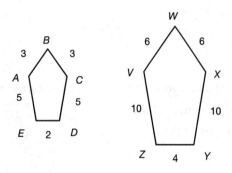

$\angle A = \angle V = 140°$
$\angle B = \angle W = 60°$
$\angle C = \angle X = 140°$
$\angle D = \angle Y = 100°$
$\angle E = \angle Z = 100°$

$$\frac{AB}{VW} \quad \frac{BC}{WX} \quad \frac{CD}{XY} \quad \frac{DE}{YZ} \quad \frac{EA}{ZV}$$

$$\frac{3}{6} = \frac{3}{6} = \frac{5}{10} = \frac{5}{10} = \frac{2}{4}$$

These two polygons are similar because their angles are congruent and the ratios of the corresponding sides are in proportion.

Quadrilaterals

A **quadrilateral** is a four-sided polygon. Since a quadrilateral can be divided by a diagonal into two triangles, the sum of its interior angles will equal 180 + 180 = 360 degrees.

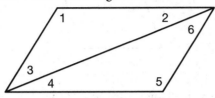

$$m\angle 1 + m\angle 2 + m\angle 3 + m\angle 4 + m\angle 5 + m\angle 6 = 360°$$

Parallelograms

A parallelogram is a quadrilateral with two pairs of parallel sides.

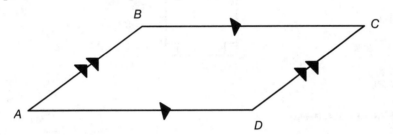

In the figure above, $\overline{AB} \parallel \overline{CD}$ and $\overline{BC} \parallel \overline{AD}$. Parallel lines are symbolized with matching numbers of triangles or arrows.

A parallelogram has:

- opposite sides that are congruent ($\overline{AB} = \overline{CD}$ and $\overline{BC} = \overline{AD}$)
- opposite angles that are congruent ($m\angle A = m\angle C$ and $m\angle B = m\angle D$)
- consecutive angles that are supplementary ($m\angle A + m\angle B = 180°$, $m\angle B + m\angle C = 180°$, $m\angle C + m\angle D = 180°$, $m\angle D + m\angle A = 180°$)
- diagonals (line segments joining opposite vertices) that bisect each other (divide each other in half)

SPECIAL TYPES OF PARALLELOGRAMS

- A **rectangle** is a parallelogram that has four right angles.

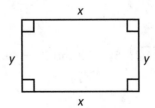

- A **rhombus** is a parallelogram that has four equal sides.

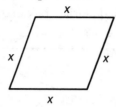

- A **square** is a parallelogram in which all angles are equal to 90 degrees and all sides are congruent. A square is a special case of a rectangle where all the sides are congruent. A square is also a special type of rhombus where all the angles are congruent.

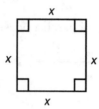

DIAGONALS OF PARALLELOGRAMS

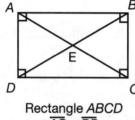
Rectangle *ABCD*
$\overline{AC} \cong \overline{BD}$

Rhombus *ABCD*
$\overline{AC} \perp \overline{BD}$

Square *ABCD*
$\overline{AB} \perp \overline{CD}, \overline{AC} \cong \overline{BD}$

In this diagram, parallelogram *ABCD* has diagonals $\overline{AC}$ and $\overline{BD}$ that intersect at point *E*. The diagonals of a parallelogram bisect each other, which means that $\overline{AE} \cong \overline{EC}$ and $\overline{BE} \cong \overline{ED}$.

In addition, the following properties hold true:

- The diagonals of a rhombus are perpendicular.
- The diagonals of a rectangle are congruent.
- The diagonals of a square are both perpendicular and congruent.

Example

In parallelogram *ABCD*, the diagonal $\overline{AC} = 5x + 10$ and $\overline{BC} = 9x$. Determine the value of *x*.

Since the diagonals of a parallelogram are congruent, the lengths are equal. We can then set up and solve the equation $5x + 10 = 9x$ to determine the value of x.

$5x + 10 = 9x$	Subtract x from both sides of the equation.
$10 = 4x$	Divide 4 from both sides of the equation.
$2.5 = x$	

AREA AND VOLUME FORMULAS

The area of any parallelogram can be found with the formula $A = bh$, where b is the base of the parallelogram, and h is the height. The base and height of a parallelogram is defined the same as in a triangle.

Note: Sometimes b is called the length (l) and h is called the width (w) instead. If this is the case, the area formula is $A = lw$.

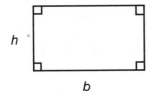 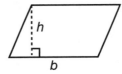

A **rectangular prism** (or **rectangular solid**) is a prism that has rectangles as bases. Recall that the formula for any prism is $V = A_b h$. Since the area of the rectangular base is $A = lw$, we can replace lw for A_b in the formula giving us the more common, easier to remember formula, $V = lwh$. If a prism has a different quadrilateral-shaped base, use the general prisms formula for volume.

Note: A cube is a special rectangular prism with six congruent squares as sides. This means that you can use the $V = lwh$ formula for it, too.

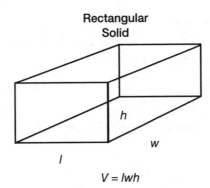

Rectangular
Solid

$V = lwh$

Circles

TERMINOLOGY

A **circle** is formally defined as the set of points a fixed distance from a point. The more sides a polygon has, the more it looks like a circle. If you consider a polygon with 5,000 small sides, it will look like a circle, but a circle is not a polygon. A circle contains 360 degrees around a center point.

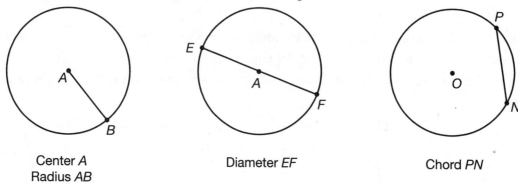

Center *A*
Radius *AB*

Diameter *EF*

Chord *PN*

- The midpoint of a circle is called the **center**.
- The distance around a circle (called **perimeter** in polygons) is called the **circumference**.
- A line segment that goes through a circle, with its endpoints on the circle, is called a **chord**.
- A chord that goes directly through the center of a circle (the longest line segment that can be drawn) in a circle is called the **diameter**.
- The line from the center of a circle to a point on the circle (half of the diameter) is called the **radius**.
- A **sector** of a circle is a fraction of the circle's area.
- An **arc** of a circle is a fraction of the circle's circumference.

CIRCUMFERENCE, AREA, AND VOLUME FORMULAS

The area of a circle is $A = \pi r^2$, where r is the radius of the circle. The circumference (perimeter of a circle) is $2\pi r$, or πd, where r is the radius of the circle and d is the diameter.

Example

Determine the area and circumference of the circle below:

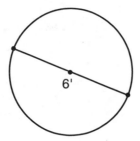

6'

We are given the diameter of the circle, so we can use the formula $C = \pi d$ to find the circumference.

$C = \pi d$

$C = \pi(6)$

$C = 6\pi \div 18.85$ feet

The area formula uses the radius, so we need to divide the length of the diameter by 2 to get the length of the radius: $6 \div 2 = 3$. Then we can just use the formula.

$A = \pi(3)2$

$A = 9\pi \div 28.27$ square feet.

Note: *Circumference* is a measure of length, so the answer is measured in *units*, where the *area* is measured in *square units*.

AREA OF SECTORS AND LENGTHS OF ARCS

The area of a sector can be determined by figuring out what the percentage of the total area the sector is, and then multiplying by the area of the circle.

The length of an arc can be determined by figuring out what the percentage of the total circumference of the arc is, and then multiplying by the circumference of the circle.

Example

Determine the area of the shaded sector and the length of the arc *AB*.

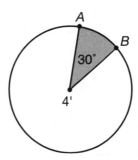

Since the angle in the sector is 30°, and we know that a circle contains a total of 360°, we can determine what fraction of the circle's area it is: $\frac{30°}{360°} = \frac{1}{12}$ of the circle.

The area of the entire circle is $A = \pi r^2$, so $A = \pi(4)^2 = 16\pi$.

So, the area of the sector is $\frac{1}{12} \times 16\pi = \frac{16\pi}{12} = \frac{4}{3}\pi \approx 4.19$ square inches.

We can also determine the length of the arc *AB*, because it is $\frac{30°}{360°} = \frac{1}{12}$ of the circle's circumference.

The circumference of the entire circle is $C = 2\pi r$, so $C = 2\pi(4) = 8\pi$.

This means that the length of the arc is $\frac{1}{12} \times 8\pi = \frac{8\pi}{12} = \frac{2}{3\pi} \approx 2.09$ inches.

A prism that has circles as bases is called a **cylinder**. Recall that the formula for any prism is $V = A_b h$. Since the area of the circular base is $A = \pi r^2$, we can replace πr^2 for A_b in the formula, giving us $V = \pi r^2 h$, where r is the radius of the circular base, and h is the height of the cylinder.

Cylinder

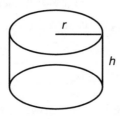

$$V = \pi r^2 h$$

A sphere is a three-dimensional object that has no sides. A basketball is a good example of a sphere. The volume of a sphere is given by the formula $V = \frac{4}{3}\pi r^3$.

Example

Determine the volume of a sphere whose radius is 1.5'.

Replace 1.5' in for r in the formula $V = \frac{4}{3}\pi r^3$.
$V = \frac{4}{3}\pi r^3$

$V = \frac{4}{3}\pi(1.5)^3$

$V = \frac{4}{3}(3.375)\pi$

$V = 4.5\pi \approx 14.14$
The answer is approximately 14.14 cubic feet.

Example

An aluminum can is 6" tall and has a base with a radius of 2". Determine the volume the can holds.

Aluminum cans are cylindrical in shape, so replace 2" for r and 6" for h in the formula $V = \pi r^2 h$.
$V = \pi r^2 h$
$V = \pi(2)^2(6)$
$V = 24\pi \approx 75.40$ cubic feet

▶ Data Analysis

Data analysis simply means reading graphs, tables, and other graphical forms. You should be able to:

- read and understand scatter plots, graphs, tables, charts, figures, etc.
- interpret scatter plots, graphs, tables, charts, figures, etc.
- compare and interpret information presented in scatter plots, graphs, tables, charts, figures, etc.
- draw conclusions about the information provided
- make predictions about the data

It is important to read tables, charts, and graphs very carefully. Read all of the information presented, paying special attention to headings and units of measure. This section will cover tables and graphs. The most common types of graphs are scatter plots, bar graphs, and pie graphs. What follows is an explanation of each, with examples for practice.

Tables

All tables are composed of **rows** (horizontal) and **columns** (vertical). Entries in a single row of a table usually have something in common, and so do entries in a single column. Look at the table below that shows how many cars, both new and used, were sold during particular months.

Month	New Cars	Used Cars
June	125	65
July	155	80
August	190	100
September	220	115
October	265	140

Tables are very concise ways to convey important information without wasting time and space. Just imagine how many lines of text would be needed to convey the same information. With the table, however, it is easy to refer to a given month and quickly know how many total cars were sold. It would also be easy to compare month to month. In fact, practice by comparing the total sales of July with October.

In order to do this, first find out how many cars were sold in each month. There were 235 cars sold in July ($155 + 80 = 235$) and 405 cars sold in October ($265 + 140 = 405$). With a little bit of quick arithmetic it can quickly be determined that 170 more cars were sold during October ($405 - 235 = 170$).

Scatter Plots

Whenever a variable depends continuously on another variable, this dependence can be visually represented in a **scatter plot**. A scatter plot consists of the horizontal (x) axis, the vertical (y) axis, and collected data points for variable y, measured at variable x. The variable points are often connected with a line or a curve. A graph often contains a legend, especially if there is more than one data set or more than one variable. A legend is a key for interpreting the graph. Much like a legend on a map lists the symbols used to label an interstate highway, a railroad line, or a city, a legend for a graph lists the symbols used to label a particular data set. Look at the sample graph below. The essential elements of the graph—the x- and y-axis—are labeled. The legend to the right of the graph shows that diamonds are used to represent the variable points in data set 1, while squares are used to represent the variable points in data set 2. If only one data set exists, the use of a legend is not essential.

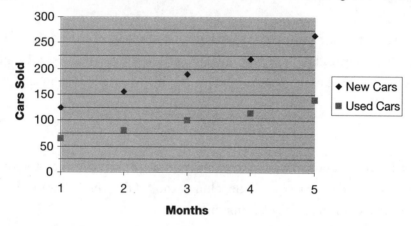

(Note: This data was used in the above example for tables.)

The x-axis represents the months after new management and promotions were introduced at an automobile dealership. The y-axis represents the number of cars sold in the particular month after the changes were made. The diamonds reflect the New Cars sold and the squares show the number of Used Cars sold. What conclusions can be drawn about the sales? Note that the New and Used car sales are both increasing each month at a pretty steady rate. The graph also shows that New Cars increase at a higher rate and that there are many more New Cars sold per month.

Try to look for scatter plots with different trends—including:

- increase
- decrease
- rapid increase, followed by leveling off
- slow increase, followed by rapid increase
- rise to a maximum, followed by a decrease
- rapid decrease, followed by leveling off
- slow decrease, followed by rapid decrease
- decrease to a minimum, followed by a rise
- predictable fluctuation (periodic change)
- random fluctuation (irregular change)

Bar Graphs

Whereas scatterplots are used to show change, **bar graphs** are often used to indicate an amount or level of occurrence of a phenomenon for different categories. Consider the following bar graph. It illustrates the number of employees who were absent due to illness during a particular week in two different age groups.

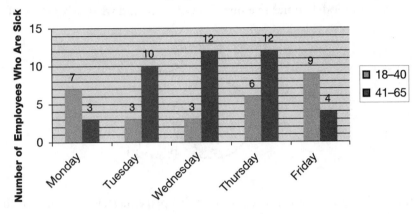

In this bar graph, the categories are the days of the week, and the frequency represents the number of employees who are sick. It can be immediately seen that younger employees are sick before and after the weekend. There is also an inconsistent trend for the younger employees with data ranging all over the place. During mid-week the older crowd tends to stay home more often.

How many people on average are sick in the 41–65 age group? To find the average you first must find out how many illnesses occur each week in the particular age group. There are a total of 41 illnesses for a five-day period ($3 + 10 + 12 + 12 + 4 = 41$). To calculate the average, just divide the total illnesses by the number of days for a total of 8.2 illnesses ($\frac{41}{5} = 8.2$) or more realistically 8 absences per day.

Pictographs

Pictographs are very similar to bar graphs, but instead of bars indicating frequency, small icons are assigned a key value indicating frequency.

Number of Students at the Pep Rally	
Freshmen	🧍🧍🧍🧍🧍🧍🧍🧍🧍🧍🧍🧍
Sophmores	🧍🧍🧍🧍🧍🧍
Juniors	🧍🧍🧍🧍🧍
Seniors	🧍🧍🧍
Key: 🧍 indicates 10 people	

In this pictograph, the key indicates that every icon represents 10 people, so it is easy to determine that there were $12 \times 10 = 120$ freshman, $5.5 \times 10 = 55$ sophomores, $5 \times 10 = 50$ juniors, and $3 \times 10 = 30$ seniors.

Pie Charts and Circle Graphs

Pie graphs are often used to show what percent of a total is taken up by different components of that whole. This type of graph is representative of a whole and is usually divided into percentages. Each section of the chart represents a portion of the whole, and all of these sections added together will equal 100% of the whole. The chart below shows the three styles of model homes in a new development and what percentage of each there is.

Models of Homes

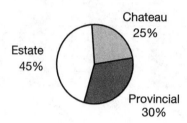

Find the percentage of Estate homes. In order to find this percentage, look at the pie chart. The categories add up to 100% (25 + 30 + 45 = 100). From the actual chart you can visually see that 45% of the homes are done in the Estate model.

Broken Line Graphs

Broken-line graphs illustrate a measurable change over time. If a line is slanted up, it represents an increase, whereas a line sloping down represents a decrease. A flat line indicates no change.

In the broken line graph below, the number of delinquent payments is charted for the first quarter of the year. Each week the number of outstanding bills is summed and recorded.

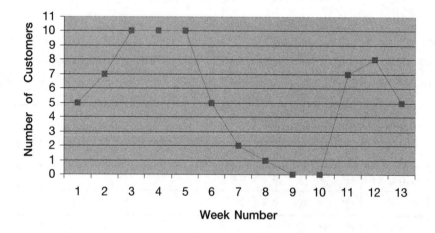

There is an increase in delinquency for the first two weeks and then it maintains for an additional two weeks. There is a steep decrease after week 5 (initially) until the ninth week, where it levels off again but this time at 0. The 11th week shows a radical increase followed by a little jump up at week 12, and then a decrease to week 13. It is also interesting to see that the first and last weeks have identical values.

Now, take the skills you have learned or honed in this review and apply them to the next practice test.

CHAPTER

6 ▶ THEA Writing Review

CHAPTER SUMMARY

This chapter covers the topics that will help you succeed on the multiple-choice and essay portions of the Writing test. You will learn about grammar, organization, as well as how to recognize your audience.

Unlike math, writing is flexible. There are many different ways to convey the same meaning. The THEA Writing section tests your writing skills in two ways. First, it asks you approximately 50 multiple-choice questions related to writing. You do not need to write out any sentences or paragraphs for these questions; you simply need to answer the questions correctly by choosing the answer **a**, **b**, **c**, or **d**.

Each question is based on a passage (you are already familiar with the test format of a passage followed by questions from the Reading section, no doubt). However, the passages in the multiple-choice Writing section are shorter than most of those in the Reading section. Another difference is that each part of a passage in the Writing section is assigned a number, so you can identify specific sentences or sentence fragments.

The second part of the Writing section asks you to write an essay. This essay is evaluated based on your ability to communicate effectively in writing. You will need to express yourself clearly and correctly in an essay of approximately 300–600 words. Keep in mind that an average page of handwritten material is approximately 225 words. More important than the essay's length are its content and organization.

As you study, you may be tempted to focus more on the multiple-choice questions than on the essay, simply because it's easier to tell whether you're correct on a multiple-choice question. This would be a mistake. Your score on the essay basically determines whether or not you pass the whole Writing section. The test scorers will not even look at your multiple-choice questions unless your essay earns a borderline score of 5, exactly in between passing and failing. In that case, the multiple-choice questions are the determining factor in whether you pass or fail. But if your essay doesn't earn a 5, the multiple-choice questions don't count at all. So you should concentrate most of your study time on learning how to write a good essay.

You can achieve a passing score on the written essay with a logical arrangement of paragraphs and ideas that are clearly communicated. Most THEA makers and English instructors recommend a five-paragraph essay, which is an easy and acceptable formula. The five-paragraph essay format helps you to logically and effectively arrange your ideas, and it gives you a chance to develop three complete ideas in the middle three paragraphs.

You will learn more about how to write an effective essay throughout the next six lessons. However, before getting into the details of how to communicate effectively through writing, let us step back and take a look at the big picture. Before you sit down to write anything, whether it be an essay for English class, a shopping list, or a letter to a friend, you need to know what your purpose for writing that piece is. Not only do you need to know your purpose for writing, you also need to recognize your audience. Taking a closer look at these two keys to effective communication will help you get off to the right start on any writing task. Understanding purpose and audience will also help you to correctly answer several multiple-choice questions on the THEA.

Purpose

Every piece of writing has a purpose. Your task as a writer is to understand why you are writing something; what is your purpose? You may answer, "It's to get a good grade" or "It's to pass a standardized test" or something similar. But you have to dig deeper than

these types of responses. Look carefully at the writing task and ask yourself questions about why you are writing. Is it to inform someone of something? Is it to persuade someone or a group of people? Do you want to entertain your readers? Do you want to describe something? If you decide to write a letter to a friend, think about your purpose. Is it to inform that person of what is going on in your life? Is it to persuade that person to accompany you on a date or a trip? Is it to entertain that person with humorous tales of high school life? As you can probably see from these examples, a combination of purposes is often at work in a piece of writing. However, in most pieces of writing, one main purpose exists.

If you know your main purpose and keep that purpose in mind throughout a writing task, the end result will be much more organized and cohesive than if you sat down and randomly tossed thoughts onto a piece of paper without a purpose. Having a purpose is similar to having a goal. It's something that you can work toward throughout the planning, writing, and revising stages of writing an essay. So, write down your purpose and keep it in front of you as you write your essay—it will help you to avoid shifts or conflicts in purpose.

Maintaining Purpose

Maintaining your purpose in an essay is paramount because if you shift purposes midway through the essay, your audience will become confused. The key is to be consistent with your original purpose all the way through the essay to the very end. For example, say you start writing an essay with the purpose of persuading your audience to vote for expanded library privileges for students. Then, in the middle of the essay you get overcome with emotion about how upsetting the voting process is because hardly anyone votes anymore. Finally, in your conclusion you state that democracy has failed. Do you think that this essay would achieve the purpose you set out to achieve at the beginning? Most likely, the readers of this essay would throw their hands up in despair and say, "How can I possibly effect any change in library privileges since democracy has failed, and no one is voting anyway?"

Sample Purpose Question

Read the passage below, written in the style of an introductory anthropology textbook. Then answer the question that follows.

(1) Anthropology is generally considered to be a social science that interprets and describes the development and cultural interactions of humans. (2) However, some scholars have dubbed it a behavioral science. (3) This is because anthropology studies the individual in her or his culture. (4) This study of humans is constantly changing because humans are constantly changing.

1. Which of the following sentences, if added between Parts 3 and 4 of the paragraph, would be most consistent with the writer's purpose and intended audience?
   a. Margaret Mead was a prominent and influential anthropologist whom I deeply respect.
   b. Regardless of what type of science anthropology is, most academics agree that it consists of the study of humans.
   c. Some anthropologists specialize in and publish articles about linguistics.
   d. Radiocarbon dating is sometimes used by anthropologists who specialize in archaeology studies.

Answer

The correct answer is **b.** Several aspects of this sentence show that it is the correct answer choice. For example, its beginning transition word, *regardless*, ties Part 3 and Part 4 together by claiming that it doesn't matter what science anthropology is called (either social or behavioral) since academics agree that it consists of the study of humans. The term *academics* echoes the phrasing of the word *scholars* in Part 2. The sentence

serves as a cohesive bridge between Part 3 and Part 4. None of the other answer choices does so. Choice **a** is not consistent with the author's audience—an educational textbook—because the first person *I* is used. Choices **c** and **d** mention completely different topics related to anthropology instead of contributing to a general overview of the science of anthropology, which is the writer's purpose.

If you find that you have several purposes for writing an essay, rank them in importance, and keep the main purpose as your overall goal. Each of your purposes should enhance each other and not detract from each other. In addition to knowing and maintaining your purpose in writing, you need to know who your audience is.

► Audience

The audience for your writing is closely tied into your purpose for writing. If your purpose is to persuade readers to do something, you need to know who your readers are. That way, you can specifically target your message to that audience. For example, if your purpose is to get people to eat more ice cream, then you need to know who your audience is. If you are writing to a group of young children who love to eat ice cream, your purpose will be quite easily achieved. You won't need to include much research or many statistics about the benefits of eating ice cream. You can instead offer detailed descriptions of how pleasant it is to eat ice cream.

On the other hand, if your audience is a group of adults who are on a diet, you will need to bring in more elevated powers of persuasion. In fact, you will probably need to cite several studies and show proof of how eating ice cream, in balance, is good for them. Perhaps you can prove that low-fat ice cream has fewer calories than a hamburger, or you can cite studies of people who occasionally eat ice cream and still stay slim. Your writing's tone, content, and even organization is greatly determined by your audience. Therefore, keeping your audience in mind throughout the writing process will help you to become a more effective communicator.

Practice

Think about the difference in tone, content, and organization in the following writing tasks. Write down examples for each task that show the particular tone, type of content, and overall organization for each. After you finish, take a moment to think about how different each writing task is merely because of the audience.

2. You jot down a quick e-mail to a friend.

3. You carefully compose an essay for a college professor.

Answers

Answers will vary, but here are some examples.

2. E-mail messages are often written hurriedly and normally lack formal organization. The e-mail's content will vary widely depending on your purpose for sending it. It could be a short, chatty e-mail that asks a friend a question or makes a request such as, "Can you help me pick out a new sweater?"

3. You probably wouldn't say things like "Therefore, only the electrons in the outermost shell are involved" to your friend because the tone is too formal and the content too academic for light conversation. However, you could very well write such a sentence in a formal essay that you hand in to a college professor because you know that academic writing takes a formal tone and uses a standard form of English. Your paragraphs will be organized, and the final essay will appear in a standard format for academic writing.

Audience Questions

Each multiple-choice question in the Writing section on the THEA that asks about a writer's purpose and audience should be looked at carefully. Refer back to the heading of each passage to see what style it is written in to help you determine the writer's purpose and audience. Additionally, when you take the essay writing portion of the THEA, be sure to keep your purpose and audience in mind throughout the writing process.

▶ Purpose and Audience in Your Essay

Before you begin to write your essay for the THEA, you should spend the first four or five minutes of the allowed time to define your purpose for writing the essay, to identify your audience, and to establish the appropriate level of formality. Three questions that will help you to do this are:

1. What is the purpose of my essay?
2. Who is my audience?
3. What level of formality should I use?

The answers to these three questions regarding a topic on the THEA essay writing section will likely yield answers, such as:

1. My purpose for writing this essay is to defend my position on the topic or to persuade my audience that my position is best.
2. My audience is one or more THEA evaluators, who are probably English instructors.
3. I should use a formal tone and structure in writing for this audience and topic.

Now that you are aware of purpose and audience, the next step is to focus on ideas and ways of organizing those ideas.

► Main Ideas and Organizational Patterns

Now that you've mastered purpose and audience, it's time to examine main ideas and how to organize those ideas in a piece of writing. Recognizing main ideas and organizational patterns will help you to correctly answer multiple-choice questions on the THEA and using one or more organizational patterns to order your main ideas in your essay will help you ace that portion of the test.

Main Ideas

The main idea in a paragraph is often called a *topic sentence*. The topic sentence normally appears in the first or last sentence of a paragraph. However, at other times, the main idea is not specifically stated, but it is implied in the overall paragraph. In those instances, readers need to determine the main idea by inference. Without clear main ideas, an essay will flounder and flop. Let's take a look at how you can unify, develop, and support main ideas to make your essay a sweeping success.

Keeping Main Ideas Unified

A good essay contains main ideas that are unified. This means that when you write down a main idea in a paragraph, all the other sentences in that paragraph are related to that main idea. This creates unity in an essay. If you write down a main idea and then interject a completely unrelated sentence in that paragraph, you will lose your audience, and that will defeat your purpose. So, be sure to maintain unity in your paragraphs.

Developing and Supporting Main Ideas

Developing main ideas to support your overall purpose for writing is a challenge. But it is a challenge you can meet successfully. If you develop your ideas in an organized way, you will help your readers understand what you are trying to communicate.

Here are ways you can develop and support main ideas:

- **Give specific examples.** Examples help readers to understand what writers mean. Examples can also enhance a reader's understanding of a complex subject. Look back through the past few lessons for the phrase *for example*, to see this step in action.
- **Supply facts, statistics, or survey results.** This is concrete information that readers will understand. Facts support your case, so use them often.
- **Include anecdotes or personal experiences.** Anecdotes tell a story, and they can illustrate a point you want to make in an essay. You may also use personal experience to illuminate a point. However, don't rely solely on anecdotes and personal experience—you need to include other support as well.
- **Mention specific details.** If your main idea is a sentence that is a general statement, you can support it by offering several specific details that show how the general statement is true.

It is essential that you offer support for all main ideas in the essay that you write for the THEA. You also need to recognize and use methods for organizing main ideas, so read on.

Organizational Patterns

An organizational pattern is a way of sequencing or ordering your ideas in a piece of writing. This section shows you several organizational patterns that you will find on the THEA. You should use one or more of them in your essay. You may be asked to identify them or to understand their use in a passage on the multiple-choice portion of the test.

Be aware that organizational patterns related to writing are also known by other terms, such as "patterns of development" and "methods of organization." So if a question asks, "What pattern of development is the author using?" you will know that the question is also asking "What organizational pattern is the author using?" since they mean the same thing.

Comparison/Contrast

Using comparison/contrast as an organizational pattern enables you to focus on the similarities and differences between two or more topics. For example, you might want to compare and contrast living in a large city with living in a small town. You could first list the comparisons, such as both places have streets, commercial businesses, and residential homes. But you would probably spend more time developing the contrasts between these two subjects, such as level of crime, job opportunities, and population.

You can use a point-by-point method, in which you give examples of a similarity between each topic and then a difference between each topic. Or, you can list all the similarities between the two topics first, and then list all the differences.

Chronological

A chronological organizational pattern presents ideas or events in a linear time frame, that is, their order of occurrence. It is often used to explain a process or to tell a story. You might want to use chronological organization to describe how to bake cookies: "First you preheat the oven, then you gather the ingredients, then you mix the ingredients and put them in the pan, and finally, you bake the cookies in the oven." This shows a progression of chronological events. You can also use a chronological pattern to narrate a story, such as "This morning I woke up and rushed off to the library. After studying for several hours, I went to the dining hall to eat lunch. The afternoon was spent in classes and labs. Then, for dinner I met two friends, and we talked until nightfall." Readers can see the progression of events throughout the day, chronologically.

Classification

An essay that uses classification as an organizational pattern will likely contain items, topics, or ideas that are divided into parts or separate categories. If you choose to use classification as a method of organization, be sure that your categories are logical and that they don't overlap. For example, if you divide books into the categories of fiction, non-fiction, and romance novels, you are creating a faulty classification system because two items in the system overlap—romance novels are fiction. Each category in a classification system needs to be logical and complete. To identify a classification method of organization, look for one general category that is broken down and divided into separate categories. For instance, the topic of non-fiction books at a book sale could be broken down to the separate categories of memoir, biography, and how-to.

Cause and Effect

Cause and effect is a logical organizational pattern that explains how one thing or idea results in another thing or idea. If you use this pattern in your writing, be careful not to make leaps in your reasoning. Each step of the cause needs to be clearly explained and shown how it created the effects you describe. You don't want to leave out any steps in this process, or you may leave your readers hanging. Also, include both immediate causes or effects and long-term causes and effects.

Order of Importance

Ideas listed in their order of importance, either least important to most important or most important to least important, create an organizational pattern. The most effective use of this pattern is to list ideas from least important to most important because the idea that is stated last has the most impact on the reader. To use this pattern of organization, you need to spend time thinking about the importance of your ideas before you can determine which idea should be placed in front of the other. Save the strongest assertion for last.

General to Specific

The general to specific organizational pattern uses deductive reasoning. Writers who use this pattern move from a general statement to specific examples or ideas that support that general statement. For example, you might write that Americans need to cultivate better money-saving habits. This general statement would then need to be supported by specific examples, such as: only five percent of Americans save money out of every paycheck, most Americans do not have enough money saved to retire comfortably, and Americans save 70% less than Europeans do.

Specific to General

The specific to general organizational pattern uses inductive reasoning. Writers who use this pattern move from specific examples or ideas to a general statement that logically follows the specific examples. For example, you might list several specific examples, such as: only five percent of Americans save money out of every paycheck, most Americans do not have enough money saved to retire comfortably, and Americans save 70% less than Europeans do. Then, you sum up this discussion by stating the general idea that Americans need to cultivate better money-saving habits.

Definition

Offering a definition of a term, idea, or concept is another method of organization. Writers using this organizational pattern offer an explanation of something or list the many different definitions of what is being defined. Sometimes you can help define something by stating what it is not. This is called *negation* or *exclusion*.

Sample Organizational Pattern Question

Read the passage below written in the style of a magazine article. Then answer the question that follows.

(1) The floundering dance company could no longer fill their theater with patrons. (2) _____. (3) Their ticket sales started to pick up. (4) The dance company began advertising the fact that the new choreographer was now working on their team. (5) More and more seats became full until there was standing room only.

4. Which of the following sentences, used in place of the blank line labeled (2), would best fit the writer's pattern of development in the paragraph?
   a. The reason can be classified into three distinct categories: lack of advertising, the public's disinterest in classical ballet, and lack of a good choreographer.
   b. This saddened both the artistic director and the dancers in the company.
   c. Even though they were located in a busy downtown district.
   d. Therefore, they hired a new choreographer who had an excellent reputation.

Answer

The correct answer is **d**. The paragraph uses the cause and effect organizational pattern. The word *therefore* signals the change in the paragraph from lack of sales to booming sales. The cause of the low attendance is implied to be that the dance company didn't have a good choreographer. You can infer this because after the new choreographer with the excellent reputation was hired, sales began booming. Choice **a** suggests the organizational pattern in the paragraph is classification; however, the paragraph does not support this method. Choice **b** does not make sense because there is no logical connection between the sadness of the dancers and the sudden increase in sales. Choice **c** is a sentence fragment.

Now that you recognize main ideas and organizational patterns, it's time to dig into the details of how to plan and write an essay.

► Essay Planning and Introductions

This section covers how to plan an essay and write an introduction for the essay portion of the THEA. The first step in writing an essay is to evaluate the assignment. You should spend the first four or five minutes of the allowed time to define your purpose for writing the essay, to identify your audience, and to establish the appropriate level of formality. After you evaluate the assignment, you will next want to plan or outline your essay.

Planning Your Essay

Below are some tips on how to use the first four or five minutes to plan your essay, based on an essay topic similar to one that could appear on the THEA. Take extra care in answering this sample question because this topic will appear many times in the next few lessons.

Sample Persuasive Essay Question

5. In your opinion, should public schools require student uniforms?

After you read the question carefully, choose your side of the issue. If there is a side of the issue you are passionate about, the choice will be easy. If you know very little about a subject and do not have an opinion, just choose the side that you think you can best support. The test scorers don't care which side you take.

Brainstorming

After you choose a side to support for this topic, jot down as many ideas as you can that directly relate to and support your position. Following are some examples of questions that can help you frame your opinions for a persuasive essay. Note the suggested answers to the questions for the topic of school uniforms.

1. Do you know anyone who might feel strongly about the subject?

   parents of school-age children, children, uniform companies, local children's clothing shops

2. What reasons might they give for feeling the way they do?

   Parents will not have to worry about what clothing to buy for their children for school. Children will not feel peer pressure to dress a certain way. Some children will not feel that their clothing is less fashionable than that of the more affluent children. Uniform companies and fabric shops will receive more business.

3. If your side won the argument, who would benefit?

   teachers and principals, because uniforms may help keep discipline in the school; parents, because clothing costs will be lower; and children, because they'll feel more accepted by their peers

4. If the opposing side won, who would be hurt?

   Take the arguments you came up with in question 3 and negate them.

5. What might happen in your city, state, country, and in the world should your side win? If your side was the law, what good might happen next and why? If the opposite side was the law, what bad might happen and why?

   Here you take your position and extend it to the larger community. For instance, imposing school uniforms will lead to a greater sense of order and equality among children across the United States.

6. How does your side affect, for the better, other current issues your readers might be passionate about; i.e., the environment, freedom of speech, and so on?

Requiring uniforms will preserve natural resources, since children will buy fewer clothes.

7. Should your side win, what senses—taste, smell, sight, touch, sound, and feelings—might be affected?

Think about the sight of hundreds of orderly-looking children quietly studying in an organized classroom . . . or whatever fits your topic. If you can appeal to one or more of the five senses, you will have a more persuasive essay.

Organize

When you have finished brainstorming, organize your notes into three or more topics. For instance, if you have three groups of people the proposal would affect, you would write how each group would be affected, whether any of the groups would take a financial loss, and what else might happen to them. Here's an example of how the notes above might be organized into topics:

Parents—Save money, children can use hand-me-downs, save wear on good clothes, buying clothes easier, less pressure from children and fewer fights over money for clothes.

Children—All children feel as well dressed as peers, feel more of a sense of belonging, easier and faster to dress in morning, don't have to worry about what others think, more disciplined and calmer at school.

School staff—Fewer fights at school, less bullying and teasing, more school loyalty among children so builds school community, parents less stressed so fewer calls for advice, frees officials to do other things like academics.

Conclusion: In the end, children, families, and school employees benefit.

Your essay doesn't absolutely have to have just three body paragraphs, though it shouldn't have fewer than three. It's just that three is a good, solid number of main points, so start practicing with three right from the start. You wouldn't want to be in the middle of your fourth body paragraph when time runs out.

Practice

Try outlining the following essay topic using the organizational guidelines.

6. In the last three decades, environmental issues have received increasing amounts of attention. Teaching materials on this subject are abundant and some are even offered free to school districts. Taking into consideration that some environmental issues should be covered, do you believe too much emphasis is being placed on environmental issues in our schools?

▶ Giving Life to an Introduction

If you feel your introductions are dull, or that they lack sparkle, there is hope. One way to enliven your introductions is to make them fun. Get creative. Indeed, the introduction can be the most fun of all the paragraphs of your essay because you have the opportunity to be creative about drawing readers into your essay. A surefire formula for a strong introduction has three parts: an attention-grabber, an orientation for the reader, and a thesis statement (using parallel structure). The thesis statement is indispensable; you can play around with the other parts a bit.

The purpose of the first sentence or two of your introduction is to get your reader's attention. You may start your introduction with a question or statement that engages the reader's imagination, such as:

Imagine a school auditorium full of alert children, all dressed neatly in blue and white uniforms. Imagine these alert children happily running out to play in their blue shorts and white oxford shirts, playing tag and flying on swings.

You will then need one or more sentences to orient your reader. Introduce your topic and give some background information. Here's an example:

Over 98% of our nation's schools have some kind of dress code for their students. Twenty percent of these codes designate a certain color and style of dress. Some of these uniform regulations even include specifics on shoes, socks, sweaters, and jackets. Over 1,000 schools each year are added to the ranks of those that have adopted stricter uniform policies for their children.

State Your Thesis

The most important part of your introduction includes a sentence that states your three or more main points in parallel form; this is called the thesis, or thesis statement. The purpose of this sentence is to tell readers what you are going to tell them in the rest of the essay. The thesis sentence is taken from the three main points of your outline: parents, children, and school staff. Put these in order from the least persuasive or important to the most persuasive or most important. Look at your arguments for each topic and put last the argument for which you can make the best case. Do you feel you can make the most convincing case for school staff and the least convincing case for parents? If so, write about parents first, then children, and finally, staff.

The trick here is to put the three in parallel form. You can always just state the three topics as they are:

Adopting a school uniform policy will benefit parents, children, and school staff.

Alternatively, you can use any number of words in phrases or even whole sentences that summarize the ideas you are going to write about. This is not the place to give much detail, however, or you will have nothing to develop in the next paragraphs.

Uniform policies provide relief for parents, enhance self-esteem in children, and facilitate learning at school.

Parallelism

Your thesis statement should use parallel form. Parallel writing serves to aid casual readers, impress test evaluators, and excite English teachers. The preceding sentence is an example of parallel writing. Parallel writing occurs when a series of phrases or sentences follow the same form. In the second sentence of this paragraph, there are three phrases that are parallel in form: verb, adjective, noun.

VERB	ADJECTIVE	NOUN
aid	casual	readers
impress	test	evaluators
excite	English	teachers

Practice

Test and strengthen your skills at parallelism. Change each sentence to correct faulty parallelism.

7. Simple, cheerful, and having trust, children are a joy to be around.

8. Being happy is more desirable than to be rich.

9. Succeeding as a teacher requires patience, caring, and having a tolerant attitude.

Answers

7. Simple, cheerful, and trusting, children are a joy to be around.
8. Being happy is more desirable than being rich.
9. Succeeding as a teacher requires patience, caring, and tolerance.

Body and Conclusion

Once you have your outline and your introduction, you need not concentrate so much on ideas; you already have them written down. In the body and conclusion of the essay, show off your writing style. Each of the three paragraphs after the introduction should contain a topic sentence and at least four supporting sentences. Your conclusion should restate your thesis and offer a few closing words.

Extra Practice

The sample paragraphs on pages 186 and 187 contain mistakes in grammar, punctuation, diction, and even organization. See whether you can find all the errors, and try to correct them.

You may need to simply rewrite some of the paragraphs. Then, compare your revisions to the ones you will find on pages 195 and 196. There are many ways to rewrite the paragraphs; maybe you will find a better way than the ones given. If you can do that, you're sure to pass the writing portion of the THEA.

► Topic Sentence and Supporting Sentences

Each paragraph should have a topic sentence. Usually the topic sentence begins the paragraph and states the main idea of the paragraph in general. For each of the three or more paragraphs that will make up the body of your essay, one of the points from your outline should be used. That is why you made the outline. The points you wrote down will be the subject of the rest of the sentences in the paragraph.

After composing the topic sentence, uphold and explain your main idea with supporting sentences. These sentences should be as detailed and descriptive as possible.

Let's go back to the uniform example and write some topic sentences and supporting sentences. Remember, the outline looks like this:

Parents—Save money, children can use hand-me-downs, save wear on good clothes, buying clothes easier, less pressure from children and fewer fights over money for clothes.

Children—All children feel as well dressed as peers, feel more of a sense of belonging, easier and faster to dress in morning, don't have to worry about what others think, more disciplined and calmer at school.

School staff—Fewer fights at school, less bullying and teasing, more school loyalty among children so builds school community, parents less stressed so fewer calls for advice, frees officials to do other things, like academics.

Conclusion: In the end, children, families, and school employees benefit.

These are the thesis statement examples:

- Adopting a school uniform policy will benefit parents, children, and school staff.
- Uniform policies provide relief for parents, enhance self-esteem in children, and facilitate learning at school.

Your first reason in favor of uniforms is that parents benefit. To make things easier, you can copy the first part of the thesis statement. This provides you with a transition (see below) as well as a topic sentence:

In my opinion, a uniform policy will benefit parents.

Next, add your detailed reasons. Here is one possible way to write the first body paragraph. (Remember, the paragraphs in this lesson have mistakes in them. Can you correct them?)

In my opinion, a uniform policy will benefit parents. Because they are all the same style and shape and usually very well made, children can use the hand-me-downs of older siblings or even used ones bought from another child. Parents they were also able to save money by buying fewer school clothes for their children. Children, who are often demanding, will have already agreed on what clothes their parents will need to buy so there will be fewer arguments over clothes for school their parents will need to buy. Children and teachers like it too. Parents are generally in favor of uniforms because you do not have to provide your children with a different matched set of clothes for each day. After buying uniforms the first year, more peace was reportedly experienced by 95% of the parents interviewed and many surveys reported that it saved them an average of $100–$200 in clothing costs.

Notice how this paragraph has used some statistics—completely made-up ones—to provide support for the topic sentence. Lots of descriptive detail and maybe even some quotations, when appropriate, will help support your main point and make your essay clear and compelling to your reader.

Now, how about a topic sentence for each of the other two body paragraphs?

- Children benefit from a school uniform policy.
- Uniforms cost no extra money for teachers and administrators, yet the benefits are great.

These sentences are fine for now, but your essay needs transitions from one paragraph to another. The first topic from your thesis statement gives your first body paragraph an automatic transition from the introduction. Now you need something that will link the first body paragraph to the second and the second to the third.

▶ Transitions

A transition sentence joins two paragraphs together in some way. Usually, an idea taken from one paragraph is linked with an idea in the second paragraph. This is done all in one sentence. Sometimes you can do this at the end of one paragraph to link it to the next, but often it's effective to build your transition right into your topic sentence, as you did with the first body paragraph.

For instance, take the topic sentence for your second body paragraph:

Children benefit from a school uniform policy.

How can you link parents, the subject of your first body paragraph, to children? Try something like this:

Not only are parents happy to see a uniform policy in place, but their children benefit as well.

A transition links together body paragraphs one and two. You can also put your transition at the end of the previous paragraph, rather than at the beginning of the new one.

Now add the points from your outline to your second and third body paragraphs. (Are you still looking for the mistakes in these paragraphs?)

Not only are parents happy to see a uniform policy in place, but their children benefit as well. If you were not very wealthy wouldn't you feel bad if you were not dressed as well as your peers. Children who dress differently are alienated from cliques at school and left to feel like outsiders and are teased unmercifully and end up losing a lot of self-esteem. Dressing in uniform eliminates that problem. Instead you feel a sense of belonging. You are less distractd by cumparing your clothes to others so you are more apd to be relaxed and queiter in school. This enables them to learn more. Children might be happy with the school uniform policy but not as happy as their teachers and principals

Uniforms cost no extra money for teachers and administrators yet the benefits are great. There is less competition in school so there is less fights. The reason is because there is less bullying and teasing and there is a lot less complaints. Instead, principals and teachers were able to use uniforms to build school pride and loyalty. Administrators and teachers will be able to concentrate on what they love to do most teach instead of dealing with problems from children and parents.

Practice

Strengthen your transition skills by using each of the following transition words in a sentence. In addition, create a sentence that goes just before the sentence the transition appears in to show how the transition is being used.

10. However

11. First

12. For example

13. Therefore

14. Indeed

Answers

Answers will vary, but here are some sample sentences.

10. I like blue. However, blue doesn't look good on me.

11. Here are the steps. First, go to the store.

12. Eat a healthy diet. For example, eat vegetables and fruit every day.

13. I want to pass the THEA. Therefore, I am carefully studying this book.

14. She is a good basketball player. Indeed, she made the Olympic team.

▶ The Conclusion

A good format to follow for writing a conclusion is to first restate your thesis, and then try for a conclusion, something that will leave your readers with a sense of closure, indicating that they really have finished.

So, in the first sentence or two, restate your thesis. Do not add any new ideas here. This is a good place to try out parallel form.

> Adopting a uniform policy will lighten the burden of parents. It will promote cheerfulness and scholarship in children. Lastly, it will free the time and talents of teachers and administrators.

The last sentence or two should contain the conclusion. Its purpose is to end the paragraph gracefully and leave the reader with a sense of finality.

The last sentence of a persuasive essay may be a call to action, a question, a prediction, or a personal comment. You might add one of these clinchers to the thesis summary on school uniforms:

- What are we waiting for? We need to talk to our teachers, principals, and school boards, and give our children ALL the tools we can that are essential for their growth and development.

■ Since school uniforms do so much good for parents, students, and faculty, would you want your school to miss out?

Practice
Try writing a conclusion for the following topic:

15. It has been suggested that elementary students should attend school six days a week instead of the standard five. That way, each school day could be shorter. Do you think this is a beneficial and workable idea or not?

Answer
Answers will vary, but here is a sample conclusion.

15. Parents, students, and teachers will all benefit if elementary schools continue to meet five days a week instead of six. The five-day week enables parents to align their work schedules with the school's, and it allows children and teachers a necessary and welcome break between school days. We cannot stand idly by and allow the six-day school week to come into effect.

Once you have your ideas down on paper, it's important to see that they are clearly and correctly expressed—unlike some of the paragraphs found in this lesson.

▶ Sentence Structure

Several elements are needed to create effective sentences. You will need to be able to recognize these elements on the multiple-choice portion of the THEA, and you will need to be able to effectively incorporate them into your essay. The content of your essay is even more important than its logical structure. Generalizations need to be supported with exact and specific details, which you are free to make up. Your choice of words needs to be precise, your sentences varied, and your paragraphs unified. Your paragraphs should have connections between them so that your whole essay flows from one thought to another. Let's look at some of the sentence elements that make up good paragraphs, so you can identify them in the multiple-choice section and use them in the essay section.

Varied Sentence Structure
Within a paragraph, sentences should be varied. This is important when you write your essay because varied sentence structure makes your essay more interesting and shows the test evaluators that you have mastered different sentence structures.

There are two types of sentence variation: sentence length and sentence structure. Sentence length should not be a problem. Use some long sentences and some short ones. As for varying the structure of a sentence, you might need to brush up on parts of speech and different types of clauses and phrases. If this is the case, go to your local library and check out a book on grammar. The idea is not to be able to name all the different types of clauses, but only to be able to place some variety in your writing. The following exercise demonstrates a few examples of various sentence structure.

Practice
Rewrite the sentences beginning with the part of speech indicated.

16. The hostess greeted her special guests graciously. (Adverb)

17. The proprietor, hard as nails, demanded the rent. (Adjective)

18. One must learn how to breathe to swim well. (Infinitive)

19. The white stallion leapt over the hurdles. (Preposition)

20. An octogenarian was playing with the children. (Participle)

21. The schools will not be state funded if they do not hire certified teachers. (Adverb clause)

For additional practice, try writing sentences that begin with these words:

After	Unless
Although	Where
As	Wherever
Because	While
Since	

Answers
16. Graciously, the hostess greeted her special guests.
17. Hard as nails, the proprietor demanded the rent.
18. To swim well, one must learn how to breathe.
19. Over the hurdles leapt the white stallion.
20. Playing with the children was an octogenarian.
21. If they do not hire certified teachers, the schools will not be state funded.

▶ Dangling Clauses

You will need to recognize dangling clauses in the multiple-choice section of the THEA. You should also avoid including them in your essay. Dangling clauses mix up who's doing what:

If they do not hire certified teachers, state funds will not be sent to the schools.

It sounds as if the funds were doing the hiring. Instead you should write:

If they do not hire certified teachers, the schools will not receive state funding.

If you start off with a clause, make sure that the who or what referred to in the clause begins the next part of the sentence.

Misplaced Modifiers
Misplaced modifiers are closely related to dangling clauses—they also can creep in and corrupt the sentence structure in a piece of writing. You should recognize what a misplaced modifier is, so you can identify it in a multiple-choice question. It's also important that you do not misplace modifiers in your essay. Before you hand in your essay, take a minute to look for misplaced modifiers in your sentences. Simply put, modifiers need to be placed as close as possible to the words they modify. Modifiers may be adjectives, adverbs, or other phrases or clauses that are used as adjectives or adverbs. If the modifier is only one word, then place it directly in front of the word it is modifying. Here are some modifiers that are often misplaced in sentences:

nearly	only
almost	hardly
merely	just

▶ Opinions

Never start a sentence with "In my opinion" or "I think." If you didn't think it, you wouldn't be writing it. In the school uniform essay, the sentence "In my opinion, a uniform policy will benefit parents" should read simply:

A uniform policy will benefit parents.

► Redundancy

Avoid redundancy. Try to keep your sentences as succinct as possible without losing meaning. Make every word and phrase count.

Take a look at the following examples of redundant phrases and replacement words you can use for concise writing:

NOT	BUT
during the course of	during
in the event that	if
in the near future	soon
plan in advance	plan
past history	past
green in color	green
true facts	facts

► Unecessary Sentences and Sentence Order

In the multiple-choice writing portion of THEA, you will need to identify sentences in a passage that do not support the main idea. On the essay portion, you should avoid writing sentences that are not on the same general topic as the rest of the paragraph.

The order of the sentences in a paragraph is just as important as the order of the paragraphs in an essay. For example, if you are writing about money parents will save, put all the sentences on money together. Provide transitions for your sentences, just as you did with your paragraphs. You can join sentences with transition words such as *besides, second, lastly*, or you can put in topic sentences.

Try rearranging the paragraph on parents in a logical order. You have two topics: money and peace in the family. So add a topic sentence to announce the first idea:

First, uniforms would save parents money.

The fake survey you added at the end of the paragraph reports statistics on both money and peace, so that's a great way to tie the two topics together. The rest of the sentences should all fit under one of the two topics. If you have something that doesn't fit, just leave it out.

► Run-On Sentences

Before you move on to problems with words in the next lesson, take a look at a problem sentence from the second body paragraph on school uniforms.

Children who dress differently are alienated from cliques at school and left to feel like outsiders and are teased unmercifully and end up losing a lot of self-esteem.

Do you see that this sentence goes on and on? It should have been divided into at least two sentences.

If you wanted to join the two above sentences, you could do it with a semicolon; if you used a comma, you'd have a sentence fault called a *comma splice*. The same is true of the sentence you just read. For more on fixing your punctuation and word problems, keep reading.

► The Punctuation, Capitalization, and Word Doctor

You will need to know correct punctuation for both the multiple-choice and the essay portions of the Writing section. In the multiple-choice section of the THEA, you will need to be able to identify punctuation errors. In the essay section of the THEA, you will need to be able to use punctuation correctly. This lesson will help you do both.

There are dozens of different punctuation marks in the English language; those covered in this section are the ones that present the most challenges to their users.

The Apostrophe

Apostrophes (') are used to indicate ownership and to form contractions. Eight rules cover all of the situations in which they may appear.

1. Add *'s* to form the singular possessive, even when the noun ends in *s*:

   The *school's* lunchroom needs to be cleaned.

   The *drummer's* solo received a standing ovation.

   Mr. Perkins's persuasive essay was very convincing.

2. A few plurals, not ending in *s*, also form the possessive by adding *'s*:

   The *children's* toys were found in every room of the house.

   The line for the *women's* restroom was too long.

   Men's shirts come in a variety of neck sizes.

3. Possessive plural nouns already ending in *s* need only the apostrophe added:

   The *customers'* access codes are confidential.

   The *students'* grades improved each semester.

   The flight *attendants'* uniforms were blue and white.

4. Indefinite pronouns show ownership by the addition of *'s*:

   Everyone's hearts were in the right place.

   Somebody's dog was barking all night.

   It was *no one's* fault that we lost the game.

5. Possessive pronouns never have apostrophes, even though some may end in *s*:

   Our car is up for sale.

   Your garden is beautiful.

   His handwriting is difficult to read.

6. Use an *'s* to form the plurals of letters, figures, and numbers used as words, as well as certain expressions of time and money. The expressions of time and money do not indicate ownership in the usual sense:

   She has a hard time pronouncing *s's*.

   My street address contains three *5's*.

   He packed a *week's* worth of clothing.

   The project was the result of a *year's* worth of work.

7. Show possession in the last word when using names of organizations and businesses, in hyphenated words, and in joint ownership:

   Sam and Janet's graduation was three months ago.

   I went to visit my *great-grandfather's* alma mater.

   The Future Farmers of America's meeting was moved to Monday.

8. Apostrophes form contractions by taking the place of the missing letter or number. Do not use contractions in highly formal written presentations:

   Poor form: *We're* going out of town next week.
   Good form: *We are* going out of town next week.

   Poor form: *She's* going to write the next proposal.
   Good form: *She is* going to write the next proposal.

Poor form: My supervisor was in the class of '89.

Good form: My supervisor was in the class of 1989.

Its vs. It's

Unlike most possessives, *its* does not contain an apostrophe. The word *it's* is instead a contraction of the words *it is*. The second *i* is removed, and replaced by an apostrophe. When revising your writing, say the words *it is* when you come across *it's* or *its*. If they make sense, you should be using the contraction. If they don't, you need the possessive form, *its*, without an apostrophe.

The Comma

Correct usage of commas (,) is not as critical to the meaning of your sentences as it is with other punctuation marks. However, they can be used to convey your voice as they speed up or slow down the pace of your sentences. Consider the difference in tone of the following example:

Sentence A: During my junior year, I attended a conference in Washington, D.C., in which student delegates from every state presented their ideas.

Sentence B: During my junior year I attended a conference in Washington, D.C. in which student delegates from every state presented their ideas.

Sentence A sounds more deliberate, giving a little more information with each clause. Sentence B reads quicker, conveying the information faster and with equal weight on each part.

In addition to helping to convey your voice and personality, commas are often used misused. There are two common errors that all college-bound students should be aware of: the comma splice, and the serial comma.

Comma Splice

A comma splice is the incorrect use of a comma to connect two complete sentences. It creates a *run-on sentence*. To correct a comma splice, you can:

- replace the comma with a period, forming two sentences
- replace the comma with a semicolon
- join the two clauses with a conjunction such as *and, because,* or *so*

Comma splice: Our school received an award, we raised the most money for the local charity.

Corrected sentence: Our school received an award. We raised the most money for the local charity.
OR
Our school received an award; we raised the most money for the local charity.
OR
Our school received an award because we raised the most money for the local charity.

Serial Comma

A serial comma is the one used last in a list of items, after the word *and*. For instance, in the following example, the comma after *apples* is the serial comma:

At the store, I bought bananas, apples, and oranges.

The lack of a serial comma can cause confusion. In the sentence, *Cindy, Ann, and Sally were hired to work in the college counselor's office*, the message is straightforward. But if the serial comma is dropped, it could be understood as Cindy being told that Ann and Sally were hired.

Cindy, Ann and Sally were hired to work in the college counselor's office.

While its use has been debated for centuries, the serial comma clarifies the meaning of sentences. Therefore, you should use it consistently whenever writing a list.

The Colon

Colons (:) appear at the end of a clause and can introduce:

- a list when the clause before the colon can stand as a complete sentence on its own

Incorrect:	The classes he signed up for include: geometry, physics, American literature, and religion.
Correct:	He signed up for four classes: geometry, physics, American literature, and religion.

- a restatement or elaboration of the previous clause

Incorrect:	Shari is a talented hairdresser: she is also the mother of two children.
Correct:	Shari is a talented hairdresser: she attends a seminar each month and has been a professional for over twenty years.
Incorrect:	My teacher wasn't in class today: he graduated Summa Cum Laude.
Correct:	My teacher wasn't in class today: he had to fly to Houston to present a paper.

Colons have the effect of sounding authoritative. They present information more confidently and forcefully than if the sentence were divided in two other types of punctuation marks. Consider the following:

My teacher wasn't in class today: he had to fly to Houston to present a paper.

My teacher wasn't in class today. He had to fly to Houston to present a paper.

The first example, with the colon, has the tone that conveys, "I know why this happened, and I am going to tell you." It sounds more authoritative. This can be effective in your essay, but because you never want to appear pompous, it should be used sparingly.

The Semicolon

Semicolons (;) may be used in two ways: to separate independent clauses, and to separate the items in a list when those items contain commas.

- Use semicolons to separate independent clauses.

Case:	Use a semicolon to separate independent clauses joined without a conjunction.
Example:	Four people worked on the project; only one received credit for it.
Case:	Use a semicolon to separate independent clauses that contain commas, even if the clauses are joined by a conjunction.
Example:	The strays were malnourished, dirty, and ill; but Liz had a weakness for kittens, so she adopted them all.

Case: Use a semicolon to separate independent clauses that are connected with a conjunctive adverb that expresses a relationship between clauses.

Example: Victoria was absent frequently; therefore, she received a low grade.

- Use semicolons to separate items in a series that contain commas.

Case: Use a semicolon to show which sets of items go together.

Examples: The dates for our meetings are Monday, January 10; Tuesday, April 14; Monday, July 7; and Tuesday, October 11.

She has lived in Omaha, Nebraska; Nutley, New Jersey; Amherst, Massachusetts; and Pensacola, Florida.

Capitalization

Capitalization is necessary both for specific words and to start sentences and quotes. However, many writers overuse it, and thus appear overly casual. There are just six occasions that require capitalization:

1. the first word of a sentence
2. proper nouns (names of people, places, and things)
3. the first word of a complete quotation, but not a partial quotation
4. the first, last, and any other important words of a title
5. languages
6. the pronoun *I*, and any contractions made with it

Point of View

Keep a consistent point of view throughout your essay. If you're referring to your subject as *they*, use *they, them,* and *their* throughout, don't start using forms of *you* instead.

Spelling Errors

You will encounter few, if any, spelling questions in the multiple-choice section of the THEA. However, you will need to make sure you spell words correctly in your essay. You will have to write quickly during the exam, so save a couple of minutes at the end to check your work for spelling errors.

Double Negatives and Problem Words

Remember to use problem words correctly. Avoid double negatives. If you must use them, make sure you are saying what you really mean. If you have time, you may want to brush up on other problem words such as *lay* and *lie, all together* and *altogether*, and so on. Discussions on these topics can be found in detail in most grammar books.

Proofread

Spend the last few minutes of the exam proofreading to see whether you included everything you had to say, whether you used the same verb tense and person throughout, and whether your words are clear. There is no time for big revisions, but check for such details as periods or questions marks after sentences and spelling.

As you proofread, check to see whether your essay flows well. If additional punctuation is necessary to get your point across, use it—but don't go overboard by throwing in commas where they are not necessary.

Verb Tenses

Unless there is a very good reason for doing otherwise, the same tense should be used throughout your essay. You may use perfect tenses when appropriate, but try to avoid using future, past, and present in one paragraph. See whether you can find the tense mistakes in the following paragraph.

Uniforms cost no extra money for teachers and administrators, yet the benefits are great. Because there is less competition in school, teachers and administrators report that there are fewer fights, less bullying, and fewer complaints from the students. Instead, principals and teachers were able to use uniforms to build school pride and loyalty. Administrators and teachers will be able to concentrate on what they love to do most, teach, instead of dealing with problems from children and parents.

The first part of the paragraph is in present tense. The past tense verb *were able* in the third sentence should be changed to the present *are able*. In the last sentence, the future tense *will be able* should also be changed to the present *are able*.

Instead, principals and teachers are able to use uniforms to build school pride and loyalty. Administrators and teachers are able to concentrate on what they love to do most, teach, instead of dealing with problems from children and parents.

Finalizing

Notice how the few remaining problems with transitions have been cleaned up in this final version of the essay on school uniforms. The body paragraph on teachers and administrators ended with too strong a statement—no one will believe that school personnel will have no problems from children just because of uniforms—so that statement has been softened.

Imagine a school auditorium full of alert children, all dressed neatly in blue and white uniforms.

Imagine these same children happily running out to play in their blue shorts and white oxford shirts, playing tag, and flying on swings. Whether or not to dress public school children alike has been the subject of much controversy in recent decades. Opponents suggest that requiring uniforms will stifle children's ability to choose, squash necessary individuality, and infringe on the rights of children and families. Although there is some justification for these arguments, the benefits of uniforms far outweigh the disadvantages. Adopting a uniform policy will benefit parents, children, and the school staff.

A uniform policy will benefit parents. Uniforms save parents money. Parents will not have to provide their children with a different matched set of clothes for each day, so fewer school clothes will be needed. Because uniforms are all the same style and shape and usually very well made, they can be passed down from an older child to a younger one, or even sold. On a recent survey, parents new to school uniforms estimated they saved up to $1,000 on school clothes per child the first year alone. The survey also reported that 95% of parents attributed an increased feeling of peace to the adoption of the uniform policy. Children will have already agreed on what clothes their parents will need to buy, so there will be fewer arguments on this often touchy subject.

Not only are parents happy to see a uniform policy in place, but their children benefit as well. If you were poor, wouldn't you feel badly if you were not dressed as well as your peers? Children who dress differently are usually alienated from cliques at school and left to feel like outsiders. Often they are teased unmercifully. Dressing in uniform eliminates that problem. Instead, uniformed children feel an increased sense of belonging that enables them to be more relaxed and quiet in school. Children do not need to compare their clothing with that of others, so they have fewer distractions during their learning time. Children like the policy because there is less nagging at home, and dressing for school is much easier.

Parents and children are not the only ones who are better off with school uniforms. Teachers and administrators love them too. Uniforms cost no extra money, yet the benefits are great. Because there is less competition in school, teachers and administrators report that less time is spent mediating because there are fewer fights, less bullying, and fewer complaints from students. Administrators and teachers can use the time they save to do what they are paid to do—build school loyalty, form young minds, and teach basic skills. Teachers report a more peaceful classroom, and administrators report a more cooperative student body.

Adopting a uniform policy will lighten the burden of parents. It will promote cheerfulness and scholarship in children. Lastly, it will free the time and talents of teachers and administrators. What are we waiting for? We need to talk to our teachers, principals, and school boards, and give our children all the tools we can that will enhance their growth and development.

Now that you have reviewed these writing strategies, apply them to the essays in the practice exams that follow.

THEA Practice Exam 2

CHAPTER SUMMARY

Here is another practice test based on the Texas Higher Education Assessment (THEA). After working through the review lessons in Chapters 4, 5, and 6 take this test to see how much your score has improved.

Like the real THEA, the exam that follows is made up of three sections: a Reading section, a Mathematics section, and a two-part Writing section that consists of multiple-choice questions and one essay topic.

For this practice exam, you should simulate the actual test-taking experience as closely as you can. Find a quiet place to work where you won't be disturbed. You can use the answer sheet on the following page. You should write your essay on a separate piece of paper. Allow yourself five hours for the entire exam. Don't worry about how long it takes to do each section. On the actual THEA, you may move from section to section as you please, go back and forth between sections, or even decide to do only one section. Since you should decide beforehand how many sections you will take and in what order, use this practice test to find out how you work best. Perhaps, for example, you can do your writing sample first, while you are fresh.

After the exam, review the answer explanations to find out what questions you missed and why.

▶ Answer Sheet

SECTION 1: READING	SECTION 2: MATH	SECTION 3: WRITING PART A
1. (a) (b) (c) (d)	1. (a) (b) (c) (d)	1. (a) (b) (c) (d)
2. (a) (b) (c) (d)	2. (a) (b) (c) (d)	2. (a) (b) (c) (d)
3. (a) (b) (c) (d)	3. (a) (b) (c) (d)	3. (a) (b) (c) (d)
4. (a) (b) (c) (d)	4. (a) (b) (c) (d)	4. (a) (b) (c) (d)
5. (a) (b) (c) (d)	5. (a) (b) (c) (d)	5. (a) (b) (c) (d)
6. (a) (b) (c) (d)	6. (a) (b) (c) (d)	6. (a) (b) (c) (d)
7. (a) (b) (c) (d)	7. (a) (b) (c) (d)	7. (a) (b) (c) (d)
8. (a) (b) (c) (d)	8. (a) (b) (c) (d)	8. (a) (b) (c) (d)
9. (a) (b) (c) (d)	9. (a) (b) (c) (d)	9. (a) (b) (c) (d)
10. (a) (b) (c) (d)	10. (a) (b) (c) (d)	10. (a) (b) (c) (d)
11. (a) (b) (c) (d)	11. (a) (b) (c) (d)	11. (a) (b) (c) (d)
12. (a) (b) (c) (d)	12. (a) (b) (c) (d)	12. (a) (b) (c) (d)
13. (a) (b) (c) (d)	13. (a) (b) (c) (d)	13. (a) (b) (c) (d)
14. (a) (b) (c) (d)	14. (a) (b) (c) (d)	14. (a) (b) (c) (d)
15. (a) (b) (c) (d)	15. (a) (b) (c) (d)	15. (a) (b) (c) (d)
16. (a) (b) (c) (d)	16. (a) (b) (c) (d)	16. (a) (b) (c) (d)
17. (a) (b) (c) (d)	17. (a) (b) (c) (d)	17. (a) (b) (c) (d)
18. (a) (b) (c) (d)	18. (a) (b) (c) (d)	18. (a) (b) (c) (d)
19. (a) (b) (c) (d)	19. (a) (b) (c) (d)	19. (a) (b) (c) (d)
20. (a) (b) (c) (d)	20. (a) (b) (c) (d)	20. (a) (b) (c) (d)
21. (a) (b) (c) (d)	21. (a) (b) (c) (d)	21. (a) (b) (c) (d)
22. (a) (b) (c) (d)	22. (a) (b) (c) (d)	22. (a) (b) (c) (d)
23. (a) (b) (c) (d)	23. (a) (b) (c) (d)	23. (a) (b) (c) (d)
24. (a) (b) (c) (d)	24. (a) (b) (c) (d)	24. (a) (b) (c) (d)
25. (a) (b) (c) (d)	25. (a) (b) (c) (d)	25. (a) (b) (c) (d)
26. (a) (b) (c) (d)	26. (a) (b) (c) (d)	26. (a) (b) (c) (d)
27. (a) (b) (c) (d)	27. (a) (b) (c) (d)	27. (a) (b) (c) (d)
28. (a) (b) (c) (d)	28. (a) (b) (c) (d)	28. (a) (b) (c) (d)
29. (a) (b) (c) (d)	29. (a) (b) (c) (d)	29. (a) (b) (c) (d)
30. (a) (b) (c) (d)	30. (a) (b) (c) (d)	30. (a) (b) (c) (d)
31. (a) (b) (c) (d)	31. (a) (b) (c) (d)	31. (a) (b) (c) (d)
32. (a) (b) (c) (d)	32. (a) (b) (c) (d)	32. (a) (b) (c) (d)
33. (a) (b) (c) (d)	33. (a) (b) (c) (d)	33. (a) (b) (c) (d)
34. (a) (b) (c) (d)	34. (a) (b) (c) (d)	34. (a) (b) (c) (d)
35. (a) (b) (c) (d)	35. (a) (b) (c) (d)	35. (a) (b) (c) (d)
36. (a) (b) (c) (d)	36. (a) (b) (c) (d)	36. (a) (b) (c) (d)
37. (a) (b) (c) (d)	37. (a) (b) (c) (d)	37. (a) (b) (c) (d)
38. (a) (b) (c) (d)	38. (a) (b) (c) (d)	38. (a) (b) (c) (d)
39. (a) (b) (c) (d)	39. (a) (b) (c) (d)	39. (a) (b) (c) (d)
40. (a) (b) (c) (d)	40. (a) (b) (c) (d)	40. (a) (b) (c) (d)
41. (a) (b) (c) (d)	41. (a) (b) (c) (d)	
42. (a) (b) (c) (d)	42. (a) (b) (c) (d)	
	43. (a) (b) (c) (d)	
	44. (a) (b) (c) (d)	
	45. (a) (b) (c) (d)	
	46. (a) (b) (c) (d)	
	47. (a) (b) (c) (d)	
	48. (a) (b) (c) (d)	

► Section 1: Reading

Questions 1–6 are based on the following passage.

The following is taken from a case that came before the Supreme Court in 1954: "347 US 483 (1954) Brown v. Board of Education."

(1) These cases come to us from the States of Kansas, South Carolina, Virginia, and Delaware. . . . Argument was heard in the 1952 Term and reargument was heard this Term on certain questions propounded by the Court.

(2) Reargument was largely devoted to the circumstances surrounding the adoption of the 14th Amendment in 1868. It covered exhaustively consideration of the Amendment in Congress, ratification by the states, then existing practices in racial segregation, and the views of proponents and opponents of the Amendment. These sources and our own investigation convince us that, although these sources cast some light, it is not enough to resolve the problem with which we are faced. At best, they are inconclusive. The most avid proponents of the post-War Amendments undoubtedly intended them to remove all legal distinctions among "all persons born or naturalized in the United States." Their opponents, just as certainly, were antagonistic to both the letter and the spirit of the Amendments and wished them to have the most limited effect. What others in Congress and the state legislatures had in mind cannot be determined with any degree of certainty.

(3) An additional reason for the inconclusive nature of the Amendment's history, with respect to segregated schools, is the status of public education at that time. In the South, the movement toward free common schools, supported by general taxation, had not yet taken hold. . . . Even in the North, the conditions of public education did not approximate those existing today. The curriculum was usually rudimentary; ungraded schools were common in rural areas; compulsory school attendance was virtually unknown. As a consequence, it is not surprising that there should be so little in the history of the 14th Amendment relating to its intended effect on public education. . . .

(4) In approaching this problem, we cannot turn the clock back to 1868, when the [14th] Amendment was adopted. . . . We must consider public education in the light of its full development and its present place in American life throughout the Nation. . . . Today, education is perhaps the most important function of state and local governments. Compulsory school attendance laws and the great expenditures for education both demonstrate our recognition of the importance of education to our democratic society. It is required in the performance of our most basic public responsibilities, even service in the armed forces. It is the very foundation of good citizenship. Today it is a principal instrument in awakening the child to cultural values, in preparing him for later professional training, and in helping him to adjust normally to his environment. In these days, it is doubtful that any child may reasonably be expected to succeed in life if he is denied the opportunity of an education. Such an opportunity, where the state has undertaken to provide it, is a right which must be made available to all on equal terms. . . .

(5) We conclude that in the field of public education . . . [s]eparate educational facilities are inherently unequal. Therefore, we hold that the plaintiffs and others similarly situated for whom the actions have been brought are . . . deprived of equal protection.

1. The passage indicates that the plaintiffs referred to in paragraph 5 were
  a. not represented by attorneys.
  b. public school students.
  c. school board members.
  d. public school teachers.

2. In paragraph 2, the phrase *post-War Amendments* refers to
  a. Constitutional amendments dealing with education.
  b. the Bill of Rights.
  c. Constitutional amendments dealing with the military.
  d. the 14th and other Constitutional amendments adopted after the Civil War.

3. Use of the term *reargument* in paragraphs 1 and 2 would indicate that
  a. on occasion, the U.S. Supreme Court hears arguments on the same case more than once.
  b. the plaintiffs were not adequately prepared the first time they argued.
  c. one or more Justices was absent during the first argument.
  d. the membership of the Supreme Court changed after the first argument.

4. According to paragraph 3 of the passage, the Court determined that it is not clear what impact Congress intended the 14th Amendment to have on public education because
  a. Congress generally does not deal with public education.
  b. public education was not universally available or standardized at the time.
  c. in 1868, no transcripts of Congressional debates were kept.
  d. the Court disagreed with Congress' intentions.

5. Which of the following sets of topics would best organize the information in the passage?
  a.   I.   the Supreme Court's role in public education
       II. the role of state government in public education
  b.   I.   the history of the 14th Amendment
       II. the cost of public education
  c.   I.   the 14th Amendment and public education
       II. the importance of public education for individuals and the country
  d.   I.   the role of Congress in funding public education
       II. the evolution of public education

6. At the time of the adoption of the 14th Amendment, little attention was paid to the subject of mandatory school attendance. According to paragraph 3 of the passage, this was because, at that time, mandatory attendance was
  a. impossible to enforce.
  b. enforced unequally with regard to race.
  c. practically non-existent.
  d. supported only by public taxation.

Questions 7–12 are based on the following passage.

(1) A recent government report addressing concerns about the many implications of genetic testing outlined policy guidelines and legislative recommendations intended to avoid involuntary and ineffective testing and to protect confidentiality.

(2) The report identified urgent concerns, such as quality control measures (including federal oversight for testing laboratories) and better genetics training for medical practitioners. It recommended voluntary screening; urged couples in high-risk populations to consider carrier screening; and advised

caution in using and interpreting pre-symptomatic or predictive tests as certain information could easily be misused or misinterpreted.

(3) About three in every 100 children are born with a severe disorder presumed to be genetic or partially genetic in origin. Genes, often in concert with environmental factors, are being linked to the causes of many common adult diseases such as coronary artery disease, hypertension, various cancers, diabetes, and Alzheimer's disease. Tests to determine predisposition to a variety of conditions are under study, and some are beginning to be applied.

(4) The report recommended that all screening, including screening of newborns, be voluntary. Citing results of two different voluntary newborn screening programs, the report said these programs can achieve compliance rates equal to or better than those of mandatory programs. State health departments could eventually mandate the offering of tests for diagnosing treatable conditions in newborns; however, careful pilot studies for conditions diagnosable at birth need to be done first.

(5) Although the report asserted that it would prefer that all screening be voluntary, it did note that if a state requires newborn screening for a particular condition, the state should do so only if there is strong evidence that a newborn would benefit from effective treatment at the earliest possible age. Newborn screening is the most common type of genetic screening today. More than four million newborns are tested annually so that effective treatment can be started in a few hundred infants.

(6) Prenatal testing can pose the most difficult issues. The ability to diagnose genetic disorders in the fetus far exceeds any ability to treat or cure them. Parents must be fully informed about risks and benefits of testing procedures, the nature and variability of the disorders they would disclose, and the options available if test results are positive.

(7) Obtaining informed consent—a process that would include educating participants, not just processing documents—would enhance voluntary participation. When offered testing, parents should receive comprehensive counseling, which should be nondirective. Relevant medical advice, however, is recommended for treatable or preventable conditions.

(8) Genetics also can predict whether certain diseases might develop later in life. For single-gene diseases, population screening should only be considered for treatable or preventable conditions of relatively high frequency. Children should be tested only for disorders for which effective treatments or preventive measures could be applied early in life.

7. The word *predisposition*, as it is used in the passage, most nearly means
   a. willingness.
   b. susceptibility.
   c. impartiality.
   d. composure.

8. The report stressed the need for caution in the use and interpretation of
   a. predictive tests.
   b. newborn screening.
   c. informed consent.
   d. pilot studies.

9. According to the passage, how many infants are treated for genetic disorders as a result of newborn screening?
   a. dozens
   b. hundreds
   c. thousands
   d. millions

10. One intention of the policy guidelines was to
 a. implement compulsory testing.
 b. minimize concerns about quality control.
 c. endorse the expansion of screening programs.
 d. preserve privacy in testing.

11. According to the report, states should implement mandatory infant screening only
 a. if the compliance rate for voluntary screening is low.
 b. for mothers who are at high risk for genetic disease.
 c. after meticulous research is undertaken.
 d. to avoid the abuse of sensitive information.

12. The most prevalent form of genetic testing is conducted
 a. on high-risk populations.
 b. on adults.
 c. on fetuses prior to birth.
 d. on infants shortly after birth.

Questions 13–17 are based on the following passage.

(1) If you have ever made a list of pros and cons to help you make a decision, you have used the utilitarian method of moral reasoning. One of the main ethical theories, utilitarianism posits that the key to deciding what makes an act morally right or wrong is its consequences. Whether our intentions are good or bad is irrelevant; what matters is whether the result of our actions is good or bad. To utilitarians, happiness is the ultimate goal of human beings and the highest moral good. Thus, if there is great unhappiness because of an act, then that action can be said to be morally wrong. If, on the other hand, there is great happiness because of an action, then that act can be said to be morally right.

(2) Utilitarians believe that we should carefully weigh the potential consequences of an action before we take it. Will the act lead to things that will make us, or others, happy? Will it make us, or others, unhappy? According to utilitarians, we should choose to do that which creates the greatest amount of good (happiness) for the greatest number of people. This can be difficult to determine, though, because sometimes an act can create short-term happiness but misery in the long term. Another problematic aspect of utilitarianism is that it deems it acceptable—indeed, even necessary—to use another person as a means to an end and sacrifice the happiness of one or a few for the happiness of many.

13. In the first sentence, the author refers to a list of pros and cons in order to
 a. show that there are both positive and negative aspects of utilitarianism.
 b. suggest that making a list of pros and cons is not an effective way to make a decision.
 c. emphasize that utilitarians consider both the good and the bad before making a decision.
 d. show readers that they are probably already familiar with the principles of utilitarian reasoning.

14. The word *posits* in the second sentence means
 a. agrees.
 b. asserts.
 c. places.
 d. chooses.

15. According to the definition of utilitarianism in paragraph 1, stealing bread to feed hungry children would be
 a. morally right because it has good intentions.
 b. morally wrong because it violates the rights of another.
 c. morally right because it has positive consequences.
 d. morally wrong because stealing is illegal.

16. According to the utilitarian principles described in paragraph 2, we should
   a. do what will bring us the most happiness.
   b. always think of others first.
   c. make our intentions clear to others.
   d. do what will make the most people the most happy.

17. In the last sentence, the author's purpose is to show that
   a. using utilitarianism to make a moral decision is not always easy.
   b. sacrifice is necessary in life.
   c. long-term consequences are more important than short-term consequences.
   d. a pro/con list is the most effective technique for making an important decision.

Questions 18–22 are based on the following passage.

(1) Jazz, from its early roots in slave spirituals and the marching bands of New Orleans, had developed into the predominant American musical style by the 1930s. In this era, jazz musicians played a lush, orchestrated style known as *swing.* Played in large ensembles, also called *big bands,* swing filled the dance halls and nightclubs. Jazz, once considered risqué, was made more accessible to the masses with the vibrant, swinging sounds of these big bands. Then came bebop. In the mid-1940s, jazz musicians strayed from the swing style and developed a more improvisational method of playing known as bebop. Jazz was transformed from popular music to an elite art form.

(2) The soloists in the big bands improvised from the melody. The young musicians who ushered in bebop, notably trumpeter Dizzy Gillespie and saxophonist Charlie Parker, expanded on the improvisational elements of the big bands. They played with advanced harmonies, changed chord structures, and made chord substitutions. These young musicians got their starts with the leading big bands of the day, but during World War II—as older musicians were drafted and dance halls made cutbacks—they started to play together in smaller groups.

(3) These pared-down bands helped foster the bebop style. Rhythm is the distinguishing feature of bebop, and in small groups the drums became more prominent. Setting a driving beat, the drummer interacted with the bass, piano, and the soloists, and together the musicians created fast, complex melodies. Jazz aficionados flocked to such clubs as Minton's Playhouse in Harlem to soak in the new style. For the young musicians and their fans this was a thrilling turning point in jazz history. However, for the majority of Americans, who just wanted some swinging music to dance to, the advent of bebop was the end of jazz as mainstream music.

18. The swing style can be most accurately characterized as
   a. complex and inaccessible.
   b. appealing to an elite audience.
   c. lively and melodic.
   d. lacking in improvisation.

19. According to the passage, in the 1940s you would most likely find bebop being played where?
   a. church
   b. a large concert hall
   c. in music schools
   d. small clubs

20. According to the passage, one of the most significant innovations of the bebop musicians was to
a. shun older musicians.
b. emphasize rhythm.
c. use melodic improvisations.
d. play in small clubs.

21. In the context of this passage, *aficionados* (in paragraph 3) can most accurately be described as
a. fans of bebop.
b. residents of Harlem.
c. innovative musicians.
d. awkward dancers.

22. The main purpose of the passage is to
a. mourn the passing of an era.
b. condemn bebop for making jazz inaccessible.
c. explain the development of the bebop style.
d. celebrate the end of the conventional swing style of jazz.

Questions 23–28 are based on the following passage.

(1) In 1997, Moscow, Russia, celebrated the 850th anniversary of its founding. In the more than eight centuries that Moscow has been a viable city, it has been characterized by waves of new construction. The most recent one is ongoing, as Moscow thrives as capital of the new Russia. The architecture of Moscow represents a hodgepodge of styles, as 12th-century forms mingle with elegant estates from the times of the czars and functional structures that reflect the pragmatism of the Soviet era. As Moscow grows under a new system of government, there is concern that some of the city's architectural history will be lost.

(2) Moscow has a history of chaotic periods that ended with the destruction of the largely wooden city and the building of the "new" city on top of the rubble of the old. The result is a layered city, with each tier holding information about a part of Russia's past. In some areas of the city, archaeologists have reached the layer from 1147, the year of Moscow's founding. Among the findings from the various periods of Moscow's history are carved bones, metal tools, pottery, glass, jewelry, and crosses.

(3) Russia has begun a huge attempt to salvage and preserve as much of Moscow's past as possible. New building could destroy this history forever, but Moscow has decided on a different approach. Recognizing that new building represents progress, and progress is necessary for the growth of the nation, new building is flourishing in Moscow. However, the Department of Preservation of Historical Monuments is insuring that building is done in a manner that respects the past. There are approximately 160 active archeological sites currently in Moscow; 5,000 buildings have been designated as protected locations.

(4) One example of the work done by the Department of Preservation and Historical Monuments is Manege Square, which lies just west of the Kremlin. Throughout Moscow's past, this square has been a commercial district. In keeping with that history, the area will be developed as a modern shopping mall, complete with restaurants, theaters, casinos, and a parking garage. Before construction could begin, however, the site was excavated and a wealth of Russian history was uncovered.

(5) Archaeologists working in Manege Square uncovered the commercial life of eight centuries. By excavating five meters deep, archaeologists provided a picture of the evolution of commercial Moscow. Among the finds: wooden street pavement from the time of Ivan the Terrible (16th century), a wide cobblestone road from the era of Peter the Great (early 18th century), street paving from the reign of Catherine the Great (mid- to late 18th century), and a wealthy merchant's estate (19th

century). Smaller finds—a belt and buckle, a gold chain, shoes, locks, and a horse harness—provide rich details about the lives of Muscovites of the past. The citizens of the present are determined that history will not repeat itself, and that the past will be uncovered and celebrated rather than shrouded and forgotten. As a result of this respectful approach to modernization, Moscow, a city with more and more modern structures appearing all the time, remains largely distinguished by Byzantine cathedrals, 15th- and 16th-century stone buildings, and the ostentatious estates of the 18th and 19th centuries.

23. From the information in paragraph 2, the reader can infer that
   a. the people of Moscow are more interested in modernization than in preservation.
   b. the Soviet government destroyed many old buildings, in keeping with an anti-czarist policy.
   c. there are very few 850-year-old cities in existence and fewer yet that preserve their past.
   d. Moscow has a history of invasions, with each new conqueror destroying the buildings of the previous regime.

24. Which of the following assumptions most influenced the views expressed by the writer in this passage?
   a. Progress and preservation are equally important principles of urban planning.
   b. Generally speaking, Muscovites are more interested in building new structures than in saving old ones.
   c. Architectural history has little meaning to people struggling to form a new government.
   d. Archaeologists and bureaucrats generally do not work well together.

25. What is the meaning of the word *chaotic* as used in paragraph 2 of this passage?
   a. tumultuous
   b. unformed
   c. undeveloped
   d. remarkable

26. The phrase *the citizens of the present are determined that history will not repeat itself* in paragraph 5 is most closely related to which statement in the passage?
   a. "the architecture of Moscow represents a hodgepodge of styles" (paragraph 1)
   b. "Moscow has a history of chaotic periods that ended with the destruction of the largely wooden city and the building of the 'new' city on top of the rubble of the old" (paragraph 2)
   c. "new building represents progress, and progress is necessary for the growth of the nation" (paragraph 3)
   d. "the area will be developed as a modern shopping mall, complete with restaurants, theaters, casinos, and a parking garage" (paragraph 4)

27. Which of the following is a valid conclusion based on the information in paragraph 3 of the passage?
   a. Throughout history, various Russian regimes have responded to a problem by creating a governmental agency to deal with it.
   b. The Russian government hopes to keep new building to an absolute minimum.
   c. The government of Moscow is encouraging new building while, at the same time, protecting old architecture.
   d. Builders in Moscow must apply for and receive several different permits before construction can commence.

28. According to the information included in the passage, which of the following is true of archaeologists in Moscow?

  a. They have uncovered a great number of historically significant items, both large and small.

  b. They operate under severe time constraints, as contractors wait to begin new buildings.

  c. There are not nearly enough archaeological teams to conduct all the possible research.

  d. They are concerned about preserving the artifacts of modes of transportation in particular.

Questions 29–35 are based on the following passage.

(1) In Manhattan's Eighth Avenue/Fourteenth Street subway station, a grinning bronze alligator with human hands pops out of a manhole cover to grab a bronze "baby" whose head is the shape of a moneybag. In the Bronx General Post Office, a giant 13-panel painting called *Resources of America* celebrates the hard work and industrialism of America in the first half of the twentieth century. And in Brooklyn's MetroTech Center just over the Brooklyn Bridge, several installations of art are on view at any given time—from an iron lasso resembling a giant charm bracelet to a series of wagons that play recordings of great American poems to a life-sized seeing-eye dog that looks so real people are constantly stopping to pet it.

(2) There exists in every city a symbolic relationship between the city and its art. When we hear the term *art,* we tend to think of private art—the kind displayed in private spaces such as museums, concert halls, and galleries. But there is a growing interest in, and respect for, public art: the kind of art created for and displayed in public spaces such as parks, building lobbies, and sidewalks.

(3) Although all art is inherently public—created in order to convey an idea or emotion to others—"public art," as opposed to art that is sequestered in museums and galleries, is art specifically designed for a public arena where the art will be encountered by people in their normal day-to-day activities. Public art can be purely ornamental or highly functional; it can be as subtle as a decorative door knob or as conspicuous as the Chicago Picasso. It is also an essential element of effective urban design.

(4) The more obvious forms of public art include monuments, sculptures, fountains, murals, and gardens. But public art also takes the form of ornamental benches or street lights, decorative manhole covers, and mosaics on trash bins. Many city dwellers would be surprised to discover just how much public art is really around them and how much art they have passed by without noticing, and how much impact public art has on their day-to-day lives.

(5) Public art fulfills several functions essential to the health of a city and its citizens. It educates about history and culture—of the artist, the neighborhood, the city, the nation. Public art is also a "place-making device" that instantly creates memorable, experiential landmarks, fashioning a unique identity for a public place, personalizing it and giving it a specific character. It stimulates the public, challenging viewers to interpret the art and arousing their emotions, and it promotes community by stimulating interaction among viewers. In serving these multiple and important functions, public art beautifies the area and regenerates both the place and the viewer.

(6) One question often debated in public art forums is whether public art should be created *with* or by the public rather than *for* the public. Increasingly, cities and artists are recognizing the importance of creating works with meaning for the intended audience, and this generally requires direct input from the community or from an artist entrenched in that community. At the same time, however, art created for the community by an

"outsider" often adds fresh perspective. Thus, cities, and their citizens are best served by a combination of public art created *by* members of the community, art created with input *from* members of the community, and art created by others *for* the community.

29. The primary purpose of the opening paragraph is to
   a. show how entertaining public art can be.
   b. introduce readers to the idea of public art.
   c. define public art.
   d. show the prevalence and diversity of public art.

30. The word *inherently* at the beginning of paragraph 3 most nearly means
   a. essentially.
   b. complicated.
   c. wealthy.
   d. snobby.

31. According to paragraphs 3 and 4, public art is differentiated from private art mainly by
   a. the kind of ideas or emotions it aims to convey to its audience.
   b. its accessibility.
   c. its perceived value.
   d. its importance to the city.

32. The use of the word *sequestered* in the first sentence of paragraph 3 suggests that the author feels
   a. private art is better than public art.
   b. private art is too isolated from the public.
   c. the admission fees for public art arenas prevent many people from experiencing the art.
   d. private art is more difficult to understand than public art.

33. Which sentence best sums up the main idea of the passage?
   a. Public art serves several important functions in the city.
   b. Public art is often in direct competition with private art.
   c. Public art should be created both by and for members of the community.
   d. In general, public art is more interesting than private art.

34. The author's goal in this passage include all of the following EXCEPT
   a. to make readers more aware of public artworks.
   b. to explain the difference between public art and private art.
   c. to explain how public art impacts the city.
   d. to inspire readers to become public artists.

35. Which of the following does the author NOT provide in this passage?
   a. an explanation of how the city affects art
   b. specific examples of urban art
   c. reason why outsiders should create public art
   d. a clear distinction between public and private art

Questions 36–42 are based on the following passage.

(1) Scientists have been studying radon and its effects since the turn of the last century. This inert gas has been proven to cause lung cancer and is suspected of being responsible for a range of other serious illnesses.

(2) Radon gas is created as the result of the decaying of uranium and radium. At the culmination of this lengthy process, the disintegrating matter becomes radon, which then decays further, releasing additional radiation and transforming into what are known as radon daughters. Unlike radon,

the daughters are not inert because they are highly sensitive to their surroundings and are chemically active. Thus when the daughters enter buildings, attach to clothing, mingle with dust particles, or are inhaled, health risks increase dramatically. Radon exists across the United States, with somewhat higher amounts located in areas where granite is common.

(3) Radon gas released directly into the atmosphere poses slight health risks. Conversely, when it is trapped and has the opportunity to accumulate, such as beneath houses and other structures, risks increase significantly. This colorless, tasteless, and odorless element can seep into buildings through walls, soil, water supplies, and natural gas pipelines. It can also be part of the properties of materials such as brick, wallboard, and concrete. When radon is prevalent in a building, it circulates in that building's air exchange and is inhaled by humans.

(4) The majority of the radon daughters exhibit electrostatic qualities as they attach to items such as clothing, furniture, and dust, a magnetic process known as plating out. The remainder of the daughters do not attach to anything. As an individual breathes the potentially damaging air, the attached and unattached daughters enter the body. As the daughters travel through the body, particles become attached to the respiratory tract, the bronchial region, the nose, and the throat. Some particles are expelled during exhalation, but most remain within the individual.

(5) The unattached daughters are the most dangerous as their untethered route often carries them directly to the lungs. They deposit significantly more radioactivity than the attached daughters— indeed, up to 40 times as much. Research indicates that those individuals who breathe primarily through their noses receive fewer doses than those who breathe primarily through their mouths.

(6) Alpha radiation begins penetrating the lungs and other organs after radon daughters settle there. Penetration and the subsequent depositing of radiation are the result of a continuation of the decaying process. An appreciable dose of alpha particles can lead to cell destruction. Higher doses can be fatal. One comparative study analyzed similar doses from radon, X-rays, and atom bombs, and concluded that the chances of developing lung cancer from radon were equal to those from the other two radiation sources. In the United States most incidences involve lower-level doses, however, which destroy a relatively low number of cells. The body will regenerate lost cells, so serious health problems become less likely.

(7) Serious problems materialize when cells are exposed repeatedly. The cycle of exposure-damage-regeneration-exposure can weaken cells and ultimately change their makeup. Cell alteration can lead to lung cancer, genetic changes, and a host of other medical problems.

36. Gases from an outdoor radon leak
    a. present serious health ramifications.
    b. are easy to detect.
    c. create a negligible health threat.
    d. transform into radon daughters.

37. It can be inferred from the passage that an inert gas such as radon is
    a. dormant in terms of chemical reactions.
    b. unusually likely to decay.
    c. more dangerous than radon daughters.
    d. created as the result of a distinct series of events.

38. One reason unattached daughters are more dangerous than attached daughters is that they
    a. demonstrate electrostatic qualities.
    b. are less likely to be expelled.
    c. regenerate after entering the lungs.
    d. have a free path toward internal organs.

39. *Plating out* is a term for a process of
  a. cohering.
  b. disseminating.
  c. deteriorating.
  d. permeating.

40. Health hazards from radon rise greatly when
  a. gases accumulate inside buildings.
  b. daughters leave the body via exhalation.
  c. individuals inhale mostly through their noses.
  d. regeneration takes place.

41. Radon is formed as a consequence of
  a. the alteration of cells.
  b. the breakdown of elements.
  c. exposure to the atmosphere.
  d. an electrostatic process.

42. In the United States, most cases of radon exposure involve doses that
  a. affect residents near granite formations.
  b. lead to genetic problems.
  c. cause recurring exposure.
  d. eliminate small amounts of cells.

► Section 2: Mathematics

1. Twelve less than 4 times a number is 20. What is the number?
  a. 2
  b. 4
  c. 6
  d. 8

$4x - 12 = 20$
$4x = 32$

2. Kathy was half the age of her mother 20 years ago. Kathy is 40. How old is Kathy's mother?
  a. 50
  b. 60
  c. 70
  d. 80

$20/2 = 10$

3. Body mass index (BMI) is equal to $\frac{\text{(weight in kilograms)}}{\text{(height in meters)}^2}$. A man who weighs 64.8 kilograms has a BMI of 20. How tall is he?
  a. 1.8 meters
  b. 0.9 meters
  c. 2.16 meters
  d. 3.24 meters

$20 = \dfrac{64.8}{x}$
$20x = 64.8$

4. Pediatric specialist Dr. Drake charges $36.00 for an office visit, which is $\frac{3}{4}$ of what general practitioner Dr. Jarmuth charges. How much does Dr. Jarmuth charge?
  a. $48.00
  b. $27.00
  c. $38.00
  d. $57.00

$\dfrac{3}{4} = \dfrac{36}{x}$
$3x = 144$
$x = \$48$

5. A town of 105,000 is served by 3 hospitals. How many people could be served by 4 hospitals?
  a. 140,000
  b. 145,000
  c. 130,000
  d. 135,000

6. A recipe serves four people and calls for $1\frac{1}{2}$ cups of broth. If you want to serve six people, how much broth do you need?
  a. 2 cups
  b. $2\frac{1}{4}$ cups
  c. $2\frac{1}{3}$ cups
  d. $2\frac{1}{2}$ cups

7. How much water must be added to 1 liter of a 5% saline solution to get a 2% saline solution?
  a. 1 L
  b. 1.5 L
  c. 2 L
  d. 2.5 L

8. If jogging for one mile uses 150 calories and brisk walking for one mile uses 100 calories, a jogger has to go how many times as far as a walker to use the same number of calories?

   a. $\frac{1}{2}$

   b. $\frac{2}{3}$

   c. $\frac{3}{2}$

   d. 2

$$\frac{100}{150} = \frac{2}{3}$$

9. A dosage of a certain medication is 12 cc per 100 pounds. What is the dosage for a patient who weighs 175 pounds?

   a. 21 cc

   b. 18 cc

   c. 15 cc

   d. 24 cc

10. A woman drives west at 45 miles per hour. After half an hour, her husband starts to follow her. How fast must he drive to catch up to her three hours after he starts?

   a. 52.5 miles per hour

   b. 55 miles per hour

   c. 60 miles per hour

   d. 67.5 miles per hour

$$3.5\,(45) = 157.5$$
$$\frac{3.5\,(45)}{3} = 52.5$$

11. Jason is six times as old as Kate. In two years, Jason will be twice as old as Kate is then. How old is Jason now?

   a. 3 years old

   b. 6 years old

   c. 9 years old

   d. 12 years old

$$J = 6K$$
$$J + 2 = 2(K + 2)$$
$$6K + 2 = 2K + 4$$
$$K = \tfrac{1}{2} \cdot J$$

12. A patient's hospice stay cost $\frac{1}{4}$ as much as his visit to the emergency room. His home nursing cost twice as much as his hospice stay. If his total health care bill was $140,000, how much did his home nursing cost?

   a. $10,000

   b. $20,000

   c. $40,000

   d. $80,000

13. Mike types three times as fast as Nick. Together they type 24 pages per hour. If Nick learns to type as fast as Mike, how much will they be able to type per hour?

   a. 30 pages

   b. 36 pages

   c. 40 pages

   d. 48 pages

$$M = 3N \qquad N = \tfrac{1}{3}M$$
$$24 = M + N$$
$$24 = M + \tfrac{1}{3}M$$
$$M = 18$$

14. Ron is half as old as Sam, who is three times as old as Ted. The sum of their ages is 55. How old is Ron?

   a. 5

   b. 10

   c. 15

   d. 30

Question 15 is based on the following diagram:

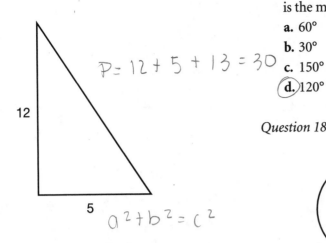

P = 12 + 5 + 13 = 30

a² + b² = c²

15. What is the perimeter of the figure?
   a. 30
   b. 20
   c. 17
   d. 60

12² + 5² = ?
144 + 25 = 169
C = 13

16. A rectangular box has a square base with an area of 9 square feet. If the volume of the box is 36 cubic feet, what is the longest object that can fit in the box?
   a. 5.8 feet
   b. 5 feet
   c. 17 feet
   d. 3 feet

Question 17 is based on the following diagram.

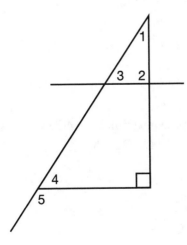

17. If angle 1 is 30°, and angle 2 is a right angle, what is the measure of angle 5?
   a. 60°
   b. 30°
   c. 150°
   d. 120°

Question 18 is based on the following diagram.

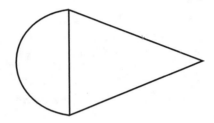

18. A half-circle is placed adjacent to a triangle, as shown in the diagram. What is the total area of the shape, if the radius of the half-circle is 3, and the height of the triangle is 4?
   a. $6(\pi + 4)$
   b. $6\pi + 12$
   c. $\frac{9}{2\pi + 24}$
   d. $\frac{9\pi}{2} + 12$

Circle: $\pi r^2 = 9\pi$
Triangle: $\frac{1}{2}bh = 4\cdot3 = 12$
$\frac{9\pi}{2} + 12$

19. If pentagon *ABCDE* is similar to pentagon *FGHIJ*, and $\overline{AB} = 10$, $\overline{CD} = 5$, and $\overline{FG} = 30$, what is $\overline{IH}$?
   a. $\frac{5}{3}$
   b. 5
   c. 15
   d. 30

20. A water tank is in the form of a right cylinder on top of a hemisphere, both with a radius of 3 feet. If the tank currently has 170 cubic feet of water in it, how high does the water level reach in the cylinder (from the top of the hemisphere)?
   a. 3 feet
   b. 2 feet
   c. 6 feet
   d. 4 feet

21. Louise wants to wallpaper a room. It has one window that measures 3 feet by 4 feet, and one door that measures 3 feet by 7 feet. The room is 12 feet by 12 feet, and is 10 feet tall. If only the walls are to be covered, and rolls of wallpaper are 100 square feet, and no partial rolls can be purchased, what is the minimum number of rolls that she will need?

  a. 4 rolls
  b. 5 rolls
  c. 6 rolls
  d. 7 rolls

Question 22 is based on the following diagram.

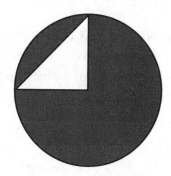

22. If the radius of the circle is 4 inches and the triangle is a right isosceles triangle with one corner in the center, what is the area of the shaded portion?

  a. $4\pi + 16$
  b. $4\pi - 16$
  c. $8\pi - 8$
  d. $16\pi - 8$

Question 23 is based on the following diagram.

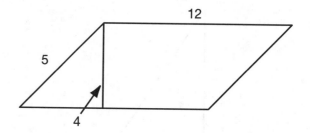

23. Find the area of the parallelogram above.
  a. 48 units^2 $(12-3)4 = 36 + 12 =$
  b. 68 units^2 48
  c. 72 units^2
  d. 240 units^2

Question 24 is based on the following diagram.

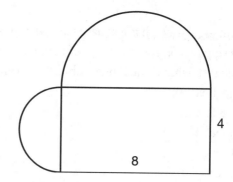

24. Find the area of the shape shown in the diagram above.
  a. $12 + 10\pi$ $32 + 10\pi$
  b. $32 + 12\pi$ $\frac{2^{2\pi}}{2} = 2\pi$
  c. $12 + 12\pi$
  d. $32 + 10\pi$ $\frac{4^{2\pi}}{2} = 8\pi$

25. What is the next number in the series below?
  3 ^{13} 16 ^{10} 6 ^{6} 12 ^{0} 12 ^{4} 8 ___
  a. 4
  b. 15
  c. 20
  d. 24

26. A pump installed on a well can pump at a maximum rate of 100 gallons per minute. If the pump runs at 50% of its maximum rate for six hours a day, how much water is pumped in one day?
  a. 3.00×10^2 gallons
  b. 1.80×10^4 gallons
  c. 3.60×10^2 gallons
  d. 7.20×10^2 gallons

27. It costs $0.75 each to make color copies at a copy center. At this price, how many copies can be purchased with $60.00?
  a. 45
  b. 60
  c. 75
  d. 80

Question 28 is based on the following diagram.

DISTANCE TRAVELED FROM CHICAGO WITH RESPECT TO TIME

TIME (HOURS)	DISTANCE FROM CHICAGO (MILES)
1	60
2	120
3	180
4	240

28. A train moving at a constant speed leaves Chicago for Los Angeles at time $t = 0$. If Los Angeles is 2,000 miles from Chicago, which of the following equations describes the distance from Los Angeles at any time t?
  a. $D(t) = 60t - 2,000$
  b. $D(t) = 60t$
  c. $D(t) = 2,000 - 60t$
  d. $D(t) = -2,000 - 60t$

2,000 - 60t

Use the table below to answer question 29.

Class Time Schedule

Period	Start Time	End Time
1	7:55	8:35
2	8:39	9:19
3		10:03
4	10:07	10:47
5	10:51	11:31
6	11:35	12:15
7	12:19	12:59
8	1:03	
9	1:47	2:27

29. According to the table, what is the starting time of period 3 and the ending time of period 8, respectively?
  a. 9:24, 1:43
  b. 9:23, 1:44
  c. 9:29, 1:59
  d. 9:23, 1:43
  e. 9:24, 1:44

30. Anne has two containers for water: a rectangular plastic box with a base of 16 square inches, and a cylindrical container with a radius of 2 inches and a height of 11 inches. If the rectangular box is filled with water 9 inches from the bottom, and Anne pours the water into the cylinder without spilling, which of the following will be true?
  a. The cylinder will overflow.
  b. The cylinder will be exactly full.
  c. The cylinder will be filled to an approximate level of 10 inches.
  d. The cylinder will be filled to an approximate level of 8 inches.

31. Roger, Lucia, Mike, and Samantha are cousins. They all practice unique sports: One enjoys skiing, one enjoys fishing, one enjoys tennis, and one enjoys volleyball.

    I. The cousin who fishes is female.

    II. Roger and Lucia dislike sports with balls.

    III. Samantha is older than the cousin who fishes.

Who likes to fish?

a. Roger
b. Mike
c. Samantha
d. Lucia

	fish	volleyball	Tenn
Lucia		X	X
Mike	X		
Sam	X		
Roger	X	X	X

32. A triangle has sides that are consecutive even integers. The perimeter of the triangle is 24 inches. What is the length of the shortest side?

a. 10 inches
b. 8 inches
c. 6 inches
d. 4 inches

$S + (S+2) + (S+4) = 24$

$3S + 6 = 24$

$S = 6$

33. Use the pattern below to answer the question that follows.

    Z26   X23   V20   T17   ____

What is the next set in the sequence?

a. R15
b. Q15
c. Q14
d. R14

34. Jamal drives 15 miles round trip to work on weekdays. On weekends, he drives an average of 20 miles per day. If Jamal gets 25 miles per gallon, and buys gas in whole gallon increments, how many gallons of gas does he have to buy in a week?

a. 3 gallons
b. 4 gallons
c. 5 gallons
d. 6 gallons

$15(5) = 75$

$20(2) = 40$

$25\overline{)115} = 4.6115$

35. The Senior High School Band is washing cars to earn money. It takes three students 5 minutes to wash a car, 7 minutes to wash a truck, and 10 minutes to wash a van. If they charge $3.00 for a car, $4.00 for a truck, and $5.00 for a van, which vehicle will earn the band the most money for the time spent working?

a. Cars
b. Trucks
c. Vans
d. There is no difference in the amount of money earned per time worked.

36. The length of a rectangle is equal to 4 inches more than twice the width. Three times the length plus two times the width is equal to 28 inches. What is the area of the rectangle?

a. 8 square inches
b. 16 square inches
c. 24 square inches
d. 28 square inches

$l = 4 + (2w)$

$3l + 2w = 28$

$6w + 12 + 2w = 28$

$8w = 16$

$w = 2 \quad l = 8$

37. A gardener on a large estate determines that the length of garden hose needed to reach from the water spigot to a particular patch of prize-winning dragonsnaps is 175 feet. If the available garden hoses are 45 feet long, how many sections of hose, when connected together, will it take to reach the dragonsnaps?

a. 2
b. 3
c. 4
d. 5

$\dfrac{175}{45} \approx 4$

38. Which number sentence is true?

a. $4.3 < 0.43$
b. $0.43 < 0.043$
c. $0.043 > 0.0043$
d. $0.0043 > 0.043$

39. Which of the following means $5n + 7 = 17$?
  a. 7 more than 5 times a number is 17
  b. 5 more than 7 times a number is 17
  c. 7 less than 5 times a number is 17
  d. 12 times a number is 17

40. Which of these is equivalent to 35° C?
  $F = \frac{9}{5}C + 32$
  a. 105° F
  b. 95° F
  c. 63° F
  d. 19° F

  $\frac{9}{5}(35°) + 32$

41. What is the value of y when $x = 3$ and $y = 5 + 4x$?
  a. 6
  b. 9
  c. 12
  d. 17

  $y = 5 + 12$
  $y = 17$

42. The radius of a circle is 13. What is the approximate area of the circle?
  a. 81.64 units squared
  b. 530.66 units squared
  c. 1,666.27 units squared
  d. 169 units squared

  $Area = \pi r^2 =$
  $\pi(13)^2 \approx 530.929$

43. What is the volume of a pyramid that has a rectangular base 5 feet by 3 feet and a height of 8 feet? ($V = \frac{1}{3}lwh$)
  a. 16 feet
  b. 30 feet
  c. 40 feet
  d. 80 feet

  $V = \frac{1}{3}(5)(3)(8)$

44. Which of these angle measures form a right triangle?
  a. 45°, 50°, 85°
  b. 40°, 40°, 100°
  c. 40°, 50°, 90°
  d. 20°, 30°, 130°

45. What is another way to write $3\sqrt{12}$?
  a. $12\sqrt{3}$
  b. $6\sqrt{3}$
  c. $2\sqrt{10}$
  d. 18

46. Third grade student Stephanie goes to the school nurse's office, where her temperature is found to be 98° Fahrenheit. What is her temperature in degrees Celsius? $C = \frac{5}{9}(F - 32)$
  a. 35.8° C
  b. 36.7° C
  c. 37.6° C
  d. 31.1° C

  $C = \frac{5}{9}(66) = 36.7°$

47. Plattville is 80 miles west and 60 miles north of Quincy. How long is a direct route from Plattville to Quincy?
  a. 100 miles
  b. 110 miles
  c. 120 miles
  d. 140 miles

  $80^2 + 60^2 = ?$
  $? = 100$

48. Each sprinkler head in a sprinkler system sprays water at an average of 16 gallons per minute. If 5 sprinkler heads are flowing at the same time, how many gallons of water will be released in 10 minutes?
  a. 80
  b. 60
  c. 320
  d. 800

▶ Section 3: Writing (Part A— Multiple-Choice)

Questions 1–3 are based on the following passage.

(1) Augustus Saint-Gaudens was born March 1, 1848, in Dublin, Ireland, to Bernard Saint-Gaudens, a French shoemaker, and Mary McGuinness, his Irish wife. (2) Six months later, the family immigrated to New York City, where Augustus grew up. (3) Upon completion of school at age thirteen, he expressed strong interest in art as a career so his father apprenticed him to a cameo cutter. (4) While working days at his cameo lathe, Augustus also took art classes at the Cooper Union and the National Academy of Design.

(5) At 19, his apprenticeship completed, Augustus traveled to Paris where he studied under Francois Jouffry at the renown Ecole des Beaux-Arts. (6) In 1870, he left Paris for Rome, where for the next five years, he <u>studies</u> classical art and architecture, and worked on his first commissions. (7) In 1876, he received his first major commission—a monument to Civil War Admiral David Glasgow Farragut. (8) Unveiled in New York's Madison Square in 1881, the monument was a tremendous success; its combination of realism and allegory was a departure from previous American sculpture. (9) Saint-Gaudens' fame grew, and other commissions were quickly forthcoming.

1. Which of the following numbered parts requires a comma to separate two independent clauses?
a. Part 9
b. Part 3
c. Part 7
d. Part 1

2. Which of the following words should replace the underlined word in Part 6?
a. studied
b. will study
c. had been studying
d. would have studied

3. Which of the following changes needs to be made to the passage?
a. Part 2: Change *where* to *when.*
b. Part 5: Change *renown* to *renowned.*
c. Part 8: Change *its* to *it's.*
d. Part 3: Change *expressed* to *impressed.*

Questions 4–6 are based on the following passage.

(1) Everglades National Park is the largest remaining sub-tropical wilderness in the continental United States. (2) It is home to abundant wildlife; including alligators, crocodiles, manatees, and Florida panthers. (3) The climate of the Everglades are mild and pleasant from December through April, though rare cold fronts may create near freezing conditions. (4) Summers are hot and humid; in summer, the temperatures often soar to around 90 degrees and the humidity climbs to over 90 percent. (5) Afternoon thunderstorms are common, and mosquitoes are abundant. (6) If you visit the Everglades, wear comfortable sportswear in winter; loose-fitting, long-sleeved shirts and pants, and insect repellent are recommended in the summer.

(7) Walking and canoe trails, boat tours, and tram tours are excellent for viewing wildlife, including alligators and a multitude of tropical and temperate birds. (8) Camping, whether in the back country or at established campgrounds, offers the opportunity to enjoy what the park offers firsthand. (9) Year-round, ranger-led activities may help you to enjoy your visit even more; such activities are offered throughout the park in all seasons.

4. Which of the following numbered parts contains a nonstandard use of a semicolon?
  a. Part 6
  b. Part 2
  c. Part 9
  d. Part 4

5. Which of the following numbered parts needs to be revised to reduce unnecessary repetition?
  a. Part 4
  b. Part 6
  c. Part 9
  d. Part 8

6. Which of the following changes is needed in the passage?
  a. Part 6: Remove the comma after *Everglades*.
  b. Part 2: Change *It is* to *Its*.
  c. Part 8: Remove the comma after *campgrounds*.
  d. Part 3: Change *are* to *is*.

Questions 7 and 8 are based on the following passage.

(1) On January 1, 1998, the Food and Drug Administration (FDA) announced that lower-fat milk products had to follow the same set of criteria as most other foods labeled "low fat." (2) This meant that such products as 2-percent milk, which contain about 5 grams of fat per serving, could no longer be labeled "low fat" because the fat content was more than 3 grams per serving, the upper limit permitted in food products labeled "low fat." (3) The Surgeon General advised that low-fat and high-fiber diets help to improve the health of Americans and reduce medical costs to the country. (4) The FDA judged that the designation "2-percent fat" on reduced fat milk products was causing consumers to imply that such products were actually low in fat content.

7. Which of the following numbered parts is least relevant to the passage?
  a. Part 4
  b. Part 1
  c. Part 3
  d. Part 2

8. Which of the following changes needs to be made to the passage?
  a. Part 4: Change *imply* to *infer*.
  b. Part 2: Change *contain* to *containing*.
  c. Part 1: Change *criteria* to *criterion*.
  d. Part 4: Change *designation* to *assignation*.

Questions 9–11 are based on the following passage.

(1) Being able to type good is no longer a requirement limited to secretaries and novelists; thanks to the computer, anyone who wants to enter the working world needs to be <u>accustomed</u> to a keyboard. (2) Just knowing your way around a keyboard does not mean that you can use one efficiently, though; while you may have progressed beyond the "hunt-and-peck" method, you may never have learned to type quickly and accurately. (3) Doing so is a skill that will not only ensure that you pass a typing <u>proficiency</u> exam, but one that is essential if you want to advance your career in any number of fields. (4) This chapter <u>assures</u> that you are familiar enough with a standard keyboard to be able to use it without looking at the keys, which is the first step in learning to type, and that you are aware of the proper <u>fingering</u>. (5) The following information will help you to increase your speed and accuracy and to do our best when being tested on timed writing passages.

9. Which of the following numbered parts contains a nonstandard use of a modifier?
  a. Part 5
  b. Part 2
  c. Part 3
  d. Part 1

10. Which of the following words, underlined in the passage, is misused in its context?
  a. assures
  b. proficiency
  c. fingering
  d. accustomed

11. Which of the following changes needs to be made in the passage?
  a. Part 3: Remove the comma after *exam.*
  b. Part 4: Insert a colon after *that.*
  c. Part 1: Change *needs* to *needed.*
  d. Part 5: Change *our* to *your.*

Questions 12 and 13 are based on the following passage.

(1) None of us knew my Uncle Elmer, not even my mother (he would have been ten years older than she) we had pictures of him in an ancient family album, a solemn, spindly baby, dressed in a white muslin shirt, ready for bed, or in a sailor suit, holding a little drum. (2) In one photograph, he stands in front of a tall chiffonier, which looms behind him, massive and shadowy, like one of the Fates in a greek play. (3) There weren't many such pictures, because photographs weren't easy to come by in those days, and in the ones we did have, my uncle had a formal posed look, as if, even then, he knew he was bound for some unique destiny. (4) It was the summer I turned thirteen that I found out what happened to him, the summer Sister Mattie Fisher, one of Grandma's evangelist friends, paid us a visit, sweeping in like a cleansing wind and telling the truth.

12. Which of the following changes needs to be made to the above passage?
  a. Part 4: Change *friends* to *friend's.*
  b. Part 4: Change *Sister* to *sister.*
  c. Part 2: Change *greek* to *Greek.*
  d. Part 3: Change *uncle* to *Uncle.*

13. Which of the following numbered parts contains a nonstandard sentence?
  a. Part 3
  b. Part 4
  c. Part 1
  d. Part 2

Questions 14–16 are based on the following passage.

(1) O'Connell Street is the main thoroughfare of Dublin City. (2) Although it is not a particularly long street Dubliners will tell the visitor proudly that it is the widest street in all of Europe. (3) This claim usually meets with protests, especially from French tourists who claim the Champs Elysees of Paris as Europe's widest street. (4) But the witty Dubliner will not <u>ensign</u> bragging rights easily and will trump the French visitor with a fine distinction: the Champs Elysees is the widest boulevard, but O'Connell is the widest street.

(5) Divided by several important monuments running the length of its center, the street is named for Daniel O'Connell, an Irish patriot. (6) An impressive monument to him towers over the entrance of lower O'Connell Street and overlooking the Liffey River. (7) O'Connell stands high above the unhurried crowds of shoppers, business people, and students on a sturdy column; he is surrounded by four serene angels seated at each corner of the monument's base.

14. Which of the following words should replace the underlined word in Part 4 of the passage?
  a. require
  b. relinquish
  c. acquire
  d. assign

15. Which of the following changes needs to be made to the second paragraph of the passage?
   a. Part 7: Replace the semicolon with a comma.
   b. Part 5: Change *Irish* to *irish*.
   c. Part 5: Change *running* to *run*.
   d. Part 6: Change *overlooking* to *overlooks*.

16. Which of the following changes needs to be made to the first paragraph of the passage?
   a. Part 2: Insert a comma after *that*.
   b. Part 3: Replace the comma after *protests* with a semicolon.
   c. Part 4: Remove the colon after *distinction*.
   d. Part 2: Insert a comma after the first *street*.

Questions 17–19 are based on the following passage.

(1) Mrs. Lake arriving twenty minutes early surprised and irritated Nicholas, although the moment for saying so slipped past too quickly for him to snatch its opportunity.

(2) She was a thin woman of medium height, not much older than he—in her middle forties he judged—dressed in a red-and-white, polka-dot dress and open-toed red shoes with extremely high heels. (3) Her short brown hair was crimped in waves, which gave a incongruous, quaint, old-fashioned effect. (4) She had a pointed nose. (5) Her eyes, set rather shallow, were light brown and inquisitive.

(6) "Dr. Markley?" she asked. (7) Nicholas nodded, and the woman walked in past him, proceeding with little mincing steps to the center of the living room where she stood with her back turned looking around. (8) "My my," she said. (9) "This is a nice house. (10) Do you live here all alone?"

17. Which of the following changes should be made in Part 3?
   a. Change *was* to *is*.
   b. Change *gave* to *gives*.
   c. Change *a* to *an*.
   d. Change *effect* to *affect*.

18. Which of the following numbered parts contains a nonstandard use of a modifier?
   a. Part 7
   b. Part 5
   c. Part 3
   d. Part 2

19. Which of the following changes needs to be made to Part 1?
   a. Insert a comma after *early*.
   b. Change *too* to *two*.
   c. Change *Lake* to *Lake's*.
   d. Change *its* to *it's*.

Questions 20–22 are based on the following passage.

(1) If your office job involves telephone work, than your faceless voice may be the first contact a caller has with your company or organization. (2) For this reason, your telephone manners have to be impeccable. (3) Always answer the phone promptly, on the first or second ring if possible. (4) Speak directly into the phone, neither too loudly nor too softly, in a pleasant, cheerful voice. (5) Vary the pitch of your voice, so that it will not sound monotonous or uninterested, and be sure to enunciate clearly. (6) After a short, friendly greeting, state your company or boss's name, then your own name.

(7) Always take messages carefully. (8) Fill out all pertinent blanks on the message pad sheet while you are still on the phone. (9) Always let the caller hang up first. (10) Do not depend in your memory for the spelling of a name or the last digit of a phone number, and be sure to write legibly. (11) When it is time to close a conversation, do so in a pleasant manner, and never hang up without saying good-bye. (12) While it is not an absolute rule, generally closing with "Good-bye" is preferable to "Bye-bye." (13) Verify the information by reading it back to the caller.

20. Which of the following editorial changes would most improve the clarity of development of ideas in the second paragraph?
  a. Delete Part 9.
  b. Reverse the order of Part 8 and Part 13.
  c. Reverse the order of Part 9 and Part 13.
  d. Add a sentence after Part 7 explaining the need to take phone messages from customers politely.

21. Which of the following changes needs to be made to the first paragraph?
  a. Part 5: Change *it* to *they*.
  b. Part 1: Change *than* to *then*.
  c. Part 2: Change *manners* to *manner*.
  d. Part 6: Change *boss's* to *bosses*.

22. Which of the following numbered parts contains a nonstandard use of a preposition?
  a. Part 1
  b. Part 2
  c. Part 8
  d. Part 10

Questions 23 and 24 are based on the following passage.

(1) Understand that your boss has problems, too. (2) This is easy to forget. (3) When someone has authority over you, it's hard to remember that they are just human. (4) Your boss may have children at home who misbehave, dogs or cats or parakeets that need to go to the vet, deadlines to meet, and bosses of his or her own (sometimes even bad ones) overseeing his or her work. (5) If your boss is occasionally unreasonable, try to keep in mind that it might have nothing to do with you. (6) He or she may be having a bad day for reasons no one else knows. (7) Of course if such behavior becomes consistently abusive, you'll have to do something about it—confront the problem or even quit. (8) But were all entitled to occasional mood swings.

23. Which of the following numbered parts contains a nonstandard use of a pronoun?
  a. Part 7
  b. Part 3
  c. Part 4
  d. Part 8

24. Which of the following changes needs to be made to the passage?
  a. Part 5: Change *unreasonable* to *unreasonably*.
  b. Part 7: Change the dash to a semicolon.
  c. Part 8: Change *were* to *we're*.
  d. Part 4: Change *deadlines* to *a deadline*.

Questions 25 and 26 are based on the following passage.

(1) Beginning next month, the Department of Sanitation will institute a program intended to remove the graffiti from sanitation trucks. (2) Any truck that finishes its assigned route before the end of the workers' shift will return to the sanitation lot, where supervisors will provide materials for workers to use in cleaning the trucks. (3) The length of time it takes to complete different routes varies, therefore, trucks will no longer be assigned to a specific route but will be rotated among the routes. (4) Therefore, workers should no longer leave personal items in the trucks, as they will not necessarily be using the same truck each day as they did in the past.

(5) It is expected that all sanitation workers will eventually participate in the cleaning up of the trucks. (6) The department estimates that the project will take approximately one month to complete.

25. Which of the following sentences, if added between Parts 2 and 3 of the first paragraph, would be most consistent with the writer's purpose and audience?

   a. Workers will be required to spend the time remaining in their shift cleaning graffiti from their trucks.

   b. During the remainder of the shift, the guys will scrub the graffiti from the trucks.

   c. Workers will be required to spend the time remaining in their shift sanitizing their filthy trucks.

   d. During the rest of the shift, the garbage men will spruce up their trucks.

26. Which of the following numbered parts in the passage contains a nonstandard sentence?

   a. Part 1

   b. Part 6

   c. Part 2

   d. Part 3

Questions 27 and 28 are based on the following passage.

(1) Beginning next month, City Transit will institute the Stop Here Program, who will be in effect every night from 10:00 P.M. until 4:00 A.M. (2) The program will allow drivers to stop the bus wherever a passenger wishes, as long as they deem it is safe to stop there. (3) This program will reduce the amount of walking that passengers will have to do after dark. (4) Passengers may request a stop anywhere along the bus route by pulling the bell cord a block ahead. (5) During the first two months of the program, when passengers attempt to flag down a bus anywhere but at a designated stop, the bus driver should proceed to the next stop and wait for them to board the bus. (6) Then the driver should give the passenger a brochure that explains the Stop Here Program.

27. Which of the following editorial changes in the passage would best help to clarify the information the paragraph intends to convey?

   a. Add a sentence between Parts 4 and 5 explaining that while the Stop Here Program allows passengers to leave the bus at almost any point, passengers may board only at designated stops.

   b. Delete Part 6.

   c. Add a sentence between Parts 5 and 6 explaining the safety advantages for passengers who flag down buses at night.

   d. Reverse the order of Parts 4 and 5.

28. Which of the following numbered parts contains a nonstandard use of a pronoun?

   a. Part 3

   b. Part 5

   c. Part 1

   d. Part 2

Questions 29 and 30 are based on the following passage.

(1) In October 1993, a disastrous wildfire swept across portions of Charlesburg. (2) Five residents were killed, 320 homes destroyed, and 19,500 acres burned. (3) A public safety task force was formed to review emergency choices. (4) The task force findings were as follows;

   (5) The water supply in the residential areas was insufficient, some hydrants could not even be opened. (6) The task force recommended a review of hydrant inspection policy.

   (7) The fire companies that responded had difficulty locating specific sites. (8) Most came from other areas and were not familiar with Charlesburg. (9) The available maps were outdated and did not reflect recent housing developments.

(10) Evacuation procedures were inadequate. (11) Residents reported being given conflicting and/or confusing information. (12) Some residents of the Hilltop Estates subdivision ignored mandatory evacuation orders, yet others were praised for their cooperation.

29. Which of the following numbered parts contains a nonstandard sentence?
a. Part 7
b. Part 5
c. Part 3
d. Part 12

30. Which of the following changes needs to be made to the passage?
a. Part 12: Change *their* to *they're*.
b. Part 12: Insert a comma after *others*.
c. Part 2: Remove the comma after *killed*.
d. Part 4: Replace the semicolon with a colon.

Questions 31–33 are based on the following passage.

(1) For years, Mt. Desert Island, particularly its major settlement, Bar Harbor, afforded summer homes for the wealthy. (2) Finally though, Bar Harbor has become a burgeoning arts community as well. (3) But, the best part of the island is the unspoiled forest land known as Acadia National Park. (4) Since the island sits on the boundary line between the temperate and sub-Arctic zones the island supports the flora and fauna of both zones as well as beach, inland, and alpine plants. (5) Lies in a major bird migration lane and is a resting spot for many birds. (6) The establishment of Acadia National Park in 1916 means that this natural monument will be preserved and that it will be available to all people, not just the wealthy. (7) Visitors to Acadia may receive nature instruction from the park naturalists as well as enjoy camping, hiking, cycling, and boating. (8) Or they may choose to spend time at the archeological museum learning about the Stone Age inhabitants of the island.

31. Which of the following sentences is a sentence fragment?
a. Part 5
b. Part 2
c. Part 4
d. Part 3

32. Which of the following adverbs should replace the words *Finally though* in Part 2?
a. Suddenly
b. Concurrently
c. Simultaneously
d. Recently

33. Which of the following changes needs to be made to Part 4?
a. Insert a comma after the word *zones*.
b. Delete the word *since* at the beginning of the sentence.
c. Delete the comma after the word *inland*.
d. Add a question mark at the end of the sentence.

Questions 34 and 35 are based on the following passage.

(1) Glaciers consist of fallen snow that compresses over many years into large, thickened ice masses. (2) Most of the world's glacial ice is found in Antarctica and Greenland, glaciers are found on nearly every continent, even Africa. (3) Presently, 10% of land area is covered with glaciers. (4) Glacial ice often appears blue because ice absorbs all other colors but reflects blue. (5) Almost 90% of an iceberg is below water; only about 10% shows above water. (6) What makes glaciers unique is their ability to move? (7) Due to sheer mass, glaciers flow like very slow rivers. (8) Some glaciers are as small as football fields, while others grow to be over one hundred kilometers long.

34. Which of the following sentences is a run-on sentence?
   a. Part 4
   b. Part 3
   c. Part 2
   d. Part 1

35. Which of the following sentences contains an error in punctuation?
   a. Part 3
   b. Part 4
   c. Part 5
   d. Part 6

Questions 36 and 37 are based on the following passage.

(1) Adolescents are at high risk for violent crimes. (2) Although they make up only 14% of the population age 12 and over, 30% of all violent crimes—1.9 million—<u>were</u> committed against them. (3) Because crimes against adolescents are likely to be committed by offenders of the same age (as well as same sex and race), preventing violence among and against adolescents is a twofold challenge. (4) Adolescents are at risk of being both victims and perpetrators of violence. (5) New violence-prevention programs in urban middle schools help reduce the crime rate by teaching both victims and perpetrators of such violence the skills of conflict resolution, how to apply reason to disputes, as well as by changing attitudes towards achieving respect through violence and towards the need to retaliate. (6) These programs provide a safe place for students to discuss their conflicts and therefore prove appealing to students at risk.

36. Which of the following sentences represents the best revision of Part 5?
   a. New violence-prevention programs in urban middle schools help reduce the crime rate by teaching both victims and perpetrators the skills of conflict resolution, by instructing how to apply reason to disputes, and by changing attitudes towards violence and towards the need to retaliate.
   b. New violence-prevention programs in urban middle schools help reduce the crime rate by teaching both victims and perpetrators of such violence the skills of conflict resolution; how to apply reason to disputes; as well as by changing attitudes towards achieving respect through violence and towards the need to retaliate.
   c. New violence-prevention programs in urban middle schools help reduce the crime rate. They teach both victims and perpetrators of such violence the skills of conflict resolution: how to apply reason to disputes, as well as by changing attitudes towards achieving respect through violence and towards the need to retaliate.
   d. New violence-prevention programs in urban middle schools help reduce the crime rate by teaching both victims and perpetrators of such violence the skills of conflict resolution, how to apply reason to disputes, as well as to change attitudes towards achieving respect through violence and towards the need to retaliate.

37. Which of the following should be used in place of the underlined word in Part 2 of the passage?
   a. will be
   b. are
   c. is
   d. was

Questions 38–40 are based on the following passage.

(1) Cuttlefish are very intriguing little animals. (2) The cuttlefish resembles a rather large squid and is, like the octopus, a member of the order of cephalopods. (3) Although they are not considered the most highly evolved of the cephalopods, cuttlefish are extremely intelligent. (4) _____. (5) While observing them, it is hard to tell who is doing the watching, you or the cuttlefish. (6) Since the eye of the cuttlefish is very similar in structure to the human eye, cuttlefish can give you the impression that you are looking into the eyes of a wizard who has metamorphosed himself into a squid with very human eyes.

(7) Cuttlefish are also highly mobile and fast creatures. (8) They come equipped with a small jet located just below the tentacles that can expel water to help them move. (9) For navigation, ribbons of flexible fin on each side of the body allow cuttlefish to hoover, move, stop, and start.

38. Which of the following sentences, if inserted into the blank numbered 4, would be most consistent with the paragraph's development and tone?
  a. Curious and friendly, cuttlefish tend, in the wild, to hover near a diver so they can get a good look, and in captivity, when a researcher slips a hand into the tanks, cuttlefish tend to grasp it with their tentacles in a hearty but gentle handshake.
  b. The cuttlefish can be cooked and eaten like its less tender relatives, the squid and octopus, but must still be tenderized before cooking in order not to be exceedingly chewy.
  c. Cuttlefish are hunted as food not only by many sea creatures, but also by people; they are delicious when properly cooked.
  d. Cuttlefish do not have an exoskeleton; instead their skin is covered with chromataphors.

39. Which of the following numbered parts should be revised to reduce its unnecessary repetition?
  a. Part 9
  b. Part 5
  c. Part 6
  d. Part 2

40. Which of the following changes should be made in the final sentence?
  a. Change *For* to *If*.
  b. Change *allow* to *allot*.
  c. Change *each* to *both*.
  d. Change *hoover* to *hover*.

▶ Section 3: Writing (Part B— Writing Sample)

Carefully read the writing topic that follows, then prepare a multiple-paragraph writing sample of 300–600 words on that topic. Make sure your essay is well-organized and that you support your central argument with concrete examples.

In his play, *The Admirable Crighton*, J. M. Barrie wrote "Courage is the thing. All goes if courage goes."

Write an essay about a time in your life when you had the courage to do something or face something difficult, or when you feel you fell short. What did you learn from the experience?

▶ Answer Explanations

Section 1: Reading

1. b. The passage discusses the negative effect of segregated schools on public school students, which indicates that the plaintiffs in the case were public school students. Though the case is called *Brown v. Board of Education,* paragraph 5 makes it clear that the plaintiffs are the winners of the case, so that public school students, not board members, prevailed.

2. d. Throughout the passage there is discussion of the 14th Amendment, and its date is given as 1868. This would indicate that the phrase *post-War Amendments* refers to the 14th and other amendments passed after the Civil War.

3. a. The word *reargument* indicates that the arguments were made at least once before. The other answer choices contain information that is not addressed in the passage and are therefore too specific to be accurate.

4. b. Paragraph 3 deals extensively with the state of public education at the time the 14th Amendment was passed. The information contained in choices **a** and **c** is not indicated by the passage; nor does it appear that the Court simply disagreed with Congress, as stated in choice **d**.

5. c. This choice provides the most complete and accurate organization of the material in this passage. The other choices contain information which is addressed only briefly, or not at all, in the passage.

6. c. Paragraph 3 states that when the 14th Amendment was being adopted, compulsory school attendance was virtually unknown. No mention is made in the paragraph of choices **a** or **b**; choice **d** is refuted in the paragraph, at least with regard to the South.

7. b. *Susceptible* means being liable to be affected by something. According to the third paragraph, some patients are genetically predisposed, or susceptible, to some diseases.

8. a. The last sentence of the second paragraph indicates that the report advised *caution in using . . . predictive tests.*

9. b. See the last sentence of the fifth paragraph, which states that *effective treatment can be started in a few hundred infants.*

10. d. The first paragraph says that the report addressed concerns about protecting confidentiality.

11. c. The last sentence of the fourth paragraph states that *careful pilot studies . . . need to be done first.* Choices **a** and **b** are not mentioned in regard to mandatory screening; choice **d** is illogical.

12. d. See the fifth paragraph: *Newborn screening is the most common type of genetic screening today.*

13. d. The opening sentence tells readers that making a list of pros and cons is a technique of utilitarian reasoning. Thus, readers who have used this technique will realize they are already familiar with the basic principles of utilitarianism.

14. b. The second sentence explains the main argument of utilitarianism—that we should use consequences to determine our course of action. Thus *posits* is used here in the sense of *asserts.*

15. c. The passage opens with an explanation that according to utilitarianism, only the consequences of our actions are morally relevant. It is further stated that an action is considered morally good if it creates good (happiness).

16. d. It is explained in paragraph 2 of the text that the utilitarian principle of choosing actions that create *the greatest amount of good (happiness) for the greatest number of people.*

17. b. The last two sentences of the passage explain two aspects of utilitarianism that complicate the decision-making process: that it is not always clear what the consequences of an action will be (whether they will bring short- or long-term happiness and to what degree), and that sometimes we must sacrifice the happiness of others.

18. c. The passage describes swing as *vibrant*, a synonym for *lively*. It is also stated that soloists in big bands *improvised from the melody*, indicating that the music was *melodic*.

19. d. In the 1940s, you would most likely hear bebop being played in clubs, such as *Minton's Playhouse in Harlem* (paragraph 3).

20. b. At the beginning of paragraph 3, the author states that *rhythm* is the *distinguishing feature of bebop*.

21. a. *Aficionado*, derived from the word *affection*, means a devotee or fan. The meaning can be inferred from the sentence, which states that *aficionados* flocked to clubs *to soak in the new style*.

22. c. The tone of the passage is neutral so only the answers beginning with *explain* or *instruct* are possible choices. The passage does not explain how to play bebop music, so **c** is the best choice.

23. d. This choice, though not stated directly, is the most logical inference from mention of Moscow's chaotic periods and of the fact that a new city has been built on the rubble of the old.

24. a. The writer speaks approvingly of both progress and preservation. See especially the middle of paragraph 5: *The citizens of the present are determined that . . . the past will be uncovered and celebrated rather than shrouded and forgotten.*

25. a. Based on the content of paragraph 2, it appears the writer is referring to a tumultuous history. In a scientific sense, *chaos* may mean matter that is unformed or undeveloped (choices **b** and **c**); however, the passage is not speaking of matter but of a city's history. The word *remarkable* (choice **d**) is not closely linked with the word *chaos*.

26. b. The content of the passage indicates that, currently, Muscovites are trying to preserve and protect old buildings; the passage further indi-

cates that this was frequently not done in the past.

27. c. The main thrust of the passage has to do with both progress and preservation.

28. a. See the descriptions of the archeological finds in paragraphs 2 and 5.

29. d. The three examples in the first paragraph show that there is a wide range of styles of public art in New York City and that public art can be found in a variety of places, including more mundane locations such as the subway and post office.

30. a. *Inherently* is an adverb that describes the essential nature of something. The context clue to answer this question is found in the same sentence. *All art is inherently public* because it is *created in order to convey an idea or emotion to others.* The author is saying that an essential characteristic of art is that it is created for others.

31. b. In paragraph 2 the author defines public art as *the kind of art created for and displayed in public spaces*, and further states in paragraph 3 that public art is *specifically designed for a public arena where the art will be encountered by people in their normal day-to-day activities.* This is in contrast to private art, which is less accessible because it is kept in specific, non-public places such as museums and galleries.

32. b. To *sequester* is to seclude or isolate. Thus, the use of this word suggests that the author feels private art is too isolated, and cut off from the public.

33. a. After defining public art, the rest of the passage discusses the functions of public art and its impact on the city.

34. d. The examples in paragraph 1 and the list of different kinds of public art will make the reader more aware of public art; paragraphs 2 and 3 explain the difference between public and private art; paragraph 5 explains how public art affects the community, and paragraph 6 discusses how public art should be created. A few readers may be inspired to create public art after reading this passage, but that is not one of its goals.

35. a. Although in paragraph 2 the author states that *there exists in every city a symbiotic relationship between the city and its art* and paragraph 5 explains how public art affects the city, there is not discussion of how the city affects art.

36. c. See the first sentence of the third paragraph. It is when the gas is trapped, as in a building, that serious ramifications can develop.

37. a. That inert gases are chemically inactive can be inferred from the second paragraph, which says that radon is unlike its chemically active daughters.

38. d. The fifth paragraph says that the unattached daughters pose danger to the lungs because they can travel directly to those organs.

39. a. The fourth paragraph says that plating out is the process by which radon daughters attach to matter.

40. a. The beginning of the third paragraph points out the relative danger posed by trapped radon as opposed to radon that is released into the atmosphere.

41. b. The beginning of the second paragraph says that radon is formed as uranium and radium decay.

42. d. See the sixth paragraph, the next-to-last sentence, which speaks of relatively low doses that eliminate a relatively small number of cells.

Section 2: Mathematics

1. d. Solve this problem with the following equation: $4x - 12 = 20$; $4x = 32$; $x = 8$.

2. b. An algebraic equation should be used: $K - 20 = \frac{1}{2}(M - 20)$; $K = 40$. Therefore, $M = 60$.

3. a. Substituting known quantities into the formula yields $20 = \frac{64.8}{x^2}$. Next, you must multiply through by x^2 to get $20x^2 = 64.8$ and then divide

through by 20 to get $x^2 = \frac{64.8}{20} = 3.24$. Now take the square root of both sides to get $x = 1.8$.

4. a. You know the ratio of Dr. Drake's charge to Dr. Jarmuth's charge is 3:4, or $\frac{3}{4}$. To find what Dr. Jarmuth charges, you use the equation $\frac{3}{4} = \frac{36}{x}$, or $3x = (4)(36)$; $4(36) = 144$, which is then divided by 3 to arrive at $x = 48$.

5. a. The ratio of 105,000 to 3 is equal to the ratio of x to 4, or $\frac{105,000}{3} = \frac{x}{4}$, where x is the population served by four hospitals. This means that $x = 4(105,000 \div 3)$, which is equal to $4(35,000)$, which is equal to 140,000.

6. b. $1\frac{1}{2}$ cups equals $\frac{3}{2}$ cups. The ratio is 6 people to 4 people, which is equal to the ratio of x to $\frac{3}{2}$. By cross multiplying, we get $6(\frac{3}{2}) = 4x$, or $9 = 4x$. Dividing both sides by 4, we get $\frac{9}{4}$, or $2\frac{1}{4}$ cups.

7. b. Five percent of 1 liter equals $(0.05)(1)$, which equals $(0.02)x$, where x is the total amount of water in the resulting 2% solution. Solving for x, you get 2.5. Subtracting the 1 liter of water already present in the 5% solution, you will find that 1.5 (which is 2.5 minus 1) liters need to be added.

8. b. $150x$ equals $(100)(1)$, where x is the part of a mile a jogger has to go to burn the calories a walker burns in 1 mile. If you divide both sides of this equation by 150, you get x equals $\frac{100}{150} = \frac{2(50)}{3(50)}$. Canceling the 50s, you get $\frac{2}{3}$. This means that a jogger has to jog only $\frac{2}{3}$ of a mile to burn the same number of calories a walker burns in a mile of brisk walking.

9. a. The ratio is $\frac{12 \text{ cc}}{100 \text{ pounds}} = \frac{x \text{ cc}}{175 \text{ pounds}}$ where x is the number of cc's per 175 pounds. You must multiply both sides by 175 to get $x = 21$.

10. a. 3.5 hours times 45 miles per hour is equal to 3 hours times x, so x equals $\frac{(3.5)(45)}{3}$, or 52.5 miles per hour.

11. a. $J = 6K$ and $J + 2 = 2(K + 2)$, so $6K + 2 = 2K + 4$, which means $K = \frac{1}{2}$. J equals $6K$, or 3.

12. c. Let E equal emergency room cost; H equal hospice cost, which is $\frac{1}{4}E$; N equal home nursing cost, which is $2H$, or $2(\frac{1}{4})E$, or $\frac{1}{2}E$. The total bill is $E + H + N$, which equals $E + \frac{1}{4}E + \frac{2}{4}E$, or 140,000. So $\frac{4}{4}E + \frac{1}{4}E + \frac{2}{4}E = 140{,}000$, so $\frac{7}{4}E = 140{,}000$. Multiplying both sides by $\frac{4}{7}$ to solve for E, we get $E = 140{,}000(\frac{4}{7})$, or 80,000. Therefore $H = \frac{1}{4}E$, or $(\frac{1}{4})80{,}000$, which equals 20,000, and $N = 2H$, or $2(20{,}000)$, or 40,000.

13. b. $M = 3N$ and $3N + N = 24$, which implies that $N = 6$ and $M = 3N = 18$. If Nick catches up to Mike's typing speed, then both M and N will equal 18, and then the combined rate will be 18 plus 18 or 36 pages per hour.

14. c. Let T equal Ted's age; S equal Sam's age, which is $3T$; R equal Ron's age, which is $\frac{S}{2}$, or $\frac{3T}{2}$. The sum of the ages is 55, which is $\frac{3T}{2} + 3T + T$, which is equal to $\frac{3T}{2} + \frac{6T}{2} + \frac{2T}{2}$, which is equal to $\frac{(3T + 6T + 2T)}{2}$ or $\frac{11T}{2}$. Now multiply both sides of $55 = \frac{11T}{2}$ by 2 to get $110 = 11T$. Divide through by 11 to get $10 = T$. That is Ted's age, so Sam is $3T$, or $3(10)$, or 30 years old, and Ron is $\frac{3T}{2}$, or 15 years old.

15. a. In order to find the perimeter, the hypotenuse of the triangle must be found. This comes from recognizing that the triangle is a 5-12-13 triangle, or by using the Pythagorean theorem. Therefore, $5 + 12 + 13 = 30$.

16. a. This uses the Pythagorean theorem. The longest object would fit on a diagonal from an upper corner to a lower corner. Since the square base is 9 feet squared, the length and width is 3 feet. Because the volume is 36 cubic feet, and the base is 9 square feet, the height must be 4 feet. First, the diagonal in the rectangular wall of the box is 5, because the other sides are 3 and 4 feet. (It is a 3-4-5 triangle.) The longest diagonal can then be found by using the Pythagorean

theorem, with a width of 5 and a height of 3 feet. This leaves 5.8 feet as the only reasonable answer.

17. d. If angle 1 is 30°, angle 3 must be 60° by right triangle geometry. Because the two lines are parallel, angles 3 and 4 must be congruent. Therefore, to find angle 5, angle 4 must be subtracted from 180 degrees. This is 120°.

18. d. Because the radius of the hemisphere is 3, and it is the same as the half the base of the triangle, the base must be 6. Therefore, the area of the triangle is $\frac{1}{2}bh = 12$. The area of the circle is πr^2, which is equal to 9π. Therefore, the half-circle's area is $\frac{9\pi}{2}$. Adding gives $\frac{9\pi}{2} + 12$.

19. c. If the pentagons are similar, then the two different pentagons will have similar proportions. Because $\overline{AB}$ is similar to $\overline{FG}$, and $\overline{AB} = 10$, and $\overline{FG} = 30$, the second pentagon is 3 times as large. Therefore, $\overline{IH}$ is 3 times as large as $\overline{CD}$, which is 15.

20. d. The volume of a sphere is $\frac{4}{3}\pi^3$. Therefore, the volume of the hemisphere is 18π. This is about 56.5. The water in the cylinder is the total water minus the water in the hemisphere, which leaves 113.5 cubic feet. Volume of a cylinder is area times height. The area of the base is 9π, or about 28.3. Divide the volume of 113.5 by the area of 28.3 to find the height, 4 feet.

21. b. The surface area of the walls is found by multiplying: 4 walls times 120 square feet = 480 square feet. The area of the door and window to be subtracted is 12 + 21 square feet = 33 square feet; $480 - 33 = 447$, so 447 square feet are needed. Louise must buy 5 rolls of wallpaper.

22. d. The total area is equal to the area of the circle minus the area of the triangle. The area of the circle is 16π, and the area of the triangle is $\frac{1}{2}bh = 8$ square feet. Therefore, the area is $16\pi - 8$.

23. a. The area of the parallelogram can be found in one of two ways. The first would be using a formula, which is not provided. The second is by splitting the parallelogram into two triangles and a rectangle. The rectangle would have an area of $(12-3)4 = 36$ square feet. The area of the triangles is $3(4)$. This gives a total area of 48.

24. d. This can be divided into a rectangle and two half-circles. The area of the rectangle is $4(8) = 32$ square feet. The diameter of the half-circles corresponds with the height and width of the rectangle. Therefore, the area of the circles is $\frac{2^{2\pi}}{2} = 2\pi$ and $\frac{4^{2\pi}}{2} = 8\pi$. Therefore, the answer is $32 + 10\pi$.

25. d. This series actually has two alternating sets of numbers. The first number is doubled, giving the third number. The second number has 4 subtracted from it, giving the fourth number. Therefore, the blank space will be 12 doubled, or 24.

26. b. The amount of water would be equal to $\frac{0.50 \times 100 \text{ gallons}}{\text{minute}} \times \frac{6 \text{ hours}}{\text{day}} \times 60$ minutes per hour. This gives 1.80×10^4.

27. d. Since the price per copy is $0.75, divide 60 by 0.75 to find the total number that can be purchased with $60; $\frac{60}{0.75} = 80$.

28. c. The speed of the train is 60 miles per hour, obtained from the table. Therefore, the distance from Chicago would be equal to $60t$. However, as the train moves on, the distance decreases from Los Angeles, so there must be a function of $-60t$ in the equation. At time $t = 0$, the distance is 2,000 miles, so the function is $2,000 - 60t$.

29. d. First, examine the table to determine that there are 40 minutes in each class period and 4 minutes of passing time between each class. To determine the starting time of period 3, add 4 minutes to the ending time of period 2. Thus, the starting time of period 3 is 9:23. To calculate the ending time of period 8, add 40 minutes to the starting time. The ending time is 1:43. The answer choice with both of these times is choice **d**.

30. a. The amount of water held in each container must be found. The rectangular box starts with 16 square inches $\times$ 9 inches = 144 cubic inches of water. The cylindrical container can hold 44π cubic inches of water, which is approximately 138 cubic inches. Therefore, the cylinder will overflow.

31. d. This problem can be solved using only statements I and III. Since the cousin who fishes is female, either Lucia or Samantha likes to fish. Statement III eliminates Samantha, which leaves Lucia.

32. c. An algebraic equation must be used to solve this problem. The shortest side can be denoted by s. Therefore, $s + (s + 2) + (s + 4) = 24$; $3s + 6 = 24$, and $s = 6$.

33. d. The letter in the sequence is decreasing by two letters, and the number is decreasing by three. This gives r14.

34. c. The total number of miles driven is 15 miles per day $\times$ 5 days + 20 miles per day $\times$ 2 days = $\frac{115 \text{ miles}}{25 \text{ miles per gallon}} = 4.6$ gallons. Five gallons must be purchased.

35. a. The earning rate must be calculated for each vehicle. A car earns $\frac{3}{5}$ dollar per minute, a truck earns $\frac{4}{7}$ dollar per minute, and a van earns $\frac{1}{2}$ dollar per minute. The cars earn the most money.

36. b. This must be solved with an algebraic equation; $L = 2W + 4$; $3L + 2W = 28$. Therefore, $6W + 12 + 2W = 28$; $8W = 16$; $W = 2$; $L = 8$; $2 \times 8 = 16$ square inches.

37. c. The answer is arrived at by dividing 175 by 45. Since the answer is 3.89, not a whole number, the gardener needs 4 sections of hose. Three sections of hose would be too short.

38. c. The farther to the right the digits go, the smaller the number.

39. a. The expression $5n$ means 5 times n. The addition sign before the 7 indicates addition.

40. b. Use 35 for C; $F = (\frac{9}{5} \times 35) + 32$. Therefore $F = 63 + 32$, or $95°$ F.

41. d. Substitute 3 for *x* in the expression 5 + 4*x* to determine that *y* equals 17.

42. b. The formula for finding the area of a circle is *A* = π*r*². First, square the radius: 13 times 13 equals 169. Then multiply by the approximate value of π, 3.14, to get 530.66.

43. c. 5 times 3 times 8 is 120; 120 divided by 3 is 40.

44. c. This is the only choice that includes a 90-degree angle.

45. b. $\sqrt{12} = \sqrt{4(3)} = \sqrt{4}\sqrt{3} = 2\sqrt{3}$. Therefore, $3\sqrt{12} = 6\sqrt{3}$.

46. b. Use the formula beginning with the operation in parentheses: 98 minus 32 equals 66. Then multiply 66 by $\frac{5}{9}$, first multiplying 66 by 5 to get 330; 330 divided by 9 is 36.66667, which is rounded up to 36.7.

47. a. The distance between Plattville and Quincy is the hypotenuse of a right triangle with sides of length 80² and 60². The length of the hypotenuse equals the square root of (80² plus 60²), which equals the square root of (6,400 plus 3,600), which equals the square root of 10,000, which equals 100 miles.

48. d. Multiply 16 times 5 to find out how many gallons all five sprinklers will release in one minute. Then multiply the result (80 gallons per minute) by the number of minutes (10) to get 800 gallons.

Section 3: Writing (Part A— Multiple-Choice)

1. b. Part 3 requires a comma before the coordinate conjunction *so*.

2. a. This answer is in the simple past tense, which is the tense used throughout the paragraph.

3. b. The context requires that the noun *renown* be replaced by the adjective *renowned*.

4. b. The semicolon in Part 2 is used incorrectly to introduce a list; it needs to be replaced with a colon. Choices **a**, **c**, and **d** are incorrect because, in each, the semicolon correctly separates two independent clauses.

5. c. The expressions *year-round* and *in all seasons* repeat the same idea. Choices **a**, **b**, and **d** are incorrect because none of these sentences contains unnecessary repetition. Part 4 may seem to, at first; however, the words *hot and humid* are expanded on the rest of the sentence and made more interesting and specific.

6. d. The subject of Part 3 is *climate* and therefore requires the third-person singular form of the verb *to be*—*is*.

7. c. Part 3 provides information about the Surgeon General's findings that are off the topic of the announcement about the FDA's ruling about the labeling of milk. All of the other sentences add information about the FDA ruling, its reasons, and its effects.

8. a. The word *imply*, meaning to express or indicate indirectly, is misused in the context of Part 4; the word *infer*, to surmise, makes sense in the context.

9. d. In Part 1, the adjective *good* is misused as an adverb; it needs to be replaced by the adverb *well*.

10. a. In Part 4, the verb *assures*, to make certain, is nonsensical in the context; it should be replaced by the verb *assumes*, to suppose or take for granted.

11. d. The paragraph consistently uses the pronoun *you*; therefore, the inconsistent use of *our* should be replaced by *your*.

12. c. The word *Greek* in Part 2 is a proper noun and should be capitalized.

13. c. Part 1 contains a run-on sentence. It requires a semicolon after the parentheses and before *we*.

14. b. The context requires a word synonymous to *surrender* or *yield*, so choice **b** is correct.

15. d. To make the pair of verbs in the sentence parallel, *overlooking* should be changed to *overlooks* to match the form of the verb *towers*.

16. d. A comma is required after an introductory dependent clause. Choice **a** would introduce a comma fault, separating a verb from its object.

Choice **b** is incorrect because the semicolon would have to be followed by a complete sentence, which is not the case. Choice **c** is incorrect because removing the colon would create a run-on sentence.

17. c. Choices **a** and **b** would cause an unwarranted shift in tense from past (in which most of the passage is written) to present. Choice **d** would change the correctly written noun, *effect*, to an incorrect verb form. (*Affect* is a verb, except when used as a noun to denote a person's emotional expression, or lack thereof, as in *He has a joyless affect.*)

18. b. The adjective *shallow* in Part 5 actually modifies the verb *set*; therefore, the adjective should be revised to be the adverb *shallowly*.

19. c. The proper noun *Lake* must be made possessive because it is followed by the gerund *arriving*.

20. c. This paragraph is about how to handle business phone calls. Reversing the order of Parts 9 and 13 would cause the paragraph to follow the natural order of the beginning to the end of a phone conversation.

21. b. This sentence requires the adverb *then* in this context.

22. d. The verb *depend* is, idiomatically, followed by the preposition *on*; in Part 10 it is wrongly followed by *in*.

23. b. The antecedent of the pronoun *they* in this sentence is *someone*. Since *someone* is singular, the subject pronoun should be *he* or *she*.

24. c. The sentence requires the contraction *we're*, short for *we are*. It is all right to use a contraction because the writer uses contractions elsewhere in the passage.

25. a. This passage's tone is the impersonal, objective style of an official announcement. Choice **a** is correct because it retains the same objective tone as the rest of the paragraph. Choice **b** is incorrect because the phrase *the guys*, referring here to sanitation workers, is too casual in tone

for the rest of the paragraph. Choice **c** is incorrect because the adjective *filthy* is too pejorative in tone for the objective style of the paragraph. Choice **d** is incorrect because the phrase *spruce up* is too colloquial for the tone of the paragraph.

26. d. Part 3 contains a run-on sentence; it requires a semicolon rather than a comma after *varies*.

27. a. Another sentence is needed to add the information that the program is only for passengers leaving the bus, not those boarding it. This information is implied in the paragraph but not directly stated; without the direct statement, the paragraph is confusing and the reader must read between the lines to get the information.

28. c. The subjective pronoun *who* is incorrectly used to refer to the Stop Here Program; the pronoun *which* would be a better choice.

29. b. Part 5 contains two sentences linked only by a comma; a semicolon is required.

30. d. In Part 4, a semicolon is used incorrectly to introduce a list; it should be replaced by a colon.

31. a. Part 5 is the only sentence fragment in this passage. It needs a subject in order to express a complete thought.

32. d. The word *Recently* is the best contrast to *Finally though* in Part 2. Choices **a**, **b**, and **c** indicate time lapses that would not necessarily take place in the context of the passage.

33. a. The comma is needed to set off the introductory clause from the independent clause. Making the changes stated in choices **b**, **c**, or **d** would create a nonstandard sentence.

34. c. Part 2 contains a comma splice; the comma should be replaced with a semicolon. Choices **a**, **b**, and **d** are incorrect because they contain standard sentences.

35. d. Even though it may look like a question, Part 6 is not an interrogatory sentence. It should not be punctuated with a question mark.

36. a. Choice **a** corrects the lack of grammatical parallelism in the list in Part 5. The other choices all fail to correct the error in parallelism.

37. d. The sentence is written in past tense, and the verb needs to be singular to agree with the singular subject of the sentence, *percent*. The other choices introduce a shift in tense.

38. a. The subject of this paragraph is the appearance and observation of cuttlefish. Choice **a** is about observing cuttlefish in the wild and the laboratory. Choices **b** and **c** are off the topic of the paragraph. Choice **d**, while having something to do with the appearance of cuttlefish, is written in jargon that is too technical to match the tone of the rest of the passage.

39. c. The double mention in Part 6 of the humanlike eyes of the cuttlefish is unnecessarily repetitious.

40. d. The correct choice is *hover*.

Section 3: Writing (Part B—Writing Sample)

Following are the criteria for scoring THEA essays.

A "4" essay is a well-formed writing sample that addresses the assigned topic and conveys a unified message to its audience. Additionally, it has the following characteristics:

- a clear purpose and focus
- controlled development of a main idea
- clear, concrete, and effective details supporting the main idea
- effective, error-free sentence structure
- precise and careful word choice
- mastery of mechanics such as punctuation and spelling

A "3" essay is an adequate writing sample that addresses the assigned topic and clearly attempts to convey a message to its audience. Generally, it has the following additional characteristics:

- a clear focus and purpose
- organization of ideas that may be vague, incomplete, or only partially effective
- an attempt at development of supporting details, which is only partly realized
- word choice and language usage that are adequate; but with minor errors in sentence structure, usage, and word choice
- mechanical mistakes such as errors in spelling and punctuation

A "2" essay is an incompletely formed writing sample that lacks clear focus. It has the following additional characteristics:

- main topic announced, but focus on it is not maintained
- unclear purpose
- use of some supporting detail but development and organization unclear
- sentences and paragraphs poorly structured
- distracting errors in sentence structure
- imprecise word usage
- distracting mechanical mistakes such as errors in spelling and punctuation

A "1" essay is an incompletely formed writing sample that fails to convey a unified message. It has the following additional characteristics:

- attempt at addressing the topic, which fails
- no clear main idea
- language and style that are inappropriate to the audience and purpose
- attempt to present supporting detail which is muddled and unclear
- attempt at organization but failure to present a clear sequence of ideas
- ineffective sentences, very few of which are free of error
- imprecise word usage
- many distracting mechanical mistakes, such as errors in spelling and punctuation

A "U" essay is a writing sample that fails because of one or more of the following:

- failure to address the assigned topic
- illegibility
- written primarily in a language other than English
- length insufficient to score

A "B" essay is a writing sample left completely blank (that is, the test-taker did not respond at all).

Following are examples of scored writing samples. (Note: There are some deliberate errors in all the essays.)

Sample "4" essay

Courage and cowardice seem like absolutes. We are often quick to label other people, or ourselves, either "brave" or "timid," "courageous," or "cowardly." However, one bright afternoon on a river deep in the wilds of the Ozark mountains, I learned that these qualities are as changeable as mercury.

During a cross-country drive, my friend Nina and I decided to stop at a campsite in Missouri and spend the afternoon on a float trip down Big Piney River, 14 miles through the wilderness. We rented a canoe and paddled happily off.

Things went fine—for the first seven or eight miles. We gazed at the overhanging bluffs, commented on the wonderful variety of trees (it was spring, and the dogwood was in bloom), and marveled at the clarity of the water. Then, in approaching a bend in the river (which we later learned was called "Devil's Elbow") the current suddenly swept us in toward the bank, underneath the low-hanging branches of a weeping willow. The canoe tipped over and I was pulled under, my foot caught for just a few seconds on the submerged roots of the willow. Just as I surfaced, taking my first frantic gulp of air,

I saw the canoe sweeping out, upright again, but empty, and Nina frantically swimming after it.

I knew I should help but I was petrified and hung my head in shame as I let my friend brave the treacherous rapids and haul the canoe back onto the gravel bar, while I stood by cravenly.

Then came the scream. Startled, I glanced up to see Nina, both hands over her eyes, dash off the gravel bar and back into the water. I gazed down into the canoe to see, coiled in the bottom of it, the unmistakable, black-and-brown, checkerboard-patterned form of a copperhead snake. It had evidently been sunning itself peacefully on the weeping willow branch when we passed by underneath.

I don't know exactly why. but the supposedly inborn terror of snakes is something that has passed me by completely. I actually find them rather charming in a scaly sort of way.

Nina was still screaming, near hysterics: "Kill it!" But I was calm in a way that must have seemed smug. "We're in its home, it's not in ours," I informed her. And gently I prodded it with the oar until it reared up, slithered over the side of the canoe, and raced away—terrified, itself—into the underbrush.

Later that night, in our cozy, safe motel room, we agreed that we each had cold chills thinking about what might have happened. Still, I learned something important from the ordeal. I know that, had we encountered only the rapids, I might have come away ashamed, labeling myself a coward, and had we encountered only the snake, Nina might have done the same. And I also know that neither of us will ever again be quite so apt to brand another person as lacking courage. Because we will always know that, just around the corner, may be the snake or the bend in the river or the figure in the shadows or something else as yet unanticipated, that will cause our own blood to freeze.

Sample "3" essay

Courage can be shown in many ways and by many kinds of people. One does not have to be rich, or educated, or even an adult to show true courage.

For example, a very heartbreaking thing happened in our family. It turned out all right but at the time it almost made us lose our faith. However, it also taught us a lesson regarding courage. In spite of our father's and my repeated warnings, my brother Matt went ice-fishing with some friends and fell through the ice into the frigid water beneath. He is prone to do things that are dangerous no matter how many times he's told. Fortunately there were grown-ups near and they were able to throw him a life line and pull him to safety. However, when they got him onto shore they discovered he was unconscious. There were vital signs but they were weak, the paramedics pronounced him in grave danger.

He is our little sisters (Nans) hero. He is 16 and she is 13, just at the age where she admires everything he does. When they took him to the hospital she insisted on going that night to see him, and she insisted on staying with me there. My father thought we should insist she go home, but it was Christmas vacation for her so there was no real reason. So he decide to let her stay. She stayed every night for the whole week just to be by Matt's side. And when he woke up she was there. Her smiling face the was first thing he saw.

In spite of the fact she was just a child and it was frightning for her to be there beside her brother she loves so much, and had to wonder, every day if he would die, she stayed. So courage has many faces.

Sample "2" essay

Courage is not something we are born with. It is something that we have to learn.

For example when your children are growing up you should teach them courage. Teach them to face lifes challanges and not to show there fear. For instance my father. Some people would say he was harsh, but back then I didnt think of it that way. One time he took me camping and I had a tent of my own. I wanted to crawl in with him but he said there was nothing to be afriad of. And I went to sleep sooner than I would have expect. He taught me not to be afriad.

There are many reasons for courage. In a war a solder has to be couragous and a mother has to be no less couragous if she is rasing a child alone and has to make a living. So, in me it is totally alright to be afriad as long as you face your fear. I have been greatful to him ever since that night.

If we dont learn from our parents, like I did from my father, then we have to learn it after we grow up. But it is better to learn it, as a child. I have never been as afriad as I was that night, and I learned a valuble lesson from it.

Sample "1" essay

Courage is important in a battle and also ordinary life. In a war if your buddy depends on you and you let him down he might die. Courage is also important in daly life. If you have sicknes in the famly or if you enconter a mugger on the street you will need all the courage you can get. There are many dangers in life that only courage will see you through.

Once, my apartment was burglerised and they stole a TV and micro-wave. I didnt have very much. They took some money to. I felt afraid when I walked in and saw things moved or gone. But I call the police and waited for them inside my apartment which was brave and also some might say stupid! But the police came and took my statement and also later caught the guy. Another time my girlfreind and I were in my apartment and we looked out the window and there was somebody suspisious out in front. It turned out to be a false alarm but she was scard and she said because I was calm it made her feel better. So courage was important to me, in my relatinship with my girlfreind.

So courage is importand not only in war but also in life.

▶ Scoring

Once again, in order to evaluate how you did on this practice exam, start by scoring the three sections of the THEA—Reading, Mathematics, and Writing—separately. You will recall that the Reading section, the Mathematics section, and the multiple-choice subsection of the Writing section are scored the same way: First find the number of questions you got right in each section. Questions you skipped or got wrong don't count; just add up the number of correct answers. Divide the number of questions you got right by the number of questions on that section of the exam to find a percentage equivalent.

In addition to achieving a passing score on the Reading section and the Mathematics section, you must receive a passing score on the writing sample subsection of the Writing section of the THEA. Your writing sample will be graded by two trained readers and their combined score used to evaluate how you did. Your score will be a combination of the two readers' judgments, somewhere between a possible high of 8 and a low of 2. The best way to see how you did on your essay for this practice exam is to give your writing sample and the scoring criteria to a teacher and ask him or her to score your essay for you.

You have probably seen improvement between your first practice exam score and this one; but keep in mind that how you did on each of the basic skills tested by the exam is more important than your overall score right now. Use your scores on this practice test to once again diagnose your strengths and weaknesses so that you can concentrate your efforts as you prepare for the exam. Turn again to the review lessons in Chapters 4, 5, and 6 that cover each of the basic skills tested on the THEA.

If you didn't score as well as you would like, ask yourself the following: Did I run out of time before I could answer all the questions? Did I go back and change my answers from right to wrong? Did I get flustered and sit staring at a difficult question for what seemed like hours? If you had any of these problems, once again, be sure to go over the LearningExpress Test Preparation System in Chapter 2 to learn how to avoid them.

After working on your reading, writing, and math skills, take the final practice exam in Chapter 8 to see how much you have improved.

THEA Practice Exam 3

CHAPTER SUMMARY

This is the third practice test in this book based on the Texas Higher Education Assessment (THEA). Use this test to see how much you have improved.

Much like the previous practice exams in this book, this one is divided into three sections: a Reading section, a Mathematics section, and a two-part Writing section that consists of multiple-choice questions and one essay topic on which you are to write from 300–600 words.

For this exam, you should simulate the actual test-taking experience as closely as you can. Work in a quiet place, away from interruptions. Use the answer sheet on the following page and, as you did before, write your essay on a separate piece of paper. Before you begin, decide in what order you are going to do the sections. Use a timer and allow yourself five hours for the entire exam.

After the exam, use the answer explanations that follow to find out which questions you missed and why.

► Answer Sheet

SECTION 1: READING

1. ⓐ ⓑ ⓒ ⓓ
2. ⓐ ⓑ ⓒ ⓓ
3. ⓐ ⓑ ⓒ ⓓ
4. ⓐ ⓑ ⓒ ⓓ
5. ⓐ ⓑ ⓒ ⓓ
6. ⓐ ⓑ ⓒ ⓓ
7. ⓐ ⓑ ⓒ ⓓ
8. ⓐ ⓑ ⓒ ⓓ
9. ⓐ ⓑ ⓒ ⓓ
10. ⓐ ⓑ ⓒ ⓓ
11. ⓐ ⓑ ⓒ ⓓ
12. ⓐ ⓑ ⓒ ⓓ
13. ⓐ ⓑ ⓒ ⓓ
14. ⓐ ⓑ ⓒ ⓓ
15. ⓐ ⓑ ⓒ ⓓ
16. ⓐ ⓑ ⓒ ⓓ
17. ⓐ ⓑ ⓒ ⓓ
18. ⓐ ⓑ ⓒ ⓓ
19. ⓐ ⓑ ⓒ ⓓ
20. ⓐ ⓑ ⓒ ⓓ
21. ⓐ ⓑ ⓒ ⓓ
22. ⓐ ⓑ ⓒ ⓓ
23. ⓐ ⓑ ⓒ ⓓ
24. ⓐ ⓑ ⓒ ⓓ
25. ⓐ ⓑ ⓒ ⓓ
26. ⓐ ⓑ ⓒ ⓓ
27. ⓐ ⓑ ⓒ ⓓ
28. ⓐ ⓑ ⓒ ⓓ
29. ⓐ ⓑ ⓒ ⓓ
30. ⓐ ⓑ ⓒ ⓓ
31. ⓐ ⓑ ⓒ ⓓ
32. ⓐ ⓑ ⓒ ⓓ
33. ⓐ ⓑ ⓒ ⓓ
34. ⓐ ⓑ ⓒ ⓓ
35. ⓐ ⓑ ⓒ ⓓ
36. ⓐ ⓑ ⓒ ⓓ
37. ⓐ ⓑ ⓒ ⓓ
38. ⓐ ⓑ ⓒ ⓓ
39. ⓐ ⓑ ⓒ ⓓ
40. ⓐ ⓑ ⓒ ⓓ
41. ⓐ ⓑ ⓒ ⓓ
42. ⓐ ⓑ ⓒ ⓓ

SECTION 2: MATH

1. ⓐ ⓑ ⓒ ⓓ
2. ⓐ ⓑ ⓒ ⓓ
3. ⓐ ⓑ ⓒ ⓓ
4. ⓐ ⓑ ⓒ ⓓ
5. ⓐ ⓑ ⓒ ⓓ
6. ⓐ ⓑ ⓒ ⓓ
7. ⓐ ⓑ ⓒ ⓓ
8. ⓐ ⓑ ⓒ ⓓ
9. ⓐ ⓑ ⓒ ⓓ
10. ⓐ ⓑ ⓒ ⓓ
11. ⓐ ⓑ ⓒ ⓓ
12. ⓐ ⓑ ⓒ ⓓ
13. ⓐ ⓑ ⓒ ⓓ
14. ⓐ ⓑ ⓒ ⓓ
15. ⓐ ⓑ ⓒ ⓓ
16. ⓐ ⓑ ⓒ ⓓ
17. ⓐ ⓑ ⓒ ⓓ
18. ⓐ ⓑ ⓒ ⓓ
19. ⓐ ⓑ ⓒ ⓓ
20. ⓐ ⓑ ⓒ ⓓ
21. ⓐ ⓑ ⓒ ⓓ
22. ⓐ ⓑ ⓒ ⓓ
23. ⓐ ⓑ ⓒ ⓓ
24. ⓐ ⓑ ⓒ ⓓ
25. ⓐ ⓑ ⓒ ⓓ
26. ⓐ ⓑ ⓒ ⓓ
27. ⓐ ⓑ ⓒ ⓓ
28. ⓐ ⓑ ⓒ ⓓ
29. ⓐ ⓑ ⓒ ⓓ
30. ⓐ ⓑ ⓒ ⓓ
31. ⓐ ⓑ ⓒ ⓓ
32. ⓐ ⓑ ⓒ ⓓ
33. ⓐ ⓑ ⓒ ⓓ
34. ⓐ ⓑ ⓒ ⓓ
35. ⓐ ⓑ ⓒ ⓓ
36. ⓐ ⓑ ⓒ ⓓ
37. ⓐ ⓑ ⓒ ⓓ
38. ⓐ ⓑ ⓒ ⓓ
39. ⓐ ⓑ ⓒ ⓓ
40. ⓐ ⓑ ⓒ ⓓ
41. ⓐ ⓑ ⓒ ⓓ
42. ⓐ ⓑ ⓒ ⓓ
43. ⓐ ⓑ ⓒ ⓓ
44. ⓐ ⓑ ⓒ ⓓ
45. ⓐ ⓑ ⓒ ⓓ
46. ⓐ ⓑ ⓒ ⓓ
47. ⓐ ⓑ ⓒ ⓓ
48. ⓐ ⓑ ⓒ ⓓ

SECTION 3: WRITING PART A

1. ⓐ ⓑ ⓒ ⓓ
2. ⓐ ⓑ ⓒ ⓓ
3. ⓐ ⓑ ⓒ ⓓ
4. ⓐ ⓑ ⓒ ⓓ
5. ⓐ ⓑ ⓒ ⓓ
6. ⓐ ⓑ ⓒ ⓓ
7. ⓐ ⓑ ⓒ ⓓ
8. ⓐ ⓑ ⓒ ⓓ
9. ⓐ ⓑ ⓒ ⓓ
10. ⓐ ⓑ ⓒ ⓓ
11. ⓐ ⓑ ⓒ ⓓ
12. ⓐ ⓑ ⓒ ⓓ
13. ⓐ ⓑ ⓒ ⓓ
14. ⓐ ⓑ ⓒ ⓓ
15. ⓐ ⓑ ⓒ ⓓ
16. ⓐ ⓑ ⓒ ⓓ
17. ⓐ ⓑ ⓒ ⓓ
18. ⓐ ⓑ ⓒ ⓓ
19. ⓐ ⓑ ⓒ ⓓ
20. ⓐ ⓑ ⓒ ⓓ
21. ⓐ ⓑ ⓒ ⓓ
22. ⓐ ⓑ ⓒ ⓓ
23. ⓐ ⓑ ⓒ ⓓ
24. ⓐ ⓑ ⓒ ⓓ
25. ⓐ ⓑ ⓒ ⓓ
26. ⓐ ⓑ ⓒ ⓓ
27. ⓐ ⓑ ⓒ ⓓ
28. ⓐ ⓑ ⓒ ⓓ
29. ⓐ ⓑ ⓒ ⓓ
30. ⓐ ⓑ ⓒ ⓓ
31. ⓐ ⓑ ⓒ ⓓ
32. ⓐ ⓑ ⓒ ⓓ
33. ⓐ ⓑ ⓒ ⓓ
34. ⓐ ⓑ ⓒ ⓓ
35. ⓐ ⓑ ⓒ ⓓ
36. ⓐ ⓑ ⓒ ⓓ
37. ⓐ ⓑ ⓒ ⓓ
38. ⓐ ⓑ ⓒ ⓓ
39. ⓐ ⓑ ⓒ ⓓ
40. ⓐ ⓑ ⓒ ⓓ

▶ Section 1: Reading

Questions 1–6 are based on the following passage.

(1) The late 1980s found the landscape of popular music in America dominated by a distinctive style of rock and roll known as *Glam Rock* or *Hair Metal*—so called because of the over-styled hair, makeup, and wardrobe worn by the genre's ostentatious rockers. Bands like Poison, White Snake, and Mötley Crüe popularized glam rock with their power ballads and flashy style, but the product had worn thin by the early 1990s. The mainstream public, tired of an act they perceived as symbolic of the superficial 1980s, was ready for something with a bit of substance.

(2) In 1991, a Seattle-based band named Nirvana shocked the corporate music industry with the release of its debut single "Smells Like Teen Spirit," which quickly became a huge hit all over the world. Nirvana's distorted, guitar-laden sound and thought-provoking lyrics were the antithesis of glam rock, and the youth of America were quick to pledge their allegiance to the brand new movement known as *grunge*.

(3) Grunge actually got its start in the Pacific Northwest during the mid 1980s, the offspring of the metal-guitar driven rock of the 1970s and the hardcore, punk music of the early 1980s. Nirvana had simply brought into the mainstream a sound and culture that got its start years before with bands like Mudhoney, Soundgarden, and Green River. Grunge rockers derived their fashion sense from the youth culture of the Pacific Northwest: a melding of punk rock style and outdoors clothing like flannels, heavy boots, worn-out jeans, and corduroys. At the height of the movement's popularity, when other Seattle bands like Pearl Jam and Alice in Chains were all the rage, the trappings of grunge were working their way to the height of American fashion. Like the music, teenagers were fast to embrace the grunge fashion because it represented defiance against corporate America and shallow pop culture.

(4) Many assume that grunge got its name from the unkempt appearance of its musicians and their dirty, often distorted guitar sounds. However, rock writers and critics have used the word "grunge" since the 1970s. While no one can say for sure who was the first to characterize a Seattle band as "grunge," the most popular theory is that it originated with the lead singer of Mudhoney, Mark Arm. In a practical joke against a local music magazine, he placed advertisements all over Seattle for a band that did not exist. He then wrote a letter to the magazine complaining about the quality of the fake band's music. The magazine published his critique, one part of which stated, "I hate Mr. Epp and the Calculations! Pure grunge!"

(5) The popularity of grunge music was ephemeral; by the mid- to late-1990s its influence upon American culture had all but disappeared, and most of its recognizable bands were nowhere to be seen on the charts. The heavy sound and themes of grunge were replaced on the radio waves by bands like NSYNC, the Backstreet Boys, and the bubblegum pop of Britney Spears and Christina Aguilera.

(6) There are many reasons why the Seattle sound faded out of the mainstream as quickly as it rocketed to prominence, but the most glaring reason lies at the defiant, anti-establishment heart of the grunge movement itself. It is very hard to buck the trend when you are the one setting it, and many of the grunge bands were never comfortable with the celebrity that was thrust upon them. One of the most successful Seattle groups of the 1990s, Pearl Jam, filmed only one music video, and refused to play large venues. Ultimately, the simple fact that many grunge bands were so against mainstream rock stardom eventually took the movement back to where it started: underground. The American mainstream public, as quick as they were to hop onto the grunge bandwagon, were just as quick to hop off, and move onto something else.

1. The author's description of glam rockers in paragraph 1 indicates that they
   a. cared more about the quality of their music than money.
   b. were mainly style over substance.
   c. were unassuming and humble.
   d. were songwriters first, and performers second.

2. The word *ostentatious* in paragraph 1 most nearly means
   a. stubborn.
   b. youthful.
   c. showy.
   d. unadorned.

3. In paragraph 3 the phrase *the trappings of grunge* refers to
   a. the distorted sound of grunge music.
   b. what the grunge movement symbolized.
   c. the unattractiveness of grunge fashion.
   d. the clothing typical of the grunge movement.

4. Which of the following is not associated with the grunge movement?
   a. Mr. Epp and the Calculations
   b. Pearl Jam
   c. Nirvana
   d. White Snake

5. Which of the following words best describes the relationship between grunge music and its mainstream popularity?
   a. solid
   b. contrary
   c. enduring
   d. acquiescent

6. In paragraph 5, the world *ephemeral* most nearly means
   a. enduring.
   b. unbelievable.
   c. a fluke.
   d. fleeting.

Questions 7–13 are based on the following passage.

(1) Without a doubt, one of the most interesting mythological characters is the Greek god Prometheus. A complex character with an undying love for the human beings he created, Prometheus embodies a rich combination of often contradictory characteristics, including loyalty and defiance, trickery and trustworthiness. He shows resilience and resolve in his actions yet weakness in his fondness for humankind.

(2) To reward Prometheus (whose name means "forethought") and his brother Epimetheus ("afterthought") for helping him defeat the Titans, Zeus, the great ruler of Olympian gods, gave the brothers the task of creating mortals to populate the land around Mount Olympus. Prometheus asked Epimetheus to give the creatures their various characteristics, such as cunning, swiftness, and flight. By the time he got to man, however, there was nothing left to give. So Prometheus decided to make man in his image: he stood man upright like the gods and became the benefactor and protector of mankind.

(3) Though Prometheus was particularly fond of his creation, Zeus didn't care for mankind and didn't want men to have the divine gift of knowledge. But Prometheus took pity on mortal men and gave them knowledge of the arts and sciences, including the healing arts and agriculture.

(4) Always seeking the best for his creation, one day Prometheus conspired to trick Zeus to give the best meat of an ox to men instead of Zeus. He cut up

the ox and hid the bones in layers of fat; then he hid the meat and innards inside the hide. When Prometheus presented the piles to Zeus, Zeus chose the pile that looked like fat and meat. He was enraged to find that it was nothing but bones.

(5) To punish Prometheus for his deceit and his fondness for humans, Zeus forbade men fire—a symbol of creative power, life force, and divine knowledge. But Prometheus would not let his children be denied this greatest of gifts. He took a hollow reed, stole fire from Mount Olympus, and gave it to men. With this divine power, creativity, ingenuity, and culture flourished in the land of mortals.

(6) Again, Zeus punished man for Prometheus's transgression, this time by sending the first woman, Pandora, to Earth. Pandora brought with her a "gift" from Zeus: a jar filled with evils of every kind. Prometheus knew Zeus to be vengeful and warned Epimetheus not to accept any gifts from Zeus, but Epimetheus was too taken with Pandora's beauty and allowed her to stay. Eventually Pandora opened the jar she'd been forbidden to open, releasing all manner of evils, including Treachery, Sorrow, Villainy, Misfortune, and Plague. At the bottom of the jar was Hope, but Pandora closed the lid before Hope could escape.

(7) Prometheus drew Zeus's greatest wrath when he refused to tell Zeus which of Zeus's sons would kill him and take over the throne. Believing he could torture Prometheus into revealing the secret, Zeus bound his flesh and ate his liver, which would regenerate each night. But Prometheus refused to reveal his knowledge of the future to Zeus and maintained his silence. Eventually, Prometheus was released by Heracles (also known as Hercules), the last mortal son of Zeus and the strongest of the mortals. Soon afterwards, Prometheus received immortality from a dying centaur, to take his place forever among the great gods of Olympus.

7. The main idea of the first paragraph is that Prometheus
   a. is disrespectful of authority.
   b. is the mythological creator of humans.
   c. has many admirable characteristics.
   d. is a fascinating character because of his complexity.

8. The author's primary purpose in this passage is to
   a. demonstrate the vengeful nature of Zeus.
   b. show how much Prometheus cared for humans.
   c. create in readers an interest in mythology.
   d. relate the story of Prometheus.

9. Based on this passage, it can be inferred that Zeus disliked humans because
   a. Prometheus spent too much time with them.
   b. Prometheus cared for humans more than he did for Zeus.
   c. humans could not be trusted.
   d. humans did not respect Zeus.

10. Zeus becomes angry at Prometheus for all of the following EXCEPT
   a. creating man.
   b. giving man fire.
   c. being excessively fond of humans.
   d. refusing to reveal which of his sons would kill him.

11. Based on this passage, the relationship between Prometheus and humans can best be described as that of
a. parent and child.
b. close friends.
c. master and servants.
d. reluctant allies.

12. The word *transgression* as used in the first sentence of paragraph 6 means
a. villainy.
b. trespass.
c. irregularity.
d. disobedience.

13. The content and style of this passage suggests that the intended audience
a. are experts on Greek mythology.
b. are religious officials.
c. is a general lay audience.
d. is a scholarly review board.

Questions 14–19 are based on the following passage.

(1) A series of studies to determine whether victims of violence and neglect later become criminals or violent offenders themselves examined the lives of child victims identified in court cases dating from 1967 to 1971. The goal of the studies was to provide data that would enable early identification and careful handling of cases to avoid an early criminal justice path.

(2) The initial study, conducted in a midwestern county, was based on documented records of 1,575 court cases of physical abuse, sexual abuse, and neglect. At the time the cases came to court, all of the children were under age eleven, and the mean age was about six. To isolate the effects of abuse and neglect from those of other variables such as gender, race, and poverty, researchers created a control group whose members matched the sample group on the basis of age, gender, race, and family social class.

(3) During the study's initial phase in 1988, researchers examined the criminal records of sample and control group members and compiled histories for all nontraffic offenses at the local, state, and federal levels. In 1994 researchers examined the arrest records again and found that, in the late 1980s, 28% of the sample group had been arrested—11% for violent crime. Of the control group, 21% had been arrested—8% for violent crime. Researchers noted that the differences in arrest rates began to emerge early, at the ages of 8 and 9. At this time, however, only 65% of the victims had passed through the peak years of violent offending (20–25).

(4) By 1994 almost half of the sample group had been arrested for some type of nontraffic offense. Eighteen percent had been arrested for violent crime—an increase of 4% in the six years since arrest records were first checked. Rates of arrest were at least 25% higher among African-American victims. Both males and females reported having made suicide attempts.

(5) Another key finding was that the rates of arrest for children who were victims of neglect (defined as an excessive failure by caregivers to provide food, shelter, clothing, and medical attention) were almost as high as the rate for physically abused children.

(6) In 1994, nearly 100% of the sample were 26 or older. After recompiling criminal histories, larger differences between the sample and control groups were found. 49% of the sample group had been arrested, 18% for violent crime; whereas only 38% of the control group had been arrested, 14% for violent crime.

(7) Preliminary findings indicate a need for criminal justice and social service agencies to take a proactive, preventive stance to stop the cycle of violence.

14. Which of the following is the most accurate definition of the term *control group* (in the second paragraph)?
  a. a group of subjects selected to make sure the results of an experiment are not caused by a factor other than the one being studied
  b. a group of scientists selected to watch the experimenter to make sure there are no serious mistakes in method
  c. a group of objective lay observers selected to make sure the experiment is not biased
  d. a group of subjects who do not know the object of the experiment

15. How did the number of arrests of physically abused youth relate to that of neglected youth?
  a. They were 25% lower.
  b. They were slightly lower.
  c. They were nearly the same.
  d. They were 25% higher.

16. What was the percentage of violent crime arrests in the control group after the first phase of the study?
  a. 4%
  b. 8%
  c. 11%
  d. 21%

17. In the late 1980s, what did researchers discover about the two study groups?
  a. The disparity of arrests materialized at young ages.
  b. Less than half of the sample group was beyond the age of 25.
  c. The average age of the participants was 11.
  d. The control group committed more violent crime than the sample group.

18. One reason for the difference in violent crime rates between the 1988 and 1994 phases of the study was that
  a. victims were closer to the age of peak violent activity in 1988.
  b. most victims who were prone to violence had already committed crimes in 1988.
  c. more victims evinced emotional problems by attempting suicide in 1994.
  d. more victims had passed through the age of peak violent activity in 1994.

19. One objective of the studies was to
  a. recommend greater participation by social service agencies.
  b. analyze statistics for traffic violations.
  c. generate information about an individual's potential crime pattern.
  d. separate physical abuse from sexual abuse.

Questions 20–24 are based on the following passage.

(1) For perhaps the tenth time since the clock struck two, Sylvia crosses to the front-facing window of her apartment, pulls back the blue curtain and looks down at the street. People hurry along the sidewalk; however, although she watches for several long moments, she sees no one enter her building.

(2) She walks back to the center of the high-ceilinged living room, where she stands frowning and twisting a silver bracelet around and around on her wrist. She is an attractive young woman, although perhaps too thin and with a look that is faintly ascetic; her face is narrow and delicate, her fine, light-brown hair caught back by a tortoiseshell comb. She is restless now, because she is being kept waiting. It is nearly two-thirty—a woman named Lola Parrish was to come at two o'clock to look at the apartment.

(3) She considers leaving a note and going out. The woman is late, after all, and besides, Sylvia is certain that Lola Parrish will not be a suitable person with whom to share the apartment. On the phone she had sounded too old, for one thing, her voice oddly flat and as deep as a man's. However, the moment for saying the apartment was no longer available slipped past, and Sylvia found herself agreeing to the two o'clock appointment. If she leaves now, as she has a perfect right to do, she can avoid the awkwardness of turning the woman away.

(4) Looking past the blue curtain, however, she sees the sky is not clear but veiled by a white haze, and the air is oppressively still. She knows that the haze and the stillness and heat are conditions that often precede a summer thunderstorm, one of the abrupt, swiftly descending electrical storms that have terrified her since she was a child. If a storm comes, she wants to be at home in her own place.

(5) She walks back to the center of the room, aware now that the idea of sharing the apartment, never appealing, born of necessity, has actually begun to repel her. Still, she knows she will have to become accustomed to the notion, because her savings are nearly gone and the small trust fund left her by her father is exhausted. She has a job, but it does not pay well, and, although she has considered seeking another (perhaps something connected with music—in her childhood she had played the flute and people had said she was gifted), lately she has found herself dragged down by a strange inertia.

(6) Besides, although her job pays poorly, it suits her. She is a typist in a natural history museum, in an office on the top floor, near the aviary. The man for whom she works, one of the curators, is rarely in, so Sylvia has the office to herself. The aviary consists of three enormous rooms, painted white, each with a high vaulted ceiling. The birds themselves, so beautifully mounted they seem alive, are displayed in elaborate dioramas. Behind glass, they perch in trees

with leaves of sculpted metal, appearing to soar through painted forests, above painted rivers and marshes. Everything is rendered in exquisite detail. And in her office there is a skylight. The location of the office, so near the open sky, suits her, too, because she is mildly claustrophobic.

20. Which of the following adjectives best describes Sylvia's mood as depicted in the story?
    a. anxious
    b. angry
    c. meditative
    d. serene

21. Based on the tone of the passage and the description of Sylvia at this moment, which of the following is the most likely reason Sylvia's job "suits her?"
    a. Her office is tastefully decorated.
    b. She is fond of her employer, the museum curator.
    c. She is musical and enjoys the singing of birds.
    d. She is able to work alone in a space that feels open.

22. When Sylvia looks out her window, the weather appears
    a. gloomy.
    b. ominous.
    c. springlike.
    d. bracing.

23. Based on the story, which of the following would most likely describe Sylvia's behavior in relationship to other people?
    a. distant
    b. overbearing
    c. dependent
    d. malicious

24. Which of the following is most likely the author's purpose in describing in detail the museum where Sylvia works?
   a. Everything in it, though beautiful and tasteful, seems frozen or removed from life and reflects some aspect of Sylvia's character.
   b. The fact that it is light and airy and filled with beautiful dioramas reflects Sylvia's youth and her wish for something better.
   c. Some part of the story, perhaps a love affair between Sylvia and her boss, will probably take place there.
   d. The killing and mounting of the beautiful birds will probably play an important part in the story.

Questions 25–31 are based on the following passage.

(1) The poet in Samuel Taylor Coleridge's "Kubla Khan" wakes from a dream or vision and announces that if people knew what he had seen they would shun him and cry out a warning:

> Beware, Beware!
> His flashing eyes, his floating hair
> Weave a circle round him thrice
> And close your eyes in holy dread,
> For he on honey-dew hath fed,
> And drunk the milk of Paradise.

Similarly, in his famous study of myth, *The Hero With a Thousand Faces*, Joseph Campbell writes about the archetypal hero who has ventured outside the boundaries of the village and, after many trials and adventures, has returned with the boon that will save or enlighten his fellows. Like Carl Jung, Campbell believes that the story of the hero is part of the collective unconscious of all humankind. He likens the returning hero to the sacred or tabooed personage described by James Frazier in *The Golden Bough*. Such an individual must, in many instances of myth, be insulated from the rest of society, "not merely for his own sake but for the sake of others; for since the virtue of holiness is, so to say, a powerful explosive which the smallest touch can detonate, it is necessary in the interest of the general safety to keep it within narrow bounds."

(2) Like Coleridge's poet, the returning hero of myth has been to a place of wonder and holiness. And, Campbell maintains, the hero, "to complete his adventure, must survive the impact of the world." He or she must return to the daylight world of ordinary human society, where he is apt to be regarded _____ as the object both of wonder and dread. As Coleridge's poem illustrates, the same fate can also befall the poet who has journeyed into the realm of imagination.

(3) There is _____ between the archetypal hero who has journeyed into the wilderness and the poet who has journeyed into the realm of imagination. Both places are dangerous and full of wonders, and both, at their deepest levels, are taken inward. They are journeys that take place into the kingdom of the mind. "The poets and philosophers before me discovered the unconscious," Sigmund Freud has said. It is into the unconscious that the poet and the hero of myth both venture. That world, writes Campbell, the "human kingdom, beneath the floor of the comparatively neat little dwelling that we call our consciousness, goes down into unsuspected Aladdin caves. There not only jewels but dangerous jinn abide. . . ."

25. Which of the following words would fit best into the blank in paragraph 2?
   a. suspiciously
   b. reluctantly
   c. unfairly
   d. ambivalently

26. Based on the passage, which of the following would best describe the hero's journey?
    a. wonderful
    b. terrifying
    c. awesome
    d. whimsical

27. The title of Campbell's book, *The Hero With a Thousand Faces*, is meant to convey
    a. the many villagers whose lives are changed by the story the hero has to tell.
    b. the fact that the hero journeys into many different imaginary countries.
    c. the universality of the myth of the hero who journeys into the wilderness.
    d. the many languages into which the myth of the hero has been translated.

28. Based on the passage, which of the following best describes the story that will likely be told by Campbell's returning hero and Frazier's sacred or tabooed personage?
    a. a radically mind-altering story
    b. a story that will terrify people to no good end
    c. a warning of catastrophe to come
    d. a story based on a dangerous lie

29. Which of the following is the most accurate definition of *boon* as the word is used in the first paragraph?
    a. gift
    b. blessing
    c. charm
    d. prize

30. The phrase that would most accurately fit into the blank in the first sentence of the third paragraph is
    a. much similarity.
    b. a wide gulf.
    c. long-standing conflict.
    d. an abiding devotion.

31. As mentioned at the end of the passage, "Aladdin's caves" are most likely to be found in
    a. the mountains.
    b. fairy tales.
    c. the fantasies of the hero.
    d. the unconscious mind.

Questions 32–36 are based on the following passage.

(1) Firefighters know that the dangers of motor-vehicle fires are too often overlooked. In the United States, one out of five fires involves motor vehicles, resulting each year in 600 deaths, 2,600 civilian injuries, and 1,200 injuries to firefighters. The reason for so many injuries and fatalities is that a vehicle can generate heat of up to 1,500° F. (The boiling point of water is 212° F and the cooking temperature for most foods is 350° F.)

(2) Because of the intense heat generated in a vehicle fire, parts of the car or truck may burst, causing debris to shoot great distances and turning bumpers, tire rims, drive shafts, axles, and even engine parts into lethal shrapnel. Gas tanks may rupture and spray highly flammable fuel. In addition, hazardous materials such as battery acid, even without burning, can cause serious injury.

(3) Vehicle fires can also produce toxic gases. Carbon monoxide, which is produced during a fire, is an odorless and colorless gas but in high concentrations is deadly. Firefighters must wear self-contained breathing devices and full protective fire-resistant gear when attempting to extinguish a vehicle fire.

32. The passage suggests that one reason firefighters wear self-contained breathing devices is to protect themselves against
    a. flying car parts.
    b. intense heat.
    c. flammable fuels.
    d. carbon monoxide.

33. The passage suggests that most injuries in motor-vehicle fires are caused by
   a. battery acid.
   b. odorless gases.
   c. extremely high temperatures.
   d. firefighters' mistakes.

34. The main focus of this passage is on
   a. how firefighters protect themselves.
   b. the dangers of motor-vehicle fires.
   c. the amount of heat generated in some fires.
   d. the dangers of odorless gases.

35. The cooking temperature for food (350° F) is most likely included in the passage mainly to show the reader
   a. at what point water boils.
   b. how hot motor-vehicle fires really are.
   c. why motor-vehicle fires produce toxic gases.
   d. why one out of five fires involves a motor vehicle.

36. One reason that firefighters must be aware of the possibility of carbon monoxide in motor-vehicle fires is that carbon monoxide
   a. is highly concentrated.
   b. cannot be protected against.
   c. can shoot great distances into the air.
   d. cannot be seen or smelled.

Questions 37–42 are based on the following passage.

(1) The composer Wolfgang Amadeus Mozart's remarkable musical talent was apparent even before most children can sing a simple nursery rhyme. Wolfgang's older sister Maria Anna, who the family called Nannerl, was learning the clavier, an early keyboard instrument, when her three-year-old brother took an interest in playing. As Nannerl later recalled, Wolfgang "often spent much time at the clavier, picking out thirds, which he was always striking, and his pleasure showed that it sounded good." Their father Leopold, an assistant concertmaster at the Salzburg Court, recognized his children's unique gifts and soon devoted himself to their musical education.

(2) Born in Salzburg, Austria, on January 27, 1756, Wolfgang was five when he learned his first musical composition—in less than half an hour. He quickly learned other pieces, and by age five composed his first original work. Leopold settled on a plan to take Nannerl and Wolfgang on tour to play before the European courts. Their first venture was to nearby Munich where the children played for Maximillian III Joseph, elector of Bavaria. Leopold soon set his sights on the capital of the Hapsburg Empire, Vienna. On their way to Vienna, the family stopped in Linz, where Wolfgang gave his first public concert. By this time, Wolfgang was not only a virtuoso harpsichord player but he had also mastered the violin. The audience at Linz was stunned by the six-year-old, and word of his genius soon traveled to Vienna. In a much-anticipated concert, the children appeared at the Schönbrunn Palace on October 13, 1762. They utterly charmed the emperor and empress.

(3) Following his success, Leopold was inundated with invitations for the children to play, for a fee. Leopold seized the opportunity and booked as many concerts as possible at courts throughout Europe. After the children performed at the major court in a region, other nobles competed to have the "miracle children of Salzburg" play a private concert in their homes. A concert could last three hours, and the children played at least two a day. Today, Leopold might be considered the worst kind of stage parent, but at the time it was not uncommon for prodigies to make extensive concert tours. Even so, it was an exhausting schedule for a child who was just past the age of needing an afternoon nap.

(4) Wolfgang fell ill on tour, and when the family returned to Salzburg on January 5, 1763,

Wolfgang spent his first week at home in bed with acute rheumatoid arthritis. In June, Leopold accepted an invitation for the children to play at Versailles, the lavish palace built by Loius XIV, king of France. Wolfgang did not see his home in Salzburg for another three years. When they weren't performing, the Mozart children were likely to be found bumping along the rutted roads in an unheated carriage. Wolfgang passed the long uncomfortable hours in the imaginary Kingdom of Back, of which he was king. He became so engrossed in the intricacies of his make-believe court that he persuaded a family servant to make a map showing all the cities, villages, and towns over which he reigned.

(5) The king of Back was also busy composing. Wolfgang completed his first symphony at age nine and published his first sonatas that same year. Before the family returned to Salzburg, Wolfgang had played for, and amazed, the heads of the French and British royal families. He had also been plagued with numerous illnesses. Despite Wolfgang and Nannerl's arduous schedule and international renown, the family's finances were often strained. The pattern established in his childhood would be the template of the rest of his short life. Wolfgang Amadeus Mozart toiled constantly, was lauded for his genius, suffered from illness, and struggled financially, until he died at age 35. The remarkable child prodigy who more than fulfilled his potential was buried in an unmarked grave, as was the custom at the time, in Vienna suburb.

37. The primary purpose of the passage is to
  a. illustrate the early career and formative experiences of a musical prodigy.
  b. describe the classical music scene in the eighteenth century.
  c. uncover the source of Wolfgang Amadeus Mozart's musical genius.
  d. prove the importance of starting a musical instrument an early age.

38. According to the passage, Wolfgang became interested in music because
  a. his father thought it would be profitable.
  b. he had a natural talent.
  c. he saw his sister learning to play.
  d. he came from a musical family.

39. What was the consequence of Wolfgang's first public appearance?
  a. He charmed the emperor and empress of Hapsburg.
  b. Leopold set his sights on Vienna.
  c. Word of Wolfgang's genius spread to the capital.
  d. He mastered the violin.

40. The author's attitude toward Leopold Mozart can best be characterized as
  a. vehement condemnation.
  b. mild disapproval.
  c. glowing admiration.
  d. incredulity.

41. In the second sentence of paragraph 4, the word *lavish* most nearly means
  a. wasteful.
  b. clean.
  c. extravagant.
  d. beautiful.

42. The author uses the anecdote about Mozart's Kingdom of Back to illustrate
  a. Mozart's admiration for the composer Johann Sebastian Bach.
  b. the role imagination plays in musical composition.
  c. that Mozart was mentally unstable.
  d. that Mozart's only friends were imaginary people and family servants.

► Section 2: Mathematics

1. A salesman drives 2,052 miles in 6 days, stopping at 2 towns each day. How many miles does he average between stops?
  a. 171
  b. 342
  c. 513
  d. 684

2. A school cafeteria manager spends $540 on silverware. If a place setting includes 1 knife, 1 fork, and 2 spoons, how many place settings did the manager buy?
  a. 90
  b. 108
  c. 135
  d. There is not enough information to solve this problem.

Question 3 is based on the following diagram.

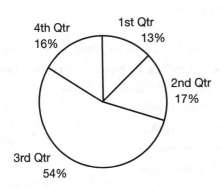

Sales for 2004

3. The pie chart above shows quarterly sales for Cool-Air's air-conditioning units. Which of the following combinations contributed 70% to the total?
  a. 1st and 2nd quarters
  b. 3rd and 4th quarters
  c. 2nd and 3rd quarters
  d. 2nd and 4th quarters

4. An office uses 2 dozen pencils and $3\frac{1}{2}$ reams of paper each week. If pencils cost 5 cents each and a ream of paper costs $7.50, how much does it cost to supply the office for a week?
  a. $7.55
  b. $12.20
  c. $26.25
  d. $27.45

5. What is the estimated product when 157 and 817 are rounded to the nearest hundred and multiplied?
  a. 160,000
  b. 180,000
  c. 16,000
  d. 80,000

6. Mr. James Rossen is just beginning a computer consulting firm and has purchased the following equipment:

3 telephone sets, each costing	$125
2 computers, each costing	$1,300
2 computer monitors, each costing	$950
1 printer costing	$600
1 answering machine costing	$50

Mr. Rossen is reviewing his finances. What should he write as the total value of the equipment he has purchased so far?
  a. $3,025
  b. $3,275
  c. $5,400
  d. $5,525

7. Roger earned $24,355 this year, and $23,000 the year before. To the nearest $100, what did Roger earn in the past two years?
  a. $47,300
  b. $47,400
  c. $47,455
  d. $47,500

8. A cafeteria has three different options for lunch.
For $2, a customer can get either a sandwich or
two pieces of fruit.
For $3, a customer can get a sandwich and one
piece of fruit.
For $4, a customer can get either two sand-
wiches, or a sandwich and two pieces of fruit.

If Jan has $6 to pay for lunch for her and
her husband, which of the following is NOT a
possible combination?
a. three sandwiches and one piece of fruit
b. two sandwiches and two pieces of fruit
c. one sandwich and four pieces of fruit
d. three sandwiches and no fruit

9. Benito earns $12.50 for each hour that he works.
If Benito works 8.5 hours per day, five days a
week, without any overtime, how much does he
earn in a week?
a. $100.00
b. $106.25
c. $406.00
d. $531.25

Question 10 is based on the following diagram.

**PRODUCTION OF TRACTORS FOR
THE MONTH OF APRIL**

FACTORY	APRIL OUTPUT
Dallas	450
Houston	425
Lubbock	
Amarillo	345
TOTAL	1,780

10. What was Lubbock's production in the month of
April?
a. 345
b. 415
c. 540
d. 560

11. Melissa can grade five of her students' papers in
an hour. Joe can grade four of the same papers in
an hour. If Melissa works for three hours grad-
ing, and Joe works for two hours, what percentage of the 50 students' papers will be graded?
a. 44%
b. 46%
c. 52%
d. 54%

12. Three students take a spelling test. Anthony takes
his test in 20 minutes. Alison finishes in 17 minutes, and Gracie finishes in just 14 minutes. What
is the average time for the three students?
a. 20 minutes
b. 19 minutes
c. 17 minutes
d. 14 minutes

13. A steel box has a base length of 12 inches and a
width of 5 inches. If the box is 10 inches tall,
what is the total volume of the box?
a. 580 cubic inches
b. 600 cubic inches
c. 640 cubic inches
d. 720 cubic inches

14. An average of 90% is needed on five tests to
receive an A in a class. If a student received scores
of 95, 85, 88, and 84 on the first four tests, what
score will the student need to achieve on the fifth
test to get an A?
a. 94
b. 96
c. 98
d. 99

15. What is the perimeter of a pentagon with three sides of 3 inches, and the remaining sides 5 inches long?
   a. 19 inches
   b. 14 inches
   c. 12 inches
   d. 9 inches

16. What is the result of multiplying 11 by 0.032?
   a. 0.032
   b. 0.0352
   c. 0.32
   d. 0.352

17. If a school buys three computers at a, b, and c dollars each, and the school gets a discount of 90%, which expression would determine the average price paid by the school?
   a. $0.9 \times \frac{(a+b+c)}{3}$
   b. $\frac{(a+b+c)}{0.9}$
   c. $(a+b+c) \times 0.9$
   d. $\frac{(a+3b+c)}{3}$

Question 18 is based on the following diagram.

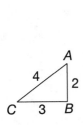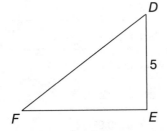

18. If the two triangles in the diagram are similar, with angle A equal to angle D, what is the perimeter of triangle DEF?
   a. 12
   b. 21
   c. 22.5
   d. 24.75

19. Roger wants to know if he has enough money to purchase several items. He needs three heads of lettuce, which cost $.99 each, and two boxes of cereal, which cost $3.49 each. He uses the expression $(3 \times \$0.99) + (2 \times \$3.49)$ to calculate how much the items will cost. Which of the following expressions could also be used?
   a. $3 \times (\$3.49 + \$.99) - \$3.49$
   b. $3 \times (\$3.49 + \$.99)$
   c. $(2 + 3) \times (\$3.49 + \$.99)$
   d. $(2 \times 3) + (\$3.49 \times \$.99)$

20. Rosa finds the average of her three most recent golf scores by using the following expression, where a, b, and c are the three scores: $\frac{(a+b+c)}{3} \times 100$. Which of the following would also determine the average of her scores?
   a. $\left(\frac{a}{3} + \frac{b}{3} + \frac{c}{3}\right) \times 100$
   b. $\frac{a+b+c}{\frac{100}{3}}$
   c. $(a+b+c) \times \frac{3}{100}$
   d. $\frac{(a \times b \times c)}{3} + 100$

21. What is $\frac{2}{3}$ divided by $\frac{5}{12}$?
   a. $\frac{13}{5}$
   b. $\frac{15}{18}$
   c. $\frac{17}{36}$
   d. $\frac{15}{6}$

22. A 15-serving recipe of a casserole must be increased by 20%. What is the new serving size?
   a. 17 servings
   b. 18 servings
   c. 20 servings
   d. 30 servings

23. City High School basketball coach Donna Green earns $26,000 a year. If she receives a 4.5% salary increase, how much will she earn?
   a. $26,110
   b. $26,450
   c. $27,170
   d. $27,260

24. In the Pinebrook school district last year, 220 students were vaccinated for measles, mumps, and rubella. Of those, 60% reported that they had the flu at some time in their lives. How many students had not had the flu previously?
   a. 36
   b. 55
   c. 88
   d. 126

25. Of the 1,125 teachers in a study of bilingual education, 135 speak fluent Spanish. What percentage of the group of teachers in the study speaks fluent Spanish?
   a. 12%
   b. 7.3%
   c. 8.3%
   d. 9.3%

Questions 26 and 27 are based on the following diagram.

MAJOR CAUSES OF HOME FIRES IN THE PREVIOUS 4-YEAR PERIOD

CAUSE	FIRES (% OF TOTAL)	CIVILIAN DEATHS (% OF TOTAL)
Heating equipment	161,500 (27.5%)	770 (16.8%)
Cooking equipment	104,800 (17.8%)	350 (7.7%)
Incendiary, suspicious	65,400 (11.1%)	620 (13.6%)
Electrical equipment	45,700 (7.8%)	440 (9.6%)
Other equipment	43,000 (7.3%)	240 (5.3%)
Smoking materials	39,300 (6.7%)	1,320 (28.9%)
Appliances, air conditioning	36,200 (6.2%)	120 (2.7%)
Exposure and other heat	28,600 (4.8%)	191 (4.2%)
Open flame	27,200 (4.6%)	130 (2.9%)
Child play	26,900 (4.6%)	370 (8.1%)
Natural causes	9,200 (1.6%)	10 (0.2%)

26. What is the percentage of the total fires caused by electrical equipment and other equipment combined?
a. 7.8%
b. 14.9%
c. 15.1%
d. 29.9%

27. Of the following causes, which one has the highest ratio of total fires to percentage of deaths?
a. heating equipment
b. smoking materials
c. exposure and other heat
d. child play

28. The snack machine in the teachers' lounge accepts only quarters. Candy bars cost 25¢, packages of peanuts cost 75¢, and cans of cola cost 50¢. How many quarters are needed to buy two candy bars, one package of peanuts, and one can of cola?
a. 8
b. 7
c. 6
d. 5

29. All of the rooms on the top floor of a government building are rectangular, with 8-foot ceilings. One room is 9 feet wide by 11 feet long. What is the combined area of the four walls, including doors and windows?
a. 99 square feet
b. 160 square feet
c. 320 square feet
d. 72 square feet

30. A child has a temperature of 40° C. What is the child's temperature in degrees Fahrenheit? $F = \frac{9}{5}C + 32$.
a. 101° F
b. 102° F
c. 103° F
d. 104° F

31. Mr. Tupper is purchasing gifts for his family. He stops to consider what else he has to buy. A quick mental inventory of his shopping bag so far reveals the following:

1 cashmere sweater valued at	$260
3 diamond bracelets, each valued at	$365
1 computer game valued at	$78
1 cameo brooch valued at	$130

Later, having coffee in the Food Court, he suddenly remembers that he has purchased only 2 diamond bracelets, not 3, and that the cashmere sweater was on sale for $245. What is the total value of the gifts Mr. Tupper has purchased so far?
a. $1,198
b. $1,183
c. $975
d. $833

Question 32 is based on the following table.

SURVEY REGARDING READING HABITS

BOOKS PER MONTH	PERCENTAGE
0	13
1–3	27
4–6	32
>6	28

32. A recent survey polled 2,500 people about their reading habits. The results are shown in the table above. According to the table, how many people surveyed had read books in the last month?
a. 700
b. 1,800
c. 1,825
d. 2,175

Questions 33 and 34 are based on the following list of ingredients needed to make 16 brownies.

> *Deluxe Brownies*
> $\frac{2}{3}$ cup butter
> 5 squares (1 ounce each) unsweetened
>   chocolate
> $1\frac{1}{2}$ cups sugar
> 2 teaspoons vanilla
> 2 eggs
> 1 cup flour

33. How much sugar is needed to make 8 brownies?
- **a.** $\frac{3}{4}$ cup
- **b.** 3 cups
- **c.** $\frac{2}{3}$ cup
- **d.** $\frac{5}{8}$ cup

34. What is the greatest number of brownies that can be made if the baker has only 1 cup of butter?
- **a.** 12
- **b.** 16
- **c.** 24
- **d.** 28

35. One lap on a particular outdoor track measures a quarter of a mile around. To run a total of three and a half miles, how many complete laps must a person complete?
- **a.** 14
- **b.** 18
- **c.** 10
- **d.** 7

36. On Monday, a kindergarten class uses $2\frac{1}{4}$ pounds of modeling clay the first hour, $4\frac{5}{8}$ pounds of modeling clay the second hour, and $\frac{1}{2}$ pound of modeling clay the third hour. How many pounds of clay does the class use during the three hours on Monday?
- **a.** $6\frac{3}{8}$
- **b.** $6\frac{7}{8}$
- **c.** $7\frac{1}{4}$
- **d.** $7\frac{3}{8}$

37. A floor plan is drawn to scale so that one quarter inch represents 2 feet. If a hall on the plan is 4 inches long, how long will the actual hall be when it is built?
- **a.** 12 feet
- **b.** 18 feet
- **c.** 24 feet
- **d.** 32 feet

38. Student track team members have to buy running shoes at the full price of $84.50, but those who were also team members last term get a 15% discount. Those who have been team members for at least three terms get an additional 10% off the discounted price. How much does a student who has been a track team member at least three terms have to pay for shoes?
- **a.** $63.38
- **b.** $64.65
- **c.** $65.78
- **d.** $71.83

Question 39 is based on the following diagram.

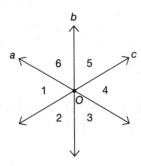

39. In the diagram above, lines *a*, *b* and *c* intersect at point *O*. Which of the following are NOT adjacent angles?
a. ∠1 and ∠6
b. ∠1 and ∠4
c. ∠4 and ∠5
d. ∠2 and ∠3

40. There are 176 men and 24 women in the local chess club. What percentage of the members is women?
a. 6%
b. 12%
c. 14%
d. 16%

41. The basal metabolic rate (BMR) is the rate at which our body uses calories. The BMR for a man in his twenties is about 1,700 calories per day. If 204 of those calories should come from protein, about what percent of this man's diet should be protein?
a. 1.2%
b. 8.3%
c. 12%
d. 16%

42. The condition Down syndrome occurs in about 1 in 1,500 children when the mothers are in their twenties. About what percent of all children born to mothers in their twenties are likely to have Down syndrome?
a. 0.0067%
b. 0.067%
c. 0.67%
d. 6.7%

43. If a population of cells grows from 10 to 320 in a period of 5 hours, what is the rate of growth?
a. It doubles its numbers every half hour.
b. It doubles its numbers every hour.
c. It triples its numbers every hour.
d. It doubles its numbers every two hours.

44. A certain water pollutant is unsafe at a level of 20 ppm (parts per million). A city's water supply now contains 50 ppm of this pollutant. What percentage of improvement will make the water safe?
a. 30%
b. 40%
c. 50%
d. 60%

45. An insurance policy pays 80% of the first $20,000 of a certain patient's medical expenses, 60% of the next $40,000, and 40% of the $40,000 after that. If the patient's total medical bill is $92,000, how much will the policy pay?
a. $36,800
b. $49,600
c. $52,800
d. $73,600

Question 46 is based on the following diagram.

RECYCLER	ALUMINUM	CARDBOARD	GLASS	PLASTIC
X	$\frac{.06}{\text{pound}}$	$\frac{.03}{\text{pound}}$	$\frac{.08}{\text{pound}}$	$\frac{.02}{\text{pound}}$
Y	$\frac{.07}{\text{pound}}$	$\frac{.04}{\text{pound}}$	$\frac{.07}{\text{pound}}$	$\frac{.03}{\text{pound}}$

46. If you take recyclables to whichever recycler will pay the most, what is the greatest amount of money you could get for 2,200 pounds of aluminum, 1,400 pounds of cardboard, 3,100 pounds of glass, and 900 pounds of plastic?
a. $409
b. $440
c. $447
d. $485

Question 47 is based on the following diagram.

BRAND	W	X	Y	Z
PRICE	0.21	0.48	0.56	0.96
WEIGHT IN OUNCES	6	15	20	32

47. Which of the brands listed on the table is the least expensive?
a. W
b. X
c. Y
d. Z

48. To lower a fever of 105°, ice packs are applied for 1 minute and then removed for 5 minutes before being applied again. Each application lowers the fever by half a degree. How long will it take to lower the fever to 99°?
a. 36 minutes
b. 1 hour
c. 1 hour and 12 minutes
d. 1 hour and 15 minutes

▶ Section 3: Writing (Part A—Multiple-Choice)

Questions 1–3 are based on the following passage.

(1) As soon as she sat down on the airplane, Rachel almost began to regret telling the travel agent that she wanted an exotic and romantic vacation; after sifting through a stack of brochures, the agent and her decided the most exotic vacation she could afford was a week in Rio. (2) As the plane hurtled toward Rio de Janeiro, she read the information on Carnival that was in the pocket of the seat in front of hers. (3) The very definition made her shiver: "from the Latin *carnavale,* meaning a farewell to the flesh." (4) She was searching for excitement, but had no intention of bidding her skin good-bye. (5) "Carnival," the brochure informed her, originated in Europe in the Middle Ages and served as a break from the requirements of daily life and society. (6) Most of all, it allowed the hard-working and desperately poor serfs the opportunity to ridicule their wealthy and normally humorless masters." (7) Rachel, a middle manager in a computer firm, wasn't entirely sure whether she was a serf or a master. (8) Should she be making fun, or would others be mocking her? (9) She was strangely relieved when the plane landed, as though her fate were decided.

1. Which of the following changes needs to be made to the above passage?
a. Part 6: Italicize *serfs.*
b. Part 2: Insert *the* before *Carnival.*
c. Part 5: Change *Middle Ages* to *middle ages.*
d. Part 9: Change *were* to *was.*

2. Which of the following numbered parts contains a nonstandard use of a pronoun?
a. Part 5
b. Part 7
c. Part 1
d. Part 8

3. Which of the following changes needs to be made to Part 5 of the passage?
a. Insert quotation marks before *originated*.
b. Remove the comma after *her*.
c. Remove the quotation marks after *Carnival*.
d. Insert quotation marks after *society*.

Questions 4–6 are based on the following passage.

(1) The Advisory Committee of the State Police has issued certain guidelines for establishing a roadblock in order to identify and apprehend drunk drivers. (2) Motorists must be able to see that a roadblock is ahead and that cars are being stopped. (3) Stops cannot be established, for example, just over a hill or around a curve. (4) Among these guidelines is the directive that the roadblock must be established in a location that gives motorists a clear view of the stop. (5) A second guideline mandates that a roadblock must display visible signs of police authority. (6) Therefore, uniformed officers in marked patrol cars should primarily staff the roadblock. (7) Plainclothes officers may <u>supplicant</u> the staff at a roadblock, but the initial stop and questioning of motorists should be conducted by uniformed officers. (8) In addition to the officers conducting the motorist stops, he or she should be present to conduct field sobriety tests on suspect drivers. (9) Finally, a command observation officer must also be present to coordinate the roadblock.

4. Which of the following changes would best clarify the order of ideas in the paragraph?
a. Delete Part 3.
b. Reverse the order of Parts 2 and 4.
c. Delete Part 8.
d. Reverse the order of Parts 5 and 6.

5. Which of the following numbered parts contains a nonstandard use of a pronoun?
a. Part 4
b. Part 5
c. Part 2
d. Part 8

6. Which of the following words or phrases should replace the underlined word in Part 7 of the paragraph?
a. supplement
b. compliment
c. supply
d. round up

Questions 7–9 are based on the following passage.

(1) Whether or not you can accomplish a specific goal or meet a specific deadline depends first on how much time you need to get the job done. (2) What should you do when the demands of the job <u>precede</u> the time you have available. (3) The best approach is to correctly divide the project into smaller pieces. (4) Different goals will have to be divided in different ways, but one seemingly unrealistic goal can often be accomplished by working on several smaller, more reasonable goals.

7. Which of the following numbered parts has an error in the verb infinitive?
a. Part 1
b. Part 2
c. Part 3
d. Part 4

8. Which of the following words should replace the underlined word in Part 2 of the passage?
a. exceed
b. succeed
c. supersede
d. proceed

9. Which of the following numbered parts in the passage needs a question mark?
a. Part 2
b. Part 3
c. Part 1
d. Part 4

Questions 10–12 are based on the following passage.

(1) Typically people think of genius, whether it manifests in Mozart composing symphonies at age five or Einstein's discovery of relativity, as having quality not just of the divine, but also of the eccentric. (2) People see genius as a "good" abnormality; moreover, they think of genius as a completely unpredictable abnormality. (3) Until recently, psychologists regarded the quirks of genius as too erratic to describe intelligibly; however, Anna Findley's ground-breaking study uncovers predictable patterns in the biographies of geniuses. (4) Despite the regularity of these patterns, they could still support the common belief that there is a kind of supernatural intervention in the lives of unusually talented men and women. (5) _____.
(6) For example, Findley shows that all geniuses experience three intensely productive periods in their lives, one of which always occurs shortly before

their deaths; this is true whether the genius lives to nineteen or ninety.

10. Which of the following sentences, if inserted in the blank numbered Part 5, would best focus the main idea of the passage?
a. These patterns are normal in the lives of all geniuses.
b. Eerily, the patterns themselves seem to be determined by predestination rather than mundane habit.
c. No matter how much scientific evidence the general public is presented with, people still like to think of genius as unexplainable.
d. Since people think of genius as a "good" abnormality, they do not really care what causes it.

11. Which of the following changes needs to be made to the passage?
a. Part 3: Change *too* to *to*.
b. Part 6: Change *geniuses* to *geniuses'*.
c. Part 1: Change *Mozart* to *Mozart's*.
d. Part 4: Change *there* to *their*.

12. Which of the following numbered parts contains a nonstandard use of a pronoun?
a. Part 4
b. Part 3
c. Part 6
d. Part 2

Questions 13–15 are based on the following passage.

(1) The English-language premiere of Samuel Beckett's play *Waiting for Godot* took place in London in August 1955. (2) *Godot* is an avant-garde play with only five characters (not including Mr. Godot, who never arrives) and a minimal setting—one rock and one bare tree. (3) The play has two acts, the second act repeating what little action occurs in the first

with few changes: the tree, for instance, acquires one leaf. (4) Famously, the critic Vivian Mercer has described Godot as "a play in which nothing happens twice." (5) Opening night critics and playgoers, greeted the play with bafflement and derision. (6) Beckett's play managed to free the theater from the grasp of detailed naturalism. (7) The line, "Nothing happens, nobody comes, nobody goes. It's awful," was met by a loud rejoinder of "Hear! Hear!" from an audience member. (8) Despite the bad notices, director Peter Hall believed so passionately in the play that his fervor convinced the backers to refrain from closing the play at least until the Sunday reviews were published. (9) Harold Hobson's review in *The Sunday Times* managed to save the play, for Hobson had the vision to recognize the play for what it history has proven it to be—a revolutionary moment in theater.

13. Which of the following changes should be made in order to improve the focus and flow of the passage?
   a. Reverse the order of Parts 6 and 7.
   b. Part 3: remove the phrase, *the tree, for instance, acquires one leaf.*
   c. Remove Part 9.
   d. Remove Part 6.

14. Which of the following changes needs to be made to the passage?
   a. Part 2: Italicize *Mr. Godot.*
   b. Part 2: Do not italicize *Godot.*
   c. Part 4: Italicize *Godot.*
   d. Part 9: Do not italicize *The Sunday Times.*

15. From which of the following numbered parts should a comma be removed?
   a. Part 5
   b. Part 9
   c. Part 3
   d. Part 4

Questions 16 and 17 are based on the following passage.

(1) The Woodstock Music and Art Fair—better known to its participants, and to history simply as "Woodstock"—should have been a colossal failure. (2) Just a month prior to its August 15, 1969 opening the fair's organizers were informed by the council of Wallkill, New York, that permission to hold the festival was withdrawn. (3) Amazingly, not only was a new site found, but word got out to the public of the fair's new location. (4) At the new site, fences that were supposed to facilitate ticket collection never materialized, all attempts at gathering tickets were abandoned. (5) Crowd estimates of 30,000 kept rising; by the end of the three days, some estimated the crowd at 500,000. (6) And then, on opening night, it began to rain. (7) Off and on, throughout all three days, huge summer storms rolled over the gathering. (8) In spite of these problems, most people think of Woodstock not only as a fond memory but as the defining moment for an entire generation.

16. In which of the following numbered parts should a comma be inserted?
   a. Part 1
   b. Part 2
   c. Part 3
   d. Part 4

17. Which of the following sentences is a run-on?
   a. Part 1
   b. Part 2
   c. Part 3
   d. Part 4

Questions 18–20 are based on the following passage.

(1) Most criminals do not suffer from anti-social personality disorder; however, nearly all persons with this disorder have been in trouble with the law. (2) Sometimes labeled "sociopaths," they are a grim

problem for society. (3) Their crimes range from con games to murder, and they are set apart by what appears to be a complete lack of conscience. (4) Often attractive and charming, and always inordinately self-confident, the sociopath nevertheless demonstrates a disturbing emotional shallowness, as if he were born without a <u>conscious</u>—a faculty as vital as sight or hearing. (5) These individuals are not legally insane, nor do they suffer from the distortions of thought associated with mental illness; however, some experts believed they are mentally ill. (6) If so, it is an illness that is exceptionally resistant to treatment, particularly since these individuals have a marked inability to learn from the past. (7) It is this final trait that makes them a special problem for law enforcement officials. (8) Their ability to mimic true emotion enables them to convince prison officials, judges, and psychiatrists that they feel remorse and have undergone rehabilitation.

18. Which of the following changes would best enhance the logical development of ideas in the passage?
   a. Remove the word *nevertheless* from Part 4.
   b. Combine Parts 1 and 2 into one sentence.
   c. Reverse the order of Parts 7 and 8.
   d. Remove Part 7.

19. Which of the following words should replace the underlined word in Part 4 of the passage?
   a. conscience
   b. consciousness
   c. ego
   d. conscientious

20. Which of the following changes needs to be made to the passage?
   a. Part 4: Change *were* to *was*.
   b. Part 5: Change *believed* to *believe*.
   c. Part 7: Change *them* to *him or her*.
   d. Part 8: Change *have* to *had*.

Questions 21 and 22 are based on the following passage.

(1) Bus operators driving buses that have wheelchair lifts are required to become familiar with wheelchair tie-down system installed in these buses. (2) After a passenger in a wheelchair enters the bus, the driver will fold up one of the front, sideways seats, and the passenger will position his or her wheelchair at the tie-downs. (3) One strap of the tie-down should be attached to each corner of the wheelchair frame. (4) Straps should not be attached to the wheelchair pedals because they may come loose. (5) The passenger should also set the brakes on the wheelchair. (6) Seat belts should be inserted under, finally, the arms of the wheelchair and fastened across the passenger's lap. (7) Most passengers in wheelchairs are familiar with the tie-down system, but it is the bus operator's responsibility to make sure the wheelchair is secured properly.

21. Which of the following numbered parts contains a misplaced modifier?
   a. Part 7
   b. Part 2
   c. Part 4
   d. Part 6

22. Which of the following changes needs to be made to the passage?
   a. Part 7: Remove the word *the* after *is*.
   b. Part 1: Insert the word *the* after *have*.
   c. Part 1: Insert the word *the* after *with*.
   d. Part 2: Remove the word *the* after *enters*.

Questions 23 and 24 are based on the following passage.

(1) A light rain was falling. (2) He drove home by his usual route. (3) It was a drive he had taken a thousand times; still, he did not know why, as he passed the park near their home, he should so suddenly and vividly picture the small pond that lay at the center

of it. (4) In winter this pond was frozen over, and he had taken his daughter Abigail there when she was small and tried to teach her how to skate. (5) She hadn't been able to catch on, and so after two or three lessons Abigail and him had given up the idea. (6) Now there came into his mind an image of such clarity it caused him to draw in his breath sharply; an image of Abigail gliding toward him on her new Christmas skates, going much faster than she should have been.

23. Which of the following changes needs to be made to the passage?
a. Part 6: Change the semicolon to a colon.
b. Part 4: Remove the word *and*.
c. Part 3: Change the semicolon to a comma.
d. Part 5: Change the comma to a semicolon.

24. Which of the following changes needs to be made to the passage?
a. Part 4: Remove the comma after *over*.
b. Part 6: Replace *Christmas* with *christmas'*.
c. Part 5: Change *him* to *he*.
d. Part 3: Replace *their* with *there*.

Questions 25–27 are based on the following passage.

(1) If a building is to be left in a safe condition after a fire is extinguished, firefighters must search for hidden fires that might <u>re-ignite</u>. (2) Typically this process known as overhaul, begins in the area of actual fire involvement. (3) Before searching for hidden fires; however, firefighters must first determine the condition of the building.

(4) The fire's intensity and the amount of water used to fight the fire are both factors that affect a building. (5) Fire can burn away floor joists and weaken roof trusses. (6) Heat from the fire can weaken concrete and the mortar in wall joints; heat can also <u>elongate</u> steel roof supports. (7) Excess water can add dangerous weight to floors and walls.

(8) Once it has been determined that it is <u>just fine</u> to enter a building, the process of overhauling begins. (9) Firefighters can often detect hidden fires by looking for discoloration, peeling paint, cracked plaster, and smoke emissions; by feeling walls and floors with the back of the hand; by listening for popping, cracking, and hissing sounds; and by using electronic sensors to detect <u>heat variance.</u>

25. Which of the underlined words or phrases in the passage should be replaced by more effective or appropriate words?
a. just fine
b. heat variance
c. elongate
d. re-ignite

26. Which of the following numbered parts contains nonstandard punctuation?
a. Part 8
b. Part 6
c. Part 9
d. Part 3

27. Which of the following changes needs to be made to the passage?
a. Part 2: Insert a comma after *process*.
b. Part 9: Remove the comma after *paint*.
c. Part 6: Replace the semicolon with a comma.
d. Part 9: Replace all the semicolons with commas.

Questions 28 and 29 are based on the following passage.

(1) The Competitive Civil Service system is designed to give candidates fair and equal treatment and ensure that federal applicants are hired based on objective criteria. (2) Hiring has to be based solely on a candidate's knowledge, skills, and abilities (which you'll sometimes see abbreviated as KSA), and not on external factors such as race, religion, sex, and so

on. (3) Whereas employers in the private sector can hire employees for subjective reasons, federal employers must be able to justify his decision with objective evidence that the candidate is qualified.

28. Which if the following numbered parts lacks parallelism?
   a. Part 2
   b. Part 3
   c. Parts 2 and 3
   d. Part 1

29. Which of the following numbered parts has an error in pronoun agreement?
   a. Part 1
   b. Part 2
   c. Part 3
   d. Parts 2 and 3

Questions 30–32 are based on the following passage.

(1) Heat exhaustion, generally characterized by clammy skin, fatigue, nausea, dizziness, profuse perspiration, and sometimes fainting, resulting from an inadequate intake of water and the loss of fluids. (2) First aid treatment for this condition includes having the victim lie down, raising the feet 8–12 inches, applying cool, wet cloths to the skin, and giving the victim sips of salt water (1 teaspoon per glass, half a glass every 15 minutes) over the period of an hour. (3) _____.

   (4) Heat stroke is much more serious; it is an immediate life-threatening condition. (5) The characteristics of heat stroke are a high body temperature (which may reach 106° F or more); a rapid pulse; hot, dry skin; and a blocked sweating mechanism. (6) Victims of this condition may be unconscious, and first aid measures should be directed at cooling the body quickly. (7) Heat stroke often occurs in poor people in urban areas. (8) The victim should be placed in a tub of cold water or repeatedly sponged with cool water until his or her temperature is lowered sufficiently. (9) Fans or air conditioners will also help with the cooling process. (10) Care should be taken, however, not to chill the victim too much once his or her temperature is below 102° F.

30. Which of the following sentences, if inserted into the blank numbered Part 3 in the passage, would best aid the transition of thought between the first and second paragraph?
   a. Heat exhaustion is a relatively unusual condition in northern climates.
   b. The typical victims of heat stroke are the poor and elderly who cannot afford air conditioning even on the hottest days of summer.
   c. Heat exhaustion is never fatal, although it can cause damage to internal organs if it strikes an elderly victim.
   d. Air conditioning units, electric fans, and cool baths can lower the numbers of people who suffer heat stroke each year in the United States.

31. Which of the following numbered parts draws attention away from the main idea of the second paragraph of the passage?
   a. Part 6
   b. Part 10
   c. Part 8
   d. Part 7

32. Which of the following numbered parts contains a nonstandard sentence?
   a. Part 8
   b. Part 1
   c. Part 5
   d. Part 3

Questions 33 and 34 are based on the following passage.

(1) Theodore Roosevelt <u>were</u> born with asthma and poor eyesight. (2) Yet this sickly child later won fame as a political leader, Rough Rider, and hero of the common people. (3) To conquer his handicaps, Teddy trained in a gym and became a light-weight boxer at Harvard. (4) Out west, he hunted buffalo and ran a cattle ranch. (5) He was civil service reformer in the east and also a police commissioner. (6) He became President McKinley's Assistant Navy Secretary during the Spanish-American War. (7) Also, he led a charge of cavalry Rough Riders up San Juan Hill in Cuba. (8) After achieving fame, he became Governor of New York and went on to become the Vice-President.

33. Which of the following sentences represents the best revision of Part 5?
   a. Back east he became a civil service reformer and police commissioner.
   b. A civil service reformer and police commissioner was part of his job in the east.
   c. A civil service reformer and police commissioner were parts of his job in the east.
   d. His job of civil service reformer and police commissioner were his jobs in the east.

34. Which of the following should be used in place of the underlined verb in Part 1 of the passage?
   a. will be
   b. are
   c. is
   d. was

Questions 35 and 36 are based on the following passage.

(1) Charles Darwin was born in 1809 at Shrewsbury England. (2) He was a biologist whose famous theory of evolution is important to philosophy for the effects it has had about the nature of man. (3) After many years of careful study, Darwin attempted to show that higher species had come into existence as a result of the gradual transformation of lower species; and that the process of transformation could be explained through the selective effect of the natural environment upon organisms. (4) He concluded that the principles of *natural selection and survival of the fittest* govern all life. (5) Darwin's explanation of these principles is that because of the food supply problem, the young born to any species complete for survival. (6) Those young that survive to produce the next generation tend to embody favorable natural changes which are then passed on by heredity. (7) His major work that contained these theories is *On the Origin of Species* written in 1859. Many religious opponents condemned this work.

35. Which of the following corrections should be made in punctuation?
   a. Part 4: Insert a comma before *and*.
   b. Part 3: Delete the comma after *study*.
   c. Part 2: Insert quotation marks around *nature of man*.
   d. Part 1: Insert a comma after *Shrewsbury*.

36. In Part 7 *On the Origin of Species* is italicized because it is
   a. a short story.
   b. the title of a book.
   c. the name of the author.
   d. copyrighted.

Question 37 is based on the following passage.

(1) Herbert was enjoying the cool, bright fall afternoon. (2) Walking down the street, red and yellow leaves crunched satisfyingly under his new school shoes.

37. Which of the following is the best revision of the passage?
  a. Herbert was enjoying the cool bright fall afternoon. Walking down the street red and yellow leaves crunched satisfyingly under his new school shoes.
  b. Herbert was enjoying the cool, bright fall afternoon. He was walking down the street, red and yellow leaves crunched satisfyingly under his new school shoes.
  c. Herbert was enjoying the cool, bright fall afternoon. Walking down the street, he crunched red and yellow leaves satisfyingly under his new school shoes.
  d. Herbert was enjoying the cool, bright fall afternoon. Walking down the street, red and yellow leaves were crunched satisfyingly under his new school shoes.

Questions 38–40 are based on the following passage.

(1) The building in which Howard Davis was to teach his undergraduate evening course, Interpretation of Poetry, was Renwick Hall, in the General Sciences Building. (2) Markham Hall, which housed the English Department offices and classrooms, was to be closed all summer for renovation.

(3) Howard's classroom was in the basement. (4) The shadowy corridor that <u>led</u> back to it was lined with glass cases containing exhibits whose titles <u>read</u>, "Small Mammals of North America," "Birds of the Central United States," and "Reptiles of the Desert Southwest." (5) The dusty specimens perched on little stands; <u>their</u> tiny claws gripped the smooth wood nervously. (6) A typewritten card, yellow with age, bearing the name of its genus and species. (7) The classroom itself was outfitted with a stainless steel sink, and behind the lectern loomed a dark-wood cabinet through whose glass doors one could see rows of jars, each holding what appeared to be an animal floating in a murky liquid. (8) The classroom <u>wreaked</u> of formaldehyde.

38. Which of the following sentences, if inserted between Parts 6 and 7, would best fit the author's pattern of development in the second paragraph of the passage?
  a. Howard would be teaching Byron, Shelley, and Keats this term.
  b. In the display case opposite Howard's classroom, a pocket gopher reared up on its hind legs, staring glassy-eyed into the open doorway.
  c. Although Markham was at least twenty-five years younger than Renwick, the administration had chosen to renovate it rather than the aging, crumbling science building.
  d. Genus and species are taxonomic categories.

39. Which of the following numbered parts contains a nonstandard sentence?
  a. Part 2
  b. Part 7
  c. Part 1
  d. Part 6

40. Which of the underlined words in the passage needs to be replaced with its homonym?
  a. led
  b. their
  c. read
  d. wreaked

▶ Section 3: Writing (Part B— Writing Sample)

Carefully read the writing topic that follows, then prepare a multiple-paragraph writing sample of 300–600 words on that topic. Make sure your essay is well-organized and that you support your central argument with concrete examples.

American students are said to have fallen behind in the sciences, and some educators believe it is because American teachers are conducting science classes ineffectively.

Write an essay in which you suggest ways science classes could be conducted so as to more effectively challenge high school and college students.

► Answer Explanations

Section 1: Reading

1. b. The author describes in paragraph 1 how glam rock musicians were characterized by their flashy hair and makeup, and refers to their music as a *product,* as if it was something packaged to be sold. The choice that best describes a musician who puts outward appearance before the quality of his or her music is choice **b**, *style over substance.*

2. c. *Ostentatious* is an adjective that is used to describe someone or something that is conspicuously vain, or *showy*. There are numerous context clues to help you answer this question: it is stated in paragraph 1 that the glam rockers had a *flashy style*, and their music was *symbolic of the superficial* 1980s.

3. d. *Trappings* usually refer to outward decoration of dress. If you did not know the definition of *trappings,* the prior sentence supplies the answer: *Grunge rockers derived their fashion sense from the youth culture of the Pacific Northwest; a melding of punk rocker style and outdoors clothing . . .* The author makes no judgment of the attractiveness of grunge fashion (choice **c**).

4. d. The author states in paragraph 1 that White Snake was a glam rock band and therefore not associated with the Seattle grunge scene. Don't be distracted by choice **a**; Mr. Epp and the Calculations may not have been a real band, but the name will nonetheless be forever associated with grunge music.

5. b. The relationship between grunge music and its mainstream popularity is best described as *contrary*. The most obvious example of this is found in the second sentence of paragraph 6, when in describing the relationship, the author states *it is very hard to buck the trend when you are the one setting it.*

6. d. *Ephemeral* is used to describe something that lasts only a short time, something that is fleeting. The context clue that best helps you to answer this question is found in the first two lines of paragraph 6, where the author states that grunge *faded out of the mainstream as quickly as it rocketed to prominence.*

7. d. In the second sentence the author states that Prometheus is a *complex character*, and in this and the following sentence, the author lists several specific examples of the *rich combination of often-contradictory characteristics* of Prometheus.

8. d. The passage relates the key episodes in the life of Prometheus. This is the only idea broad enough and relevant enough to be the main idea of the passage.

9. b. Prometheus's actions show that he cared for humans more than he cared for Zeus. He gave man knowledge of the arts and sciences although Zeus wanted men to be kept in ignorance (paragraph 3); he tricked Zeus to give mankind the best meat from an ox (paragraph 4); and he stole fire from Mt. Olympus to give mortals the fire that Zeus had denied them (paragraph 5).

10. a. Zeus had given Prometheus and his brother the task of creating humans as a reward for their help in defeating the Titans.

11. a. Prometheus helped create mortals and then became their *benefactor and protector* (second paragraph). He is thus most like a *parent* to humans.

12. d. The *transgression* refers back to the previous paragraph, which describes how Prometheus disobeyed Zeus and stole fire from Mount Olympus to give it to man.

13. c. The style is neither formal nor informal but an easy-going in between to make the material easily understood and interesting to a lay audience. In addition, the passage does not take for granted that the reader knows basic information about mythology. For example, second paragraph states that Zeus was *the great ruler of Olympian gods.*

14. a. The definition is implied in the beginning of the sentence: The control group was created for this experiment in order to isolate the effects of abuse and neglect from those of other variables such as gender, race, and poverty.

15. c. The fifth paragraph notes that rates of arrest were *almost as high,* meaning that they were nearly the same. The arrest rate for physically abused victims was slightly higher than that for neglected children, which rules out choice **b.**

16. b. As stated in the third paragraph, of the 21% of the control group arrested, 8% of arrests were for violent crimes.

17. a. The third paragraph states, *researchers noted that the differences in arrest rates began to emerge early. . . .*

18. d. The third paragraph notes that only 65% of the sample group had passed through the years of peak violent activity in 1988, while almost all had done so by 1994. This is one reason the arrest rate for violent crime was higher in 1994 than in 1988.

19. c. The last sentence of the first paragraph notes the goal of the studies.

20. a. In the second paragraph, Sylvia is described as restless, and in the fourth paragraph she is fearful of the impending storm; therefore her mood is most likely anxious.

21. d. Choices **a** and **b** may be true but are not reflected in the story. Choice **c** is wrong because the birds that surround Sylvia at work are dead and mounted and therefore aren't singing. In the final sentence, Sylvia is described as mildly claustrophobic, so the best answer is **d,** which states that she works in a space that feels open.

22. b. In paragraph four, Sylvia does not want to go outside because an electrical storm is coming,

and she has always been terrified of storms. Choice **a** is wrong because the adjective *gloomy* doesn't connote the threat of a frightening electrical storm. Since Sylvia is afraid of the weather, cheery adjectives such as *springlike* or *bracing* (choices **c** and **d**) cannot be said to describe it.

23. a. Sylvia's job suits her partly because her boss is usually gone and she's alone at work; she is mildly fearful of meeting the new person, Lola Parrish, and even thinks of leaving before their appointment. These details point to a distant kind of person, the opposite of someone who might be *overbearing* or *malicious* (choices **b** and **d**). She seems to want to be alone and so is unlikely to be *dependent* on others (choice **c**).

24. a. Sylvia does seem distant and her life somewhat cold, so choice **a** is the most logical choice. The details in the story do not connote lightness or airiness (choice **b**). There is no hint in the story that Sylvia feels anything about her boss, nor is there anything in this scene to remind us of the actual killing of the birds in the museum (choices **c** and **d**).

25. d. To be ambivalent is to hold mutually conflicting thoughts or feelings about a person, object, or idea. As the remainder of the sentence states, the returning hero is *the object both of wonder and dread.*

26. c. The word *awe* implies mingled reverence, dread, and wonder, so the adjective *awesome* is the best of all the choices to describe a place that is *dangerous and full of wonders* (second sentence of the third paragraph).

27. c. The first sentence of the passage describes Campbell's hero as *archetypal.* An archetype is a personage or pattern that occurs in literature and human thought often enough to be considered universal. Also, in the second sentence, the author of the passage mentions *the collective unconscious of all humankind.* The faces in the title belong to the hero, not to villagers, countries, languages, or adventures (choices **a**, **b**, and **d**).

28. a. The passage states that the hero's tale will *enlighten his fellows,* but that it will also be dangerous. Such a story would surely be radically mind-altering.

29. b. The definition of the word *boon* is blessing. What the hero brings back may be a kind of gift, charm, or prize (choices **a**, **c**, and **d**), but those words do not necessarily connote blessing or enlightenment.

30. a. The paragraph describes only the similarity between the hero's journey and the poet's.

31. d. The last sentence in the passage says that the kingdom of the unconscious mind goes down into unsuspected Aladdin caves. The story of Aladdin is a fairy tale (choice **b**), but neither this nor the other choices are in the passage.

32. d. The discussion of carbon monoxide in the last paragraph serves to demonstrate why a firefighter should wear breathing apparatus. The other choices are not related specifically to breathing.

33. c. The third sentence of the passage says: *The reason for so many injuries and fatalities is that a vehicle can generate heat of up to 1,500° F.*

34. b. Almost all the information in the passage relates to danger. Choices **a**, **c**, and **d** are touched on but are too narrow to be the main point.

35. b. The cooking temperature shows the more than 1,000-degree difference in heat between a motor-vehicle fire and a fire we are all familiar with, that used for cooking.

36. d. The last paragraph states that *carbon monoxide . . . is an odorless and colorless gas.*

37. a. The passage is a neutral narration of Mozart's childhood and the beginning of his musical career. Choices **c** and **d** can be eliminated because the author does not take a side or try to provide a point. Choice **b** is incorrect because

the author does not make any generalizations about the classical music "scene."

38. c. The passage clearly states that Wolfgang took an interest in the clavier when his sister was learning the instrument.

39. c. The passage states that Wolfgang's first *public* appearance was at Linz and that after this concert word of his genius traveled to Vienna. The passage states earlier that Vienna was the *capital* of the Hapsburg Empire.

40. b. The author's tone towards Leopold is *mild*—neither strongly approving nor disapproving. In a few places, however, the author conveys some disappointment, especially in the last lines of paragraph 3, where he or she states that Leopold set an exhausting schedule for Wolfgang.

41. c. *Lavish* means expended or produced in abundance. Both *wasteful* and *extravagant* are synonyms for *lavish*, but because it is modifying *palace, extravagant* is the more logical choice.

42. d. The author's language emphasizes Mozart's imagination. The phrase *engrossed in the intricacies of his make-believe court* suggests a child with a lively imagination. None of the other choices is directly supported by the text.

Section 2: Mathematics

1. a. 2,052 miles divided by 6 days equals 342 miles per day; 342 miles divided by 2 stops equals 171 miles.

2. d. There is not enough information to solve this problem. The price of one piece of silverware is needed to find the solution.

3. b. The 3rd and 4th quarters are 54% and 16% respectively. This adds to 70%.

4. d. First find the total price of the pencils: (24 pencils)($0.05) = $1.20. Then find the total price of the paper: (3.5 reams)($7.50 per ream) = $26.25. Next, add the two totals together: $1.20 + 26.25 = $27.45.

5. a. 157 is rounded to 200; 817 is rounded to 800; 200 times 800 equals 160,000.

6. d. It is important to remember to include all three telephone sets ($375 total), both computers ($2,600 total), both monitors ($1,900 total), the printer, and the answering machine in the total value for the correct answer of $5,525.

7. b. $24,355 + $23,000 = $47,355. When this is rounded to the nearest $100, the answer is $47,400.

8. a. It would cost $7 to get three sandwiches and a piece of fruit.

9. d. $12.50 per hour × 8.5 hours per day × 5 days per week is $531.25. This can be estimated by multiplying $12 × 8 × 5 = $480. Because Benito earns $0.50 more an hour and works a half-hour more per day, you know that his actual earnings are more than $480, and so the only reasonable answer is **d**.

10. d. The production for Lubbock is equal to the total minus the other productions: 1,780 − 450 − 425 − 345 = 560.

11. b. The number of papers graded is arrived at by multiplying the rate for each grader by the time spent by each grader. Melissa grades 5 papers an hour for 3 hours, or 15 papers; Joe grades 4 papers an hour for 2 hours, or 8 papers, so together they grade 23 papers. Because there are 50 papers, the percentage graded is $\frac{23}{50}$, which is equal to 46%.

12. c. To find the average time, you add the times for all the students and divide by the number of students; 20 + 17 + 14 = 51; 51 divided by 3 is 17.

13. b. The volume will equal the length times the width times the depth or height of a container: (12 inches)(5 inches)(10 inches) = 600 cubic inches.

14. c. An average of 90% is needed of a total of 500 points: 500 × 0.90 = 450, so 450 points are needed. Add all the other test scores together:

95 + 85 + 88 + 84 = 352. Now subtract that total from the total needed, in order to see what score the student must make to reach 90%: 450 − 352 = 98.

15. a. The sum of the sides equals the perimeter: (3 sides × 3 inches) + (2 sides × 5 inches) = 19 inches.

16. d. To find the answer do the following equation: 11 × 0.032 = 0.352.

17. a. The 90% discount is over all three items; therefore the total price is $(a + b + c) \times 0.9$. The average is the total price divided by the number of computers: $0.9 \times \frac{(a + b + c)}{3}$.

18. c. $\overline{DE}$ is 2.5 times greater than $\overline{AB}$, or 5; therefore, $\overline{EF}$ is 7.5 and $\overline{DF}$ is 10. Add the three sides together to arrive at the perimeter.

19. a. Because there are three at $0.99 and two at $3.49, the sum of the two numbers minus $3.49 will give the cost.

20. a. This is the same as the equation provided; each score is divided by three.

21. a. For the answer, divide $\frac{2}{3}$ by $\frac{5}{12}$, which is the same as $\frac{2}{3} \times \frac{12}{5} = \frac{24}{15} = 1\frac{3}{5}$.

22. b. Twenty percent of 15 servings equals (0.20)(15) = 3. Adding 3 to 15 gives 18 servings.

23. c. There are three steps involved in solving this problem. First, convert 4.5% to a decimal: 0.045. Multiply that by $26,000 to find out how much the salary increases. Finally, add the result ($1,170) to the original salary of $26,000 to find out the new salary, $27,170.

24. c. If 60% of the students had the flu previously, 40% had not had the disease; 40% of 220 is 88.

25. a. Divide 135 Spanish-speaking teachers by 1,125 total teachers to arrive at 0.12, or 12%.

26. b. Adding 9.6% (electrical equipment) and 5% (other equipment) is the way to arrive at the correct response of 14.9%.

27. b. Smoking materials account for only 6.7% of the fires but for 28.9% of the deaths.

28. b. Two candy bars require 2 quarters; one package of peanuts requires 3 quarters; one can of cola requires 2 quarters for a total of 7 quarters.

29. c. Each 9-foot wall has an area of $(9)(8)$ or 72 square feet. There are two such walls, so those two walls combined have an area of $(72)(2)$ or 144 square feet. Each 11-foot wall has an area of $(11)(8)$ or 88 square feet, and again there are two such walls: $(88)(2)$ is 176. Finally, add 144 and 176 to get 320 square feet.

30. d. Use the formula provided: $\frac{9}{5}(40) + 32 = 72 + 32 = 104$.

31. b. Add the corrected value of the sweater ($245) to the value of the two, not three, bracelets ($730), plus the other two items ($78 and $130), for a total of $1,183.

32. d. 13% had not read books; therefore, 87% had; 87% is equal to 0.87; $0.87 \times 2,500 = 2,175$ people.

33. a. The recipe is for 16 brownies. Half of that, 8, would reduce the ingredients by half. Half of $1\frac{1}{2}$ cups of sugar is $\frac{3}{4}$ cup.

34. c. The recipe for 16 brownies calls for $\frac{2}{3}$ cup of butter. An additional $\frac{1}{3}$ cup would make 8 more brownies, for a total of 24 brownies.

35. a. To solve this problem, you must convert $3\frac{1}{2}$ to $\frac{7}{2}$ and then divide $\frac{7}{2}$ by $\frac{1}{4}$. The answer, $\frac{28}{2}$, is then reduced to 14.

36. d. Mixed numbers must be converted to fractions, and you must use the least common denominator of 8; $\frac{18}{8} + \frac{37}{8} + \frac{4}{8} = \frac{59}{8}$, which is $7\frac{3}{8}$ after it is reduced.

37. d. Four inches is equal to 16 quarter inches, which is equal to $(16)(2 \text{ feet}) = 32$ feet.

38. b. You can't just take 25% off the original price, because the 10% discount is taken off the price that has already been reduced by 15%. Figure the problem in two steps: after the 15% discount the price is $71.83; 90% of that—subtracting 10%—is $64.65.

39. b. Angles 1 and 4 are the only ones NOT adjacent to each other.

40. b. Add the number of men and women to get the total number of members: 200. The number of women, 24, is 12% of 200.

41. c. The problem is solved by dividing 204 by 1,700. The answer, 0.12, is then converted to a percentage, 12%.

42. b. The simplest way to solve this problem is to divide 1 by 1,500, which is 0.0006667. Then, count off two decimal places to arrive at the percentage, which is 0.06667%. Since the question asks about what percentage, the nearest value is 0.067%.

43. b. You can use trial and error to arrive at a solution to this problem. After the first hour, the number would be 20, after the second hour 40, after the third hour 80, after the fourth hour 160, and after the fifth hour 320. The other answer choices do not have the same outcome.

44. d. 30 ppm of the pollutant would have to be removed to bring the 50 ppm down to 20 ppm; 30 ppm represents 60% of 50 ppm.

45. c. You must break the 92,000 into the amounts mentioned in the policy: $92,000 = 20,000 + 40,000 + 32,000$. The amount the policy will pay is $(0.8)(20,000) + (0.6)(40,000) + (0.4)(32,000) = 16,000 + 24,000 + 12,800 = 52,800$.

46. d. $2,200(0.07) = \$154$; $\$154 + 1,400(0.04) = \$210$; $\$210 + 3,100(0.08) = \$458$; $\$458 + \$900(0.03) = \$485$.

47. c. You can find the price per ounce of each brand, as follows:

BRAND	PRICE IN CENTS PER OUNCE
W	$\frac{21}{6} = 3.5$
X	$\frac{48}{15} = 3.2$
Y	$\frac{56}{20} = 2.8$
Z	$\frac{96}{32} = 3.0$

It is then easy to see that Brand Y, at 2.8 cents per ounce, is the least expensive.

48. c. The difference between 105 and 99 is 6 degrees. Application of the ice pack plus a "resting" period of 5 minutes before reapplication means that the temperature is lowered by half a degree every six minutes, or 1 degree every 12 minutes; 6 degrees times 12 minutes per degree equals 72 minutes, or 1 hour and 12 minutes.

Section 3: Writing (Part A— Multiple-Choice)

1. c. *Middle Ages* is a proper noun and should be capitalized.

2. c. The objective pronoun *her* is misused in Part 1 as a subject pronoun; *it* needs to be replaced with the pronoun *she*.

3. a. Quotation marks need to be inserted before the quotation is resumed after the interrupting phrase, *the brochure informed her*.

4. b. Part 1 states that guidelines were established, and Part 4 states specifically what one of the guidelines was, so Part 4 should follow Part 1. Also the information in Part 2 follows from the information in Part 4: Part 4 names *roadblocks* as a type of guideline; Part 2 contains specific information about roadblocks. So Part 2 should be moved to come after Part 4.

5. d. In Part 8, the pronouns *he* or *she* need to be changed to *they* to agree in number and person with the antecedent *officers*.

6. a. The context requires a word meaning to add something to complete a thing; choice **a**, *supplement*, is the only word or phrase with that meaning.

7. c. *To correctly divide* is a split infinitive. The infinitive is *to divide*. Choices **a**, **b**, and **d** do not make this kind of error.

8. a. The context requires a verb that means *to extend beyond*, not *to come before*. The words in the other choices do not have this meaning.

9. a. Part 2 in the only interrogatory sentence in the passage. Since it asks a question, it needs a question mark as punctuation.

10. b. The main idea of this paragraph is that, while genius has a recognizable pattern, the patterns are extraordinary. Choice **b** directly states that the patterns have the eerie quality of the fated.

11. c. The possessive *Mozart's* is required before the gerund *composing*.

12. a. Part 4 contains an error in pronoun/antecedent agreement; the pronoun *they* must be changed to *it* in order to agree in number and person with its antecedent, *regularity*.

13. d. Part 6 is a statement about the effect of the play in theater history in general; however, this statement is placed in the midst of a description of the reception of the opening of the play. The paragraph ends with a statement about the play's effect on theater history, so Part 6 should either be moved to the end of the paragraph or removed. Since there is no choice to move Part 6 to the end of the paragraph, choice **d** is the correct answer.

14. c. The names of works that can be published on their own should be italicized, even if only part of the title (in this case *Godot*) is used to designate the work; therefore choice **b** is incorrect. Choice **a** is incorrect because Mr. Godot names a character, not the play. Choice **d** is incorrect because the titles of newspapers must be italicized.

15. a. The comma in Part 5 separates the subject, *critics* and *playgoers*, from its verb, *greeted*.

16. b. Inserting a comma in Part 2, after the word *opening*, separates the introductory clause from the rest of the sentence. The sentences in choices **a**, **c**, and **d** are correct as they are written.

17. d. The two independent clauses in Part 2 need a conjunction in order for the sentence to be grammatically correct. Choices **a**, **b**, and **c** are incorrect because those sentences are correctly written.

18. c. Part 8 should come before Part 7. Part 7 comments on this final trait, but Part 8 details another trait. Logically, all the characteristics should be mentioned before commenting on the final one.

19. a. The context requires a noun that defines awareness of the moral or ethical side of one's conduct; the word *conscience* has this meaning. The words in the other choices do not have this meaning.

20. b. The sentence is written in present tense, so the present tense of *believe* is required.

21. d. In Part 6, the modifier *finally* is misplaced. It would be better placed at the beginning of the sentence.

22. c. The word *the* is necessary before the singular *wheelchair tie-down system*.

23. a. A semicolon should separate two complete sentences (independent clauses); the second half of Part 6 is not a complete sentence but a restatement of a portion of the first half. This makes a colon appropriate.

24. c. The pronoun is one of the subjects of the sentence, and so it should be changed from the object form *him* to the subject form *he*.

25. a. The tone of this paragraph is formal and specific; it also uses professional jargon—for instance, in referring to the parts of a house with which firefighters should be familiar. Choice **c** is correct because the phrase *just fine* is too colloquial and informal for the tone of the passage.

26. d. The semicolon after *fires* in Part 3 creates a sentence fragment, because the phrase before the semicolon is not an independent clause.

27. a. The comma is needed after *process* to set off the interruptive phrase *known as overhaul*.

28. d. Since the sentence states that the system is designed *to give*, then it needs *to ensure* as well. Choices **a**, **b**, and **c** are correct as written.

29. c. The pronoun *his* should be replaced with *their* in order to agree with *federal employers*. There are no errors in pronoun agreement in choices **a**, **b**, or **d**.

30. c. The paragraphs are related in that they both talk about the physical effects or extreme heat on people and the treatment of these conditions. Each paragraph's main subject is a different condition suffered because of extreme heat. The second paragraph begins by mentioning that heat stroke, the subject of the paragraph, is much more serious than the condition mentioned above, heat exhaustion. Choice **c** best aids the transition by ending the first paragraph with an explanation of the most serious effects of heat exhaustion, thereby paving the way for the contrasting description of the far more serious condition, heat stroke.

31. d. The main idea of this paragraph is a description of the symptoms and treatment of heat stroke. The information in Part 7 about the most common victims of heat stroke is least relevant to the topic of the paragraph.

32. b. Part 1 is a sentence fragment; it contains no main verb.

33. a. Choice **a** is written in the tone and style reflected in the passage. Choices **b**, **c**, and **d** are awkward versions of the same details.

34. d. The verb needs to be singular to agree with *Theodore Roosevelt*. Choices **a**, **b**, and **c** are incorrect because they introduce a shift in tense.

35. d. Commas are used to separate city from country. Choices **a**, **b**, and **c** would make the sentences grammatically incorrect.

36. b. Titles of books are always underlined or italicized. Short stories (choice **a**) are punctuated with quotation marks. Author's names (choice **c**) are not italicized. Copyrights do not need italics (choice **d**).

37. c. This choice adds the subject *he* in the second sentence, eliminating the dangling modifier *walking down the street.* Otherwise, the sentence reads as if the leaves are walking down the street.

38. b. This paragraph's purpose is descriptive; it describes the classroom and the corridor outside it. Choice **b** is correct because the information in the sentence adds to the description of the corridor.

39. d. Part 6 is a dependent clause with no independent clause to attach itself to; therefore, it is a sentence fragment.

40. d. The word *wreaked* should be replaced in this context by its homonym, *reeked.*

Section 3: Writing (Part B— Writing Sample)

Following are the criteria for scoring THEA essays.

A "4" essay is a well-formed writing sample that addresses the assigned topic and conveys a unified message to its audience. Additionally, it has the following characteristics:

- a clear purpose and focus
- controlled development of a main idea
- clear, concrete, and effective details supporting the main idea
- effective, error-free sentence structure
- precise and careful word choice
- mastery of mechanics such as punctuation and spelling

A "3" essay is an adequate writing sample that addresses the assigned topic and clearly attempts to convey a message to its audience. Generally, it has the following additional characteristics:

- a clear focus and purpose
- organization of ideas that may be vague, incomplete, or only partially effective

- an attempt at development of supporting details, which is only partly realized
- word choice and language usage that are adequate; but with minor errors in sentence structure, usage, and word choice
- mechanical mistakes such as errors in spelling and punctuation

A "2" essay is an incompletely formed writing sample that lacks clear focus. It has the following additional characteristics:

- main topic announced but focus on it is not maintained
- unclear purpose
- use of some supporting detail but development and organization unclear
- sentences and paragraphs poorly structured
- distracting errors in sentence structure
- imprecise word usage
- distracting mechanical mistakes such as errors in spelling and punctuation

A "1" essay is an incompletely formed writing sample that fails to convey a unified message. It has the following additional characteristics:

- attempt at addressing the topic, which fails
- no clear main idea
- language and style that are inappropriate to the audience and purpose
- attempt to present supporting detail which is muddled and unclear
- attempt at organization but failure to present a clear sequence of ideas
- ineffective sentences, very few of which are free of error
- imprecise word usage
- many distracting mechanical mistakes, such as errors in spelling and punctuation

A "U" essay is a writing sample that fails because of one or more of the following:

- failure to address the assigned topic
- illegibility
- written primarily in a language other than English
- length insufficient to score

A "B" essay is a writing sample left completely blank (that is, the test-taker did not respond at all).

Following are examples of scored writing samples. (Note: There are some deliberate errors in all the essays.)

Sample "4" essay

The best way for teachers to boost their students' science test scores is to stop worrying quite so much about the scores and start being concerned about making the students excited by science.

Before ever asking students to memorize facts, the teacher should demonstrate a scientific process or, better, teach the students how to experiment for themselves, allowing them to apprehend the process with their senses before trying to fix it in their intellect. For example, the teacher might pass around an ant farm in the class room and let the students observe the little critters skittering behind the glass, going about their complex, individual tasks, before asking the student to read that ants have a rigid social structure, just as people do. If possible, it would be even better to take them on a field trip to observe a real ant-hill or to see how other kinds of real animals behave, say on a farm or in a zoo. The teacher might allow the students to create a chemical reaction in a beaker asking them to memorize the formula.

When I was small, I had first-hand experience with this kind of teaching. My father built a telescope (a painstaking project that should only be taken on out of love because it is a very difficult,

intricate task). The telescope had a clock at its base that kept it fixed on the moon or stars rather than turning as the earth turns. When my father switched off the clock, I remember watching through the eyepiece, fascinated at how quickly the stars drifted out of my field of vision—it took only seconds—and even more fascinated to realize that what I was seeing was us floating so swiftly through space. He told me the magical names of the geological formations on the moon, such as the crater called "The Sea of Tranquillity." When I looked through the lens, the pock-marked silvery disc of the moon seemed as close as the hills behind our suburban house.

After that, I became interested in the statistics such as the rate of the rotation of the earth, the geophysical facts behind the making of the craters that form the moon's laughing face, in a way I never would have if the facts had been the starting point of a lecture.

This approach should be begun, not in high school or college, but in grade school or even in kindergarten. The facts are important, of course—without them, we can have no real understanding. But curiosity is as vital to learning as the ability to memorize—perhaps more so. Because curiosity will keep students learning long after they have passed their final test in school.

Sample "3" essay

Science is important for many reasons, but especially because today's world is based on technology. If other countries get ahead of us in science the consequences may be dire. So it is extremely important for our students to excell.

The first and best way to teach science is to make the student see the practical application of it. For example, if the teacher is teaching botony, she might explain the medical uses of plants. Or if teaching physics, she might show a diagram of a rocket ship. Field trips are a good idea, as well, perhaps to a factory that makes dolls. The point is to make it practical and interesting to boys and girls alike.

When I was in high school I had a teacher named Mr. Wiley who let us mix things in jars and watch the results. Sometimes they were unexpected! Such as a kind of mushroom we planted that was poisonous and reminded us of the horror movies we all loved in those days. Mr. Wiley made it interesting in a personal way, so that it wasn't just dry facts. And he told us the practical uses, such as this particular kind of mushroom is used in the making of certain insect poison.

In this day and age it is important for all of us to know something about science because it affects all aspects of our lives, but for young people it is vital. Their livelihoods—and even their lives—may depend on that knowledge.

Sample "2" essay

Science is a necesary skill because it can effect each one of us, such as a cure for disease. It is responsable for TV, cars, and other items we take for granted. So we all depend on it and need to learn it.

The best way to teach science is to have a good textbook and also good equiptment in the classroom. If the equiptment is poor there is no way they are going to learn it, which is why the poorer schools are behind the richer ones and also behind other countries. Its the most important factor in the classroom today.

Another way to teach science is through field trips and vidio-tapes. There are many tapes in the library and every school should have a good vidio system. Also a good library is important. And there are many places to take the class that they would find intresting.

When I was in school I thought science was boring. I wish I had learned more about it because I think it would make me understand the world of technology. If we don't understand technology we

are at it's mercy, and it is something we rely on to get us through our lives. Without science we would have no technilogical advances. If other countries are ahead of us it is our own fault for not putting science as a priority.

Sample "1" essay

Science is importnant and we should teach it to our students in the right way. A scientist coming in to talk would be one way. Also experimints that the students can do. The reason it is important, is other countrys are ahead of us and we may have a war. Then if there tecnoligy is better they will take us over. So it is dangerous not to have students that know alot about science.

If we teach our children to relay too much on science and technoligy what will happen if it fails. If the computers fail we are in serious trouble. Which shows that science cant solve everything! There is still no cure for cancer and our products cause polution. So science is important and our students should learn but it isnt everything and they should learn that they should study other things to.

If we teach science in the right way our country will be better off as well as our children when they are caught up.

▶ Scoring

Evaluate how you did on this practice exam by scoring the three sections of the THEA—Reading, Mathematics, and Writing—separately. For the Reading section, the Mathematics section, and the multiple-choice subsection of the Writing section, use the same scoring method. First, find the number of questions you got right in each section. Questions you skipped or got wrong don't count; just add up the number of correct answers. Divide your number of correct answers by the number of questions in that section to find your percentage.

THEA PRACTICE EXAM 3

In addition, as mentioned in previous chapters, you must receive a passing score on the writing sample subsection of the Writing section of the THEA. Your writing sample will be graded by two readers and their combined score used to evaluate how you did. Your score will be a combination of the two readers' judgments, somewhere between a possible high of 8 and a low of 2. To see how you did on your essay for this third and final practice exam, be sure to give it and the scoring criteria to a teacher and ask him or her to score your essay for you.

You have probably seen improvement between your first practice exam score and this one; but if you didn't improve as much as you would like, following are some options for you to consider:

- If you scored below 60%, you should seriously consider whether you are ready for the THEA at this time. A good idea would be to take some brush-up courses, either at a community college nearby or through correspondence, in the areas you feel less sure of. If you don't have time for a course, you might try private tutoring.

- If your score is in the 60% to 70% range, you need to work as hard as you can to improve your skills. Reread and pay close attention to all the information in Chapters 2, 4, 5, and 6 of this book to improve your score.

- If your score is between 70% and 80%, you could still benefit from additional work by going back to Chapters 4, 5, and 6 and by brushing up on your reading comprehension and general math skills before the exam.

- If you scored above 80%, that's great! This kind of score should make you a success in the academic program of your choice. Don't lose your edge, though; keep studying right up to the day before the exam.

The key to success in almost any pursuit is to prepare for all you are worth. By taking the practice exams in this book, you have made yourself better prepared than other people who may be taking the exam with you. You have diagnosed where your strengths and weaknesses lie and learned how to deal with the various kinds of questions that will appear on the test. Go into the exam with confidence, knowing that you are ready and equipped to do your best.

How to Use
the CD-ROM

So you think you're ready for your exam? Here's a great way to build confidence and know you are ready: using LearningExpress's Academic Skills Tester AutoExam CD-ROM software included inside the back cover of this book. This disk can be used with any PC running Windows 3.1 through Windows XP. (Sorry, it doesn't work with Macintosh.) The following description represents a typical "walk through" the software.

To install the program:

1. Insert the CD-ROM into your CD-ROM drive. The CD should run automatically. If it does not, proceed to step 2.

2. From Windows, select **Start**, then choose **Run.**

3. Type D:/Setup.

4. Click **OK.**

The screens that appear subsequently will walk you right through the installation procedure.

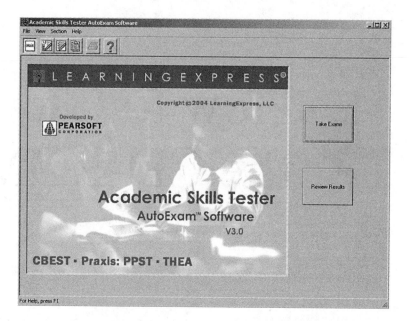

From the Main Menu, select **Take Exams.** (You can use **Review Exam Results** after you have taken at least one exam, in order to see your scores.)

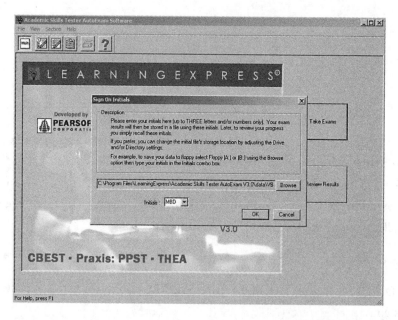

Now enter your initials. This allows you a chance to record your progress and review your performance for as many simulated exams as you'd like. Notice that you can also change the drive where your exam results are stored. If you want to save to a floppy drive, for instance, click on the "Browse" button and then choose the letter of your floppy drive.

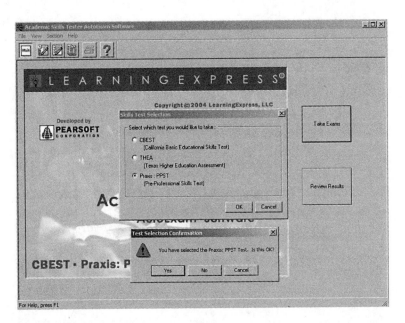

Now, since this CD-ROM supports three different academic exams, you need to select your exam of interest. Let's try CBEST, the California Basic Education Skills Test, as shown above.

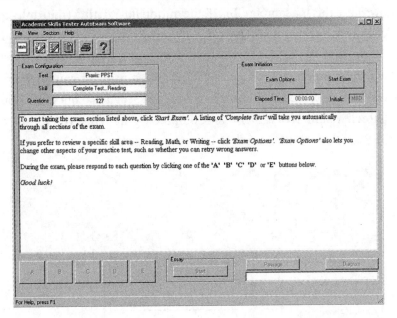

Now you're into the **Take Exams** section, as shown above. You can choose **Start Exam** to start taking your test, or **Exam Options.** The next screen shows you what your **Exam Options** are.

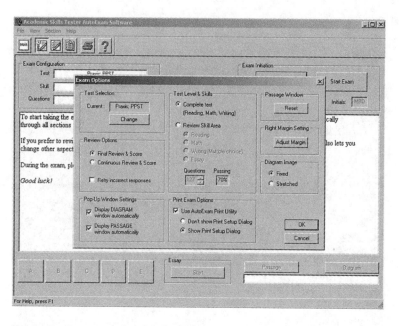

Choosing **Exam Options** gives you plenty of options to help you fine tune your rough spots. How about a little math to warm up? Click **Review Skill Area,** and then the **Math** option. Choose the number of questions you want to review right now. Since this is a sample CBEST, the button for **Writing (multiple-choice)** is gray; CBEST doesn't have multiple-choice writing questions. If you are taking a Praxis or THEA, the **Writing (multiple-choice)** button will be active. On the left you can choose whether to wait until you've finished to see how you did (**Final Review & Score**) or have the computer tell you after each question whether your answer is right (**Continuous Review & Score**). Choose **Retry incorrect responses** to get a second chance at questions you answer wrong. (This option works best with **Review Skill Area** rather than **Complete Test.**) When you finish choosing your options, click **OK.** Then click the **Start Exam** button on the main exam screen.

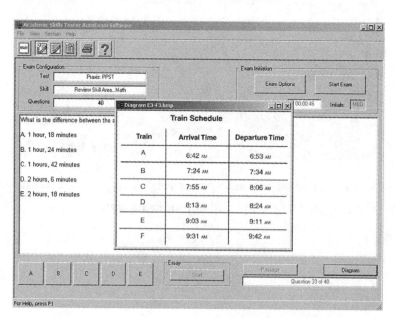

As you can see, diagrams are displayed any time a math problem calls for one. You can move the diagram window (or a passage for reading questions) by clicking on the bar at the top of the window and dragging to where you want it. You can also minimize the diagram window by clicking on the left box in the right corner. You can get the diagram back any time by clicking the **Diagram** button.

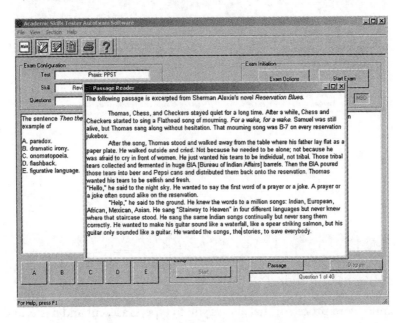

Once you've responded to all ten of the questions, go back to **Exam Options** and select a **Reading** exam; then click on **Start Exam.** AutoExam makes it easy by displaying the reading passage in its own window, which always "rides on top" of the exam window, as seen above. You can scroll through the reading passage using the scroll bar on the right, or minimize the passage so you see only the question window. To get the passage back, click the **Passage** button.

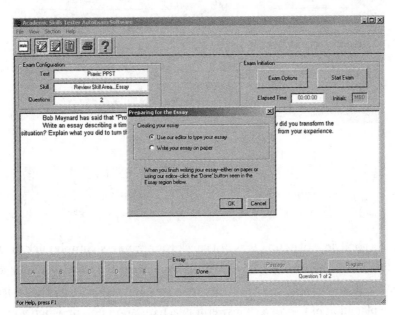

Don't forget about an essay or two for some good practice. Once again, click the **Exam Options** button, select the Essay setting, click **Start Exam,** and you're on your way again. You have the option of writing out your essay by hand or using AutoExam's built-in editor.

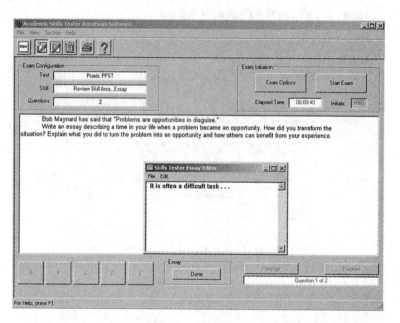

This editor is a simple word processor that allows you to type, erase, cut and paste, and save. When you finish writing your essay—by hand or on screen—click **Done.**

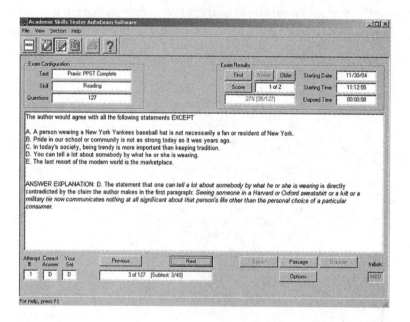

After you have had a good dose of exams, why not check your progress? Simply click the **Review Exams** menu button (as seen on the first screen) and you can review your progress in detail and check your score. You can see how many questions you got right and how long each section took you, and review individual questions. Note that you can choose to have an explanation of the correct answer for each question pop up when you review that question.

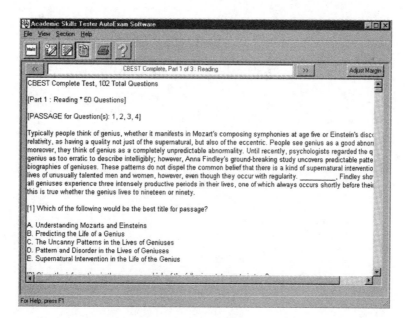

What's that? No time to work at the computer? Click the **Print Exams** menu bar button and you'll have a full-screen review of an exam that you can print out, as shown above.

For technical support, call (212) 995-2566.

NOTES

NOTES

NOTES

NOTES

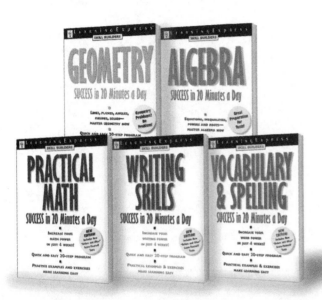